PrincetonReview.com

COLLEGE ESSAYS THAT MADE A DIFFERENCE

BY THE STAFF OF THE PRINCETON REVIEW

FOURTH EDITION

Random House, Inc.
New York

The Princeton Review, Inc.
111 Speen St., Suite 550
Framingham, MA 01701
E-mail: bookeditor@review.com

ISBN: 978-0-375-42785-5
ISSN: 2152-7830

SVP, Publisher: Robert Franek
Editor: Laura Braswell
Print Production: Best Content Solutions, LLC
Production Editor: Kristen O'Toole

ACKNOWLEDGMENTS

This book would not have been possible without the following individuals here at The Princeton Review, who granted us the opportunity to make the fourth edition of *College Essays* a reality; Robert Franek, who was instrumental in the development of this title; Scott Harris and Kristen O'Toole, who transformed the various pieces of the manuscript into the book now in your hands; and Laura Braswell, who provided much valuable input along the way.

Thirteen admissions officers kindly set aside time to speak with us about the particulars of their institution's undergraduate admissions process: Martha Allman, John Corona, Margit A. Dahl, Mark Davies, Stephen Farmer, John Latting, Mitchell Lipton, Carol Lunkenheimer, Duncan Murdoch, Parke Muth, Tom Parker, Lorne T. Robinson, and Michael Zaletel.

The folks most vital to this book, of course, are the contributors—amazing students who took time out of their busy lives to stay in touch and answer questions. To each student who participated in this project: Many thanks for your patience, hard work, and generosity. We commend you for having the guts to lay it all out there for the benefit of future generations of college applicants.

CONTENTS

INTRODUCTION

Why did we produce this book?

For a couple of reasons. First, we wanted to provide a little inspiration to students sweating over their application essays to highly selective colleges. Too many freaked-out high schoolers with outstanding academic and community service records, enviable SAT and ACT scores, and impressive sports achievements have complained that they don't know what to write about or where to start. Hopefully this book will show that there are a million different ways to approach the essay and that if a student reflects on what's most important, he or she will indeed have something to write about. Our evidence is enclosed herewith: actual essays that got living, breathing high school students—kids with crushes and acne and big feet—into the colleges of their dreams.

These students wrote about scores of things, from their love of horses to the shortcomings of being short to the importance of personal hygiene. There are sad tales full of tragedy, homesickness, and civil war, as well as funny stories involving puberty, public embarrassment, and infomercials. There are stories of achievement and of failure, of love and death, of relationships with God, and of spirituality.

Like most collections of prose featuring many diffirent authors, the pieces in this book display a range of creativity and sophistication with the written word. Some essays are so good they may intimidate you; others might make you say to yourself, "Hey, I could write something like that." Others are so strange and unexpected you may wonder how on earth some of the most discriminating colleges in the country accepted into their freshman classes the people who wrote them. Which brings us to the second reason we produced this book: to give you a better understanding of the regularities and irregularities of selective college admissions. Along with each essay in the book, you will find the high school GPA; extracurricular activities; hometown; race; and SAT, SAT Subject Test(s), and ACT scores, where applicable, of the student who wrote it—all criteria competitive schools may consider in their admit decisions. In addition, we provide the college or university each student enrolled at and their expected or actual year of graduation. Sure, you can find average SAT scores and GPAs of last year's freshman class in most college guides, but what you'll find here are the profiles of individual applicants who are currently enrolled at, or have graduated from, the most selective undergraduate schools in the nation. To top it off, we've also included interviews with admissions officers at thirteen stellar schools to help shed a little light on what happens on the other side of the admissions fence.

How can this book help you?

We don't comment on individual essays, applicants, or admissions results; we simply present the information to you. After considering the information for the applicants who enrolled at a given college (for most colleges in the book we profile more than one successful applicant—see p. xi), you'll start to get an idea of what you need—in terms of academic competitiveness, essay quality, extracurricular activities, etc.—to gain admission to it. What's more, we provide a list of the other schools to which each student profiled in the book applied and the ultimate results of those applications. By studying these results, you can start to gauge what your own success rate will be at the various mega-selective colleges in America. Even if you do not plan to apply to the same schools as the students included in this book, the quality of the essays and the strength of the students' overall applications can be used to measure your own writing and credentials.

Ideally, these essays will inspire you, supply you with paradigms for narrative and organizational structures, teach you ways to express yourself you hadn't yet considered, and help you write exactly what you wish to communicate.

This book should also help prepare you to encounter both success and failure with your college applications. You're going to be a bit perplexed when Harvard accepts, Columbia waitlists, and Stanford rejects a student in the book. As you'll see, even wunderkinds—we've profiled plenty of them—get denied admission to top-flight schools. In fact, very few of the students you will encounter in this book got into every college to which they applied. So what should this mean to you? It means that failure is a part of life, even when you've busted your hump working on whatever it was that ultimately failed. But even if you do get a rejection letter, there's no reason to feel completely bereft: a few fat envelopes are probably finding their way to you.

Why'd they do it?

Why *would* students allow us to publish their essays, test scores, grades, and personal biographical information? They realize the value their stories have for prospective college students. After all, successfully navigating the process of selective college admissions is no small feat. Many said they were honored to have been chosen for publication and to have been given the chance to help the next generation of applicants.

Which students did we accept submissions from, and why?

We only accepted submissions from current students at, or recent graduates of, colleges and universities that received very high selectivity ratings in our flagship book, *The Best 373 Colleges*. Students and alumni of the following schools appear in the book:

Amherst College
Bard College
Barnard College
Brandeis University
Brown University
Bryn Mawr College
California Institute of Technology
Carleton College
Claremont McKenna College
Columbia University
The Cooper Union for the Advancement of Science and Art
Cornell University
Dartmouth College
Davidson College
Duke University
Franklin W. Olin College of Engineering
Georgetown University
Hamilton College
Harvard College
Kenyon College
Massachusetts Institute of Technology

Middlebury College
New College of Florida
New York University
Northwestern University
Pomona College
Princeton University
Reed College
Rice University
Smith College
Stanford University
Swarthmore College
Tufts University
University of California—
   Los Angeles
University of California—San Diego
University of Notre Dame
University of Pennsylvania
Washington & Lee University
Washington University in St. Louis
Wellesley College
Wesleyan University
Whitman College
Williams College
Yale University

In limiting submissions to students who gained admission to the nation's most selective colleges and universities, we hope to give you an idea of the highest standards you may encounter in undergraduate admissions. We received many more responses than we were able to publish and, in selecting students to profile in this book, our goal was to assemble the best-possible cross-section of top applicants—a group of students who were accepted to different schools, submitted high-quality essays on a range of themes, and had varied academic and extracurricular accomplishments. We did not aim to produce line-by-line instructions of what to do and what not to do in your application to a given school. Rather, we wished simply to show you how real students fared in the admissions jungle.

THE PARTS OF THIS BOOK

Essay Fundamentals

To emphasize the role that grammar plays in essay excellence, we composed a review of the essentials. The essay's importance in an application is also discussed.

Q&A with Admissions Officers

We interviewed admissions folks at thirteen schools that received selectivity ratings of 95 or higher in *The Best 373 Colleges*. We discussed the essay, the application as a whole, and the specifics of how the admissions ship is run at each administrator's school. Their responses will give you insight into what happens after your application is signed, sealed, and delivered.

The Applicants

Each student profile is broken down into manageable chunks. The name of the student[1] and a photograph (if he or she provided one) come first. We then offer a short paragraph, summarizing the major accomplishments and activities the student highlighted on his or her application. Next, we provide the student's statistical record—test scores, high school GPA[2], high school attended—and demographic information—hometown, gender, race. We then list the school(s) that the student applied to. Finally, you will see an actual essay that the student wrote and submitted with his or her applications. If each school the student applied to did not receive the essay, we let you know which ones did. Among the essays, not every sentence is eloquent, nor every comma perfectly placed. However, these are the essays as they were submitted, read, and ultimately accepted. We think they're all solid. Some are excellent. More importantly, they all passed the ultimate test for college application soundness: Their authors gained acceptance into at least one of the top schools to which they applied. In a few cases, we printed more than one essay written by a given student; Princeton's application, for example, requires four short essays, so we included the complete set.

We did not group the applicants according to the quality of their essays, or according to the schools at which they eventually matriculated; you will find them in alphabetical order by first name. The location of the page listing each applicant's admissions decision(s) can be found at the end of his or her profile.

While you read, you may want to consult the school profiles, either in *The Best 373 Colleges* and on our website, PrincetonReview.com. In each school profile, you will find information about students who applied in the most recent academic year, including average SAT and ACT scores, the overall number of applicants, and the yield (the percentage of students accepted who enrolled). We also break down the application elements into hierarchical

1 Five students wished to remain anonymous in this edition. Their profiles can be found at the end of this section.

2 We indicate the scale a student's high school GPA is on if the student has informed us that it is not on the 4.00 scale. If they have informed us that their GPA is weighted, we also indicate that.

categories—which components of the application each school considers very important factors, important factors, and other factors; you'll see which of these categories the essay falls into for each college.

Where They Got In

This is an index of the admissions decisions each student received. Try putting yourself in the position of the admissions officer; in some cases, you may be surprised by the admissions staff's decision. This index is also alphabetized by the student's first name.

EDITOR'S NOTE

Though it goes without saying, *don't* plagiarize the essays in this book. Your response must be in your own words. We encourage you to note words, structures, and themes that you really like, but do not copy phrases, whole sentences, or paragraphs. If you're caught plagiarizing you won't get into college at all. It's just wrong.

Part 1

ESSAY
FUNDAMENTALS

GRAMMAR AND FORM

You should strive to make your college application clear, concise, candid, structurally sound, and 100 percent grammatically accurate.

Clarity and conciseness are achieved through a lot of reading, rereading, and rewriting. Without question, repeated critical revision by yourself and by others is the surest way to trim, tune, and improve your prose.

As candor cannot be impressed after the fact, your writing should be sincere from the outset. Let's be frank: You're probably pretty smart. You can probably fake candor if absolutely necessary, but don't. For one thing, it involves a lot more work. Moreover, no matter how good your insincere essay may be, we're confident that the honest and authentic one you write will be even better.

Structural soundness is the product of a well-crafted outline. Sketch out the general themes of your essay first; worry about filling in the particulars later. Many people like to start by putting ideas onto paper in the form of "bubble outlines"—they'll write down the names of things that they're passionate or know a lot about, circle the ones that they really think describe who they are, then connect with lines ideas that complement one another. Others, like movie director Paul Thomas Anderson, start writing lists of things that they like or have done—lists and lists and lists—until an overall theme starts to take shape. If you go about it this way, you have the details of your essay written down even before you decide what your theme will be. The idea is to get thinking, get your thoughts onto paper, then settle down to attack the task of building a formal outline. Pay close attention to the structure of your essay and to the fundamental message it communicates. Make sure you have a thesis statement and a well-conceived narrative. Your essay should flow from beginning to end. Use paragraphs properly and make sure they are in logical order. The sentences within each paragraph should be complete and also flow in logical order.

Grammatical accuracy is key. A thoughtful essay that offers true insight will undoubtedly stand out, but if it is riddled with poor grammar and misspelled words, it will not receive serious consideration. *It is critical that you avoid grammatical errors.* We can't stress this enough. Misspellings, awkward constructions, run-on sentences, and misplaced modifiers cast doubt on your efforts. Admissions officers will question the amount of care you put into the essay's composition. For more information, see the Appendix on page 335.

GRAMMATICAL CATEGORY	WHAT'S THE RULE?	BAD GRAMMAR	GOOD GRAMMAR
MISPLACED MODIFIER	A word or phrase that describes something should go right next to the thing it modifies.	1. Eaten in Mediterranean countries for centuries, **northern Europeans** viewed the tomato with suspicion. 2. A **former greenskeeper** now about to become the Masters champion, **tears** welled up in my eyes as I hit my last miraculous shot.	1. Eaten in Mediterranean countries for centuries, **the tomato** was viewed with suspicion by northern Europeans. 2. **I was a former greens-keeper** who was now about to become the Masters champion; **tears** welled up in my eyes as I hit my last miraculous shot.
PRONOUNS	A pronoun must refer unambiguously to a noun and it must agree (singular or plural) with that noun.	1. Though **brokers** are not permitted to know executive access **codes, they** are widely known. 2. The **golden retriever** is one of the smartest breeds of dogs but **they** often **have** trouble writing **essays** for college admission. 3. Unfortunately, both **candidates** for whom I worked sabotaged their own **campaigns** by taking **a contribution** from illegal **sources**.	1. Though **brokers** are not permitted to know executive access **codes, the codes** are widely known. 2. The **golden retriever** is one of the smartest breeds of dogs but **it** often **has** trouble writing **an essay** for college admission. 3. Unfortunately, both **candidates** for whom I worked sabotaged their own **campaigns** by taking **contributions** from illegal **sources**.
SUBJECT/VERB AGREEMENT	The subject must always agree with the verb. Make sure you don't forget what the subject of a sentence is, and don't use the object of a preposition as the subject.	1. **Each** of the men involved in the extensive renovations **were** engineers. 2. Federally imposed **restrictions** on the ability to use certain information **has** made life difficult for Martha Stewart.	1. **Each** of the men involved in the extensive renovations **was** an engineer. 2. Federally imposed **restrictions** on the ability to use certain information **have** made life difficult for Martha Stewart.
PARALLEL CONSTRUCTION	Words in lists in the same sentence need to be similar in form to the other words in the list.	1. The two main goals of the Eisenhower presidency were a **reduction** of taxes and **to increase** military strength. 2. **To provide a child** with the skills necessary for survival in modern life is **like guaranteeing their** success.	1. The two main goals of the Eisenhower presidency were **to reduce** taxes and **to increase** military strength. 2. **Providing children** with the skills necessary for survival in modern life is **like guaranteeing their** success.
COMPARISONS	You can only compare things to exactly the same things.	1. The **rules** of written English are more stringent than **spoken English**. 2. The **considerations** that led many colleges to impose admissions quotas in the last few decades **are similar to the quotas** imposed in the recent past by large businesses.	1. The **rules** of written English are more stringent than **those of spoken English**. 2. The **considerations** that led many colleges to impose admissions quotas in the last few decades **are similar to those** that led large businesses to impose quotas in the recent past.
PASSIVE/ ACTIVE VOICE	Choose the active voice, in which the subject performs the action.	1. **The ball was hit by the bat**. 2. After months **were spent** trying to keep justdillpickles.com afloat single-handedly, **resignation was chosen by me**.	1. **The bat hit the ball**. 2. After **I spent months** trying to keep justdillpickles.com afloat single-handedly, **I chose to resign**.

Good writing is writing that is easily understood. You want to get your point across, not bury it in words. Don't talk in circles. Your prose should be clear and direct. If an admissions officer has to struggle to figure out what you are trying to say, you're in trouble.

Get to the point in three pages. Don't be long-winded and boring. Admissions officers don't like long essays. Would you, if you were in their shoes? Be brief. Be focused. If there is a word limit, abide by it.

Buy and read *The Elements of Style*, by William Strunk Jr., E. B. White, and Roger Angell. We can't recommend this highly enough. It is a great investment for any undergrad. Almost every college requires its students to complete a course or two in composition, even students who major in subjects that are not writing-intensive, like chemistry. If you enroll in a major that involves a lot of writing, *The Elements of Style* will become your best friend. If you decide on a profession that requires you to put pen to paper on a daily basis, you will refer to it forever.

Proofread your essay from beginning to end, proofread it again, then proofread it some more. Read it aloud. Keep in mind, the more time you spend with a piece of your own writing, the less likely you are to spot errors. Ask friends, teachers, siblings—somebody other than yourself—to read your essay and comment on it. Ask them if it reflects your personality and tells a coherent story. If it doesn't, work on it more. Do not get content ideas from them. Then have an English teacher or another stickler for grammar to make sure your essay is clear, concise, candid, structurally sound, and 100 percent grammatically accurate.

WHAT COLLEGES WANT TO SEE IN YOUR ESSAY: WRITING ABILITY AND INSIGHT INTO WHO YOU ARE

The admissions officers reading your essay want it to show that you can write at the college level. This means you have command of the English language and can use it to craft a cogent written statement. They are not interested in your vocabulary skills, so give the thesaurus to mom and have her hide it.

You should write your essay without fancy words whose meanings you don't understand. It is painfully obvious to admissions officers when you do this; they're almost embarrassed *for* you.

Admissions officers are interested in seeing that you understand sentence and paragraph structure and can pace a narrative—and that you know what a narrative is in the first place. If you're a little unsure, a narrative is simply a story. Unless you're William Faulkner, the story your essay tells to admissions officers needs to be brief, flow logically from one event to the next, and have a convincing conclusion. People usually act consistently (even if they're consistently inconsistent), and their pattern of actions more times than not leads to consistent outcomes. You'd have to be a darn clever wordsmith, for example, to convince a reader that a chain smoker could enter the New York City Marathon and win it just because he "had a lot of heart." Your essay should not read like a work of fiction and require admissions officers to suspend disbelief. Keep it brief and coherent.

This does not mean that you or someone else should edit your essay down to nothing. It also shouldn't sound like a marketing piece. It should sound the way you talk (when you speak with correct grammar, of course).

An additional point we hope you will pick up on is that no matter how impressive your grades, test scores, and extracurriculars are, admissions decisions by these top-flight schools involve subjective elements you can't control. Always be yourself, not the person you think admissions officers want to see. That's the job of a con artist, and it almost never works. Besides, admissions officers are paid to find students who are good matches for their institution. A dishonest essay may lead you to the wrong school. Who wants to fill out transfer applications?

Time and again admissions officers tell us that they want students to write their college essays about the things they, the students, actually care about. You should write your essay about something you do, not something you would do if you were president of the United States (unless specifically asked to do so). Admissions officers want to know why you spent every Wednesday afternoon last year teaching an underprivileged boy how to use a computer, even when you didn't want to or didn't think you had time. They want to know about your hobbies and interests. They even want to know why you're passionate about Spider-Man comics.

But notice the "why." The essay isn't just an opportunity for you to show you're a character who would bring some much-needed uniqueness to campus. It's an opportunity for you to give admissions officers real insight into who you are. This means your essay absolutely must include a "why." There are no exceptions. Why do you love Spider-Man? Is it something he is or isn't? Is Spidey's story somehow an allegory for selfless service to others? If you're an artist, is it the care with which every frame is crafted? The detail? If you're a cultural anthropologist, is it Spidey's continued ability to resonate with readers, both old and young? Your essay should show that you have thought about why you love what you love, believe what you believe, or are who you are. The "why" in your essay will show that you know how to reflect and analyze in college.

TOPICS THAT WORK, TOPICS THAT DON'T

Opinion differs from college to college regarding what's a good essay topic and what isn't. More than a few opinions can be found in Part 2 of this book, which is devoted to the interviews we conducted with admissions professionals at over a dozen elite colleges. There are a few topics, however, that almost invariably send shudders down admissions officers' spines. These include sex (especially *your* sex life), drugs (especially *your* drug use), and violent events in which you participated. Admissions officers also tire of reading travelogues and stories of how you recovered from a sports injury. Want to make them groan? Rehash the extracurricular activities that you already listed on your application, or editorialize on the top news item of the day. Swearing isn't effective, either. They appreciate humor, but if you're not funny in person, you shouldn't try to be so on paper. If your essay relies on humor, you should have a teacher read it: If your humor doesn't elicit the right response from them, it most likely won't get the reaction you're looking for in the admissions office.

Admissions officers also don't want to read an essay you wrote for another school. If you use the same essay for all the schools to which you apply, make sure the correct school's name appears in each version (if applicable). It's common courtesy.

What *do* they like to read about? Curiosity, passion, and persistence. These are attributes that great college students have. Great students go on to be great alumni. Colleges that have great students and great alumni tend to attract quality applicants, and the cycle goes on. But you shouldn't *tell* the admissions office that you are curious, passionate, or persistent; you should *show* them. Let your narrative do this. How? Check out some of the essays inside.

SO HOW MUCH DOES THE ESSAY COUNT, ANYWAY?

As Jim Miller, Dean of Admissions at Brown University, once told us, "A great essay can heal the sick, but can't raise the dead." Most often (the main exception being those colleges that don't require test scores, like Bates College) the two most important factors in your application are your high school GPA and standardized test scores. If you are reading this very early in high school, make getting good grades your top priority. When it comes time to take the SAT or ACT, prepare for it, and do well. If you're reading this in the fall of your senior year and your GPA is in the toilet, this book is going to be of little use to you.

The consensus among most admissions officers is that the essay can both help and hurt you, but it can help you more. That is reason enough to put your best effort into writing it. It is, after all, the one part of your college application over which you have total control. This book is our way of preparing you to take command of that process with authority.

Part 2

Q & A With
Admissions Officers

We interviewed admissions officers at 13 highly selective schools about college applications and essays. They told us what they like and don't like to read, the number of essays they read each year, and just how much the essay counts. The following professionals dedicated their time to answering our questions:

Tom Parker, Dean of Admission and Financial Aid at Amherst College
Mark Davies, Dean of Admissions at Bucknell University
John Corona, Associate Dean of Admission at Colgate University
Mitchell Lipton, Dean of Admissions and Records at Cooper Union
Michael Zaletel, Application Committee Chair at Deep Springs College
Duncan Murdoch, Dean of Admission at Franklin W. Olin College of Engineering
John Latting, Director of Admissions at Johns Hopkins University
Lorne T. Robinson, Dean of Admissions and Financial Aid at Macalester College
Carol Lunkenheimer, Dean of Undergraduate Admissions at Northwestern University
Stephen Farmer, Director of Undergraduate Admissions at University of
    North Carolina—Chapel Hill
Parke Muth, Senior Assistant Dean of Admissions at University of Virginia
Martha Allman, Director of Admissions at Wake Forest University
Margit A. Dahl, Dean of Undergraduate Admissions at Yale University

For ease of reading, we introduce each officer's response to the questions we ask with the name of the institution he or she serves.

SUBJECT MATTER AND WRITING

Which themes continually appear in essays?

Amherst: We give four or five different options. I look for an experience or interaction that they have had that led them to a particular value or interaction, a reflection.

Bucknell: There are number of commonly used topics, but students will tend to write about meaningful experiences or key people in their lives.

Cooper Union: Human Rights/Civil Liberties, volunteerism, and most recently, involvement in the Middle-East.

UNC: Many students choose to write about school activities such as sports or band, significant people in their lives, or summer experiences such as mission trips or Governor's school. While these themes are used more often than others, the theme itself does not necessarily determine the quality of the essay.

UVA: I am not sure that theme is the correct term to describe the types of essays we often get. There are, according to the Russian Formalists, only nine plots available, so essays tend to fall into these forms. The most common of these would be the maturation plot, also known as the bildungsroman. In this plot, the student grows from having undergone an experience that challenged him or her.

Wake Forest: Personal struggle/triumph and epiphanies—often resulting from community service or international experiences—are very common.

Yale: The most common ones are probably [about] the things that students do the most in high school. Our essay topics are very open and we let [students] talk about things that are very meaningful. We're not one of those colleges that asks for offbeat topics and asks applicants to come up with a creative answer. We certainly get ones about important people, grandparents, family experiences, that sort of thing.

There are terrible essays on wonderful topics and wonderful essays on very ordinary topics. The topic itself does not make the essay.

What do you love to see?

Amherst: Pure pleasure and genuine intellectuality.

Bucknell: Honesty. Experiences that have made a significant impact on one's life always grab the reader's attention.

Cooper Union: Essays written with passion and emotion. Those which discuss a personal matter/conflict/growth. Essays with humor—they're refreshing.

Johns Hopkins: We start at the beginning. The first sentence is read carefully, the first paragraph is closely read, and then it's open-ended from there . . . if it's high quality, we'll examine everything. The very first sentence should accomplish a lot. . .the essays I remember do that—similar to a short story. Some students don't dive right in; they try to set up their case, crafting what turns out to be dry prose. They don't have time to do that.

Macalester: I enjoy reading direct, honest, concise writing.

Northwestern: Writing with a natural voice. Don't be formal if you're not formal. If you're funny, be humorous. We're trying to get a sense of what you're like; stay with your natural voice.

Olin: We love to see that students understand Olin's unique mission and want to contribute to our community.

Subtle humor done well can make a big impact in an essay. One essay we received a couple years ago from an applicant compared Olin to pizza on Thanksgiving. In his essay, he noted that while everyone has turkey, stuffing, and cranberry sauce on Thanksgiving because that's the tradition, his family realized that they didn't really like turkey, etc. all that much; what they liked best was pizza. The family started a new tradition of having pizza on Thanksgiving. The student observed that this was an applicable analogy to Olin—a new and innovative college that's a better fit for him because it's a new and different institution. He did an excellent job of using subtle humor, a great theme, and actual substance in his essay.

UNC: Creativity, honesty, humor, and an authentic voice.

UVA: I love to read essays that show rather than tell, that focus on details instead of abstractions, and that have a voice. This is, of course, quite a tall order for a short essay.

Wake Forest: Clear, descriptive, beautiful writing. Thoughtful essays that reveal a creative, serious, and engaged student.

What topics are risky? And when, if ever, is risk-taking a good idea?

Bucknell: Though it is important to be confident, excessive arguments about how qualified and talented a candidate is do not sit well with the reader. It is important to stay away from strong political and religious views because you cannot predetermine that the reader shares your beliefs. The only risk worth taking is telling the committee about overcoming a personal obstacle. If you want to write about enduring personal problems, then be sure to include how you overcome [the problem] or it may be assumed that you have not changed or achieved success.

Cooper Union: Mistakes made (even ones that had legal repercussions) and what has been learned from them. While this topic is risky, I would prefer to know the truth about an individual, his or her failures and how he or she has subsequently grown. Other risky topics include: abortion, politics, and affirmative action. Some admissions counselors will undoubtedly compare their own ideals [to the student's] and may not be as objective [as others].

Deep Springs: It's risky to use a non-essay format (e.g., a collection of poems). It had better be very good. Anything that uses tricks to avoid thinking through things in a structured, rigorous, and interesting way is bad.

Macalester: I really don't want to know about their sex lives.

UNC: Few topics are too risky, but it depends on how well the student presents the topic. If a student chooses a controversial topic such as abortion, does she support her arguments well? If a student tries to use humor, is it effective?

UVA: Any topic can be risky. I think the grand narratives (meta-narratives for the post modern crowd), are difficult to write about well in a limited amount of space. Man's inhumanity to man would fall into this category. I am being a bit tongue-in-cheek, as I do not wish to discourage students from writing about what they care about. I have seen great essays on almost any topic and terrible essays on almost any topic. (I have read over 25,000.)

Wake Forest: Shock value in college essays is not desirable. Avoid profanity, sex, violence, and gory details.

Yale: I think it's not so much the topic as it is [how the student] deals with a topic; I don't think that there's any individual topic that can't be dealt with. I think some kids do take risks in essays. They don't always work, but I appreciate the courage to try. Don't waste 50 percent of your essay space with a poem; it's ultimately going to serve you a little better to write some prose.

What experience would you like students to write about more often?

Bucknell: Stories that deal with life experiences or information that won't appear anywhere else in the application always capture our attention.

Cooper Union: Things that move them emotionally and philosophically. Experiences that they have learned from and are now richer from. Travels—who did they meet, what did they see, what did they learn? What they expect to gain by going to college other than preparation for a job.

Deep Springs: The ideas they are curious and excited about.

Johns Hopkins: Students assume we want to know about them personally—and we do—but we want the essay to be a window on their lives, their community, school, teachers, and [general] situation. Students rarely reflect on their schools or neighborhoods—more on family and friends. We want to learn about the context of the application. Where is the student coming from? We prefer the essay to talk about one's own situation; it helps us balance the traditional admissions measures—grades, scores, etc.—in the application.

UNC: There are no specific experiences we would like students to write about more often than others. We simply want students to choose experiences that are important to them, rather than ones they think we want to read.

UVA: I would encourage students to focus on what our greatest writer calls "a local habitation and a name." In other words, a student should focus on the details and on a level of language that permits details to speak.

Wake Forest: Intellectual epiphanies—the "Ah-ha" moments that made a concept or idea come to life.

What bores you?

Amherst: Students playing the college application process too safely . . . it's refreshing to see a kid being himself or herself—you don't have to climb Mount Kenya. . .as long as it's sincere.

Bucknell: How an essay is written can be boring. Think of the best teachers who can make any topic interesting. The word essay derives from the French *essayer*, "to try," so try to teach us something about yourself. A college essay needs to be unique. Tell us things about yourself that only you could say, without using too many of those thesaurus-type words that we do not use in everyday conversation. Even when writing about a common topic, present it from your own perspective with descriptions of your own reactions and perceptions, the setting, the circumstances, and so forth. Imagine yourself as an admissions officer who may have read 40 other essays that day. How will your essay stand out to keep our attention?

Cooper Union: Reading about *The Catcher in the Rye*, Holden Caulfield, *The Great Gatsby*, or Ayn Rand's *The Fountainhead*.

Deep Springs: Essays that amount to a list of activities or achievements.

Macalester: Indirect, misleading, or meandering writing.

Northwestern: The class trip to Europe. We don't tend to have repetitive stuff since we change questions.

Olin: It's always very clear when students are writing things they think we (the readers) want to hear about. Stay away from canned responses.

UNC: Essays that don't have a voice.

UVA: The standard five-paragraph essay that does not let a voice come through.

Wake Forest: The passive voice. Colloquial writing. Run-on sentences. Essays that read like book reports. Attempts to mask bad writing by being cute and clever. School essays that are reworked to fit the college essay question.

Yale: Superficiality. There are many students who, for whatever reason, do not go beyond the superficial. They'll tell us what they've been doing [and] keep it fact-based. They don't get it to a reflective level.

What's the most ridiculous achievement you've ever seen listed on an application? What's the most ridiculous essay topic? Were these students admitted?

Bucknell: One student listed that he once held his breath for 58 seconds; there was no context to it, and I think the world record is over five minutes, so I still wonder why he listed it. I do not know that there is one most ridiculous essay topic above all others, but the writer should avoid outrageous, unsubstantiated claims. I do not remember if those students were admitted, but it probably doesn't matter how good their essay is if their high school transcript doesn't show a challenging schedule and successful results.

Cooper Union: Most ridiculous essay topic: Someone wrote about olives, the different kinds and the pleasure attained from eating them—and yes they were admitted.

Deep Springs: Domesticating a stray animal. Not admitted. Our essay questions are fairly narrow and seem to discourage people from "ridiculous" essay topics.

UVA: Listing a dramatic performance in kindergarten as evidence of interest in theater.

I don't find our essays to be ridiculous. Students often try too hard to impress us with the size of their vocabulary and if they do not really comprehend the connotations of the words they took from the thesaurus it can be comic. Some of the latter types have not been offered admission.

Which mistakes appear so often they do not count as strikes against the applicant?

Amherst: [They] do count against you. The hastily and poorly done essay is pretty close to irrevocable.

Bucknell: I do not want to say what mistakes are okay, because the writer should try [to do] the best possible work he or she can, without thinking that we will let a few particular things slide. Shoot for "A" work and, if you fall a little short, you'll still get an "A-minus." If you shoot for a "B" and fall a little short, you'll get a "B-minus." Which would you rather have?

Cooper Union: Misuse of hyphens and dashes. Writing "3" instead of "three."

Macalester: Mistakes are mistakes. When they're made, they're noticed.

UNC: Readers recognize mistakes more often than not, although they do not always count as strikes against the applicant. Spelling errors, poor essay structure, and misuse of pronoun "their" and adverb "there" are some of the more common mistakes.

UVA: As a highly selective school, we don't see all that many mistakes anymore. Grammar checks and spelling checks have helped many a student in the last few years.

Wake Forest: All mistakes count as strikes against the applicant.

What writing tips would you offer to your applicant pool?

Bucknell: The essay is your one chance to be a little creative with your application, as opposed to listing your address and birth date and enclosing letters of recommendation that you will never see, written by someone else. Have fun, make your essay lively, and let us into your head a little. Make the essay about yourself so that we learn about you, not someone else. Spell-check and grammar check, to catch variations such as its/it's, to/too/two, their/there/they're, begin/being, perfect/prefect, and now/own/won. Be concise so that we know what it is you are writing about, instead of covering multiple topics with no unity. Finally, begin early, during the summer, so you can revise your essay as needed, while you are not in the hectic time of your life known as senior year of high school.

Cooper Union: Keep it personal, do not include what is already obvious—i.e., what is stated on an activity sheet or resume, and check your spelling and grammar. If you're applying to Cooper Union, make sure to remove all of the "Carnegie Mellon's" from your essays!

Deep Springs: Style is important: be engaging, interesting, and show a certain vivacity.

Johns Hopkins: Get your pen and paper or saddle up to the word processor. Don't write as if there is a correct answer [or] be too cautious. It seems to me that we work hard to craft questions that prevent that, but we see students who are too cautious. Be adventurous intellectually—write unconventionally. Applicants have more freedom than they think, and it's in their interest to use that flexibility.

Macalester: Be yourself. Use your own voice. Own your essay rather than let someone else tell you what to write. Address any questions the admissions committee may have about your application up front. Tell your story, if you have one.

Northwestern: Answer the whole question. For example, we have a question that asks what an applicant would do with five minutes of airtime—what would they talk about and why? Kids don't answer the why part; they go on about the subject but there's no analysis, no reflection.

Olin: Simple grammar, punctuation, and spelling are important. Get multiple people to proofread your application and essays.

UNC: Writing is a process. Don't expect to write your essay in one sitting. Proofread. Let your own voice come through; this is our opportunity to get to know you.

Wake Forest: Be sure that you answer the essay question. Write clearly and concisely. Check closely for spelling, grammatical, and punctuation errors. Plan your essay well in advance.

Yale: [To] try to be as honest and open about themselves as they can be. We are trying as hard as we can to get a feeling for who this person is. The pieces of paper really do represent them pretty well. And students control a piece of that through their student essays.

Who should edit a student's essay?

Amherst: Parents are awful, friends are awful, and people who advise kids for money are awful. The best person is a teacher.

Bucknell: A student should always find someone who can provide objective input. If the topic is particularly sensitive or personal, then he or she ought to seek someone trustworthy.

Cooper Union: A peer, not dad or mom—they usually have too many issues which paint the essays a terribly contrived color. A high school counselor is okay if they avoid influencing the content of the essays.

Northwestern: If you're a kid whose mom might be an English teacher, ask her. Or ask your best friend or sibling. [It's] always a good idea to have someone else read to see if your essay sounds like you.

Olin: The more people who help proof an essay and application, the better. Teachers, counselors, and parents can all provide great advice and editing tips. It is important to note that getting advice on a draft is different than getting content from others.

Students should ask those closest to them—friends, family, teachers, etc.—if the text of the essay truly expresses who they are; your personality should shine through.

UNC: Students should first edit their own essays. Word processing programs have built-in editing features (e.g., spell-check) to help facilitate this process. Students should then have another person review their essay. Whether a friend, parent, teacher, or guidance counselor, that person should never re-write the essay; their role should be minimal and should never edit out the student's voice.

UVA: A student should read [his or her] essay aloud to a friend. I think that others should read it too, but they should ask questions rather than rewrite the essay.

Wake Forest: Only the student should be involved in writing and editing the essay. The essay is used by the admissions committee to judge the applicant—not her English teacher, mother, or friend; thus it should be the exclusive work of the applicant.

Yale: These are essays that they need to write. Not their mother or their guidance counselor or a website. I think it's perfectly all right for a parent or friend to read the essay, but they shouldn't do it with a red pen in hand.

What grammatical mistakes make you cringe? What do you dislike, content-wise?

Amherst: Cutesy stuff. I look for sincerity. The ability to think abstractly produces the best essays, frankly; balancing experience and talking vividly about an experience that transpired.

A not-funny kid trying to be funny. The heavy hand of some college consultant.

Bucknell: Misuse of commas and semicolons are particularly tiresome. Also, fragments and run-on sentences do not make good lasting impressions.

Cooper Union: I love when a kid writes, "Coopers Union."

Deep Springs: All grammatical mistakes, especially the possessive form. What we dislike content-wise coincides fairly well with what bores us—a list of activities, an unreflective retelling of an incident.

Johns Hopkins: There are two things that I see regularly, two lines that are crossed.

(1) Ideological issues are best left aside. An applicant who gets too much into specific political issues just might be thrusting these views on someone who disagrees, and then [the reader] has to work at remaining objective. We train our staff to take students on their own terms, but we're all human. I don't see why an applicant would test the waters.

(2) Sometimes students come across as immature. Showing a sense of humor is great, but don't use humor in your college application that you wouldn't use with your parents!

Macalester: Misspellings, poor grammar, and typographical errors really get in the way of reading an essay, so attention to detail is important.

Northwestern: Swear words.

Olin: Simple spelling and punctuation errors show a lack of attention to detail and can send the message to application readers that you are not serious about acceptance to our institution or that your application was thrown together [at the] last minute. Take the right amount time to prepare your application and essays.

UVA: It depends on the student. A student who is not a native speaker may have problems with articles, for example, but that isn't surprising, or worth cringing about. A student who has all the top scores and all the best opportunities in the world who makes careless mistakes often makes me think that he or she does not really want to come to UVA.

All readers have inherent likes and dislikes. It might be that one reader will respond to a topic much differently than another: *De gustibus non est disputandum.* For example, some readers will see the inclusion of a Latin tag as pretentious; others will see it as an erudite addition.

Wake Forest: Incorrect use of its/it's, there/their/they're, your/you're, whose/who's, and his/her/their are the most personally bothersome.

Yale: Forced creativity, forced humor, or self-consciously trying to be different. By itself, is that going to keep somebody out? No. But it doesn't help their cause.

If a topic feels forced, they just need to put that pencil down. Students ask themselves, What does that college want to hear? And we keep telling kids that you're 180 degrees in the wrong direction if you're asking yourself that question. They do need to sit in the driver's seat and ask, What should this school know about me?

This is not the time to be particularly shy; on the other hand, you don't want to go at it with a great deal of braggadocio. You don't want to start every paragraph with the letter *I*. They should be asking themselves, What kind of essay is going to get them close to what I'm like?

How is your admissions decision affected by a perspective or opinion (expressed by an applicant in his or her essay) with which you categorically disagree? What happens if you find the content offensive?

Amherst: Can't do that. . .God awful, politically, you can't do it.

Bucknell: As admissions counselors we cannot afford to allow our personal, political or religious beliefs affect any admissions decision. The essay is examined for structure, grammar, and, of course, content, but the strength of the argument, the insights into the values of the applicant, and his or her personal qualities are what we are trying to assess. Differing values from our own cannot dictate the process, and, in some instances, could be viewed as a positive factor in evaluating each applicant from the perspective of encouraging diversity and opinions that do not necessarily reflect the majority. That's not to say that the Admissions Committee has not debated the decisions for students whose essays contained racist, misogynistic, or other distasteful views—on the contrary, we look long and hard at those students who would otherwise be easily admissible by their academic numbers when we encounter essays of such a nature. Those debates are healthy in that they allow us to examine our own priorities in making decisions and what is most important in shaping the current class.

Cooper Union: Again, the best we can do is attempt to be objective. Can I guarantee this? No. But we try our hardest.

Deep Springs: We strive to discount such considerations, so long as the opinion is thought through. Content that is truly offensive, rather than merely disagreeable, is rarely thought through.

Macalester: Students generally aren't admitted or denied by colleges based on the opinions they hold unless those opinions are so extreme as to disrupt the campus community. We don't think of our applicants as being certain types—instead, they're individuals and we read their applications as such.

UNC: [An] admissions decision [is] not affected by the perspectives or opinions expressed by the applicant in an essay.

UVA: If a student writes well on any topic then he or she will be rewarded in the process.

Could a student write well about an offensive topic? Should free speech extend to admission essays? Maybe these are topics worth thinking and writing about. Is political correctness a part of the admission process? Frankly, I think the answers will vary from school to school and reader to reader.

Wake Forest: We seek curious students with open minds who are eager to explore and debate issues.

Close-mindedness or demonstrations of racism, sexism, or disrespect in essays can result in a denial of admission.

INSIDE THE ADMISSIONS OFFICE

What work experience is required of people who review applications? Are there any particular qualities you look for in a reader?

Amherst: Full-time admissions officer.

Bucknell: While there is no particular work experience that is required of our admissions committee, they are all trained to be insightful and careful readers.

Cooper Union: All readers are either full-time admissions counselors or faculty who are members of an admissions committee.

Deep Springs: We look for prudence and judgment that can evaluate many aspects of a student, rather than just intellect. Readers are chosen from the student body as well as the wider Deep Springs community.

Northwestern: Our part-time readers tend to be retired high school guidance counselors or doctoral students.

UNC: Most people who review applications have extensive experience in undergraduate admissions. We also hire part-time readers who have varied backgrounds in the field of education (e.g., teachers, administrators, etc.). Readers must be able to make decisions, support their decisions with solid arguments, and debate their decisions with others who disagree.

UVA: We require no particular work experience. Our readers typically have experience in writing of one kind or another.

Wake Forest: At Wake Forest, our readers are admissions officers who are also almost without exception alumni of the university. In hiring admissions staff members, academic achievements [and] communication skills are important factors. To be an admissions officer, and thus an application reader at Wake Forest, one must be a reader, a thinker, and one who is comfortable in the academic world.

Do you use an academic or other index initially to sort applications into "probably," "maybe," and "long shot" piles? If not, how do you complete your initial sorting?

Bucknell: For applicants whose credentials fall in the extreme ranges of our pool, a sorting process is employed to identify the strongest group and weakest group.

Cooper Union: For sure.

Olin: We read every application and take into consideration both academic and personal qualities while ranking students. No application is denied or accepted until at least two people have reviewed it and the application reading team has discussed the candidate's likelihood of succeeding academically and socially at Olin College.

UNC: We do not use an index to sort applications. Each application receives the same review by multiple readers.

UVA: We read holistically. We do not have indexes of any sort. We read one at a time, then make a case for offer, wait list, or deny.

Do you have an overall mission statement that guides you when looking at essays and applications?

Bucknell: Our goal is to admit the best-qualified and diverse (geographic, socioeconomic, racial, ethnic, religious, and sexual orientation) class in order to build a rich and vibrant community at Bucknell.

Colgate: In our admission process we strive to find the best possible students who will contribute to academic life at Colgate as well as enhance the campus community. Students who are successful in the admission process have shown an ability to respond to challenges, develop their own ideas, use their imagination, and challenge themselves in and out of the classroom. As a result our admission staff looks for excellence in all areas; however, a strong academic record is absolutely essential.

Personal essays are an opportunity for students to showcase their unique writing talents and add depth to their application. Use this opportunity to say something new about yourself. Essays should complete the profile we gain from your grades, scores, recommendations, and talents. The quality of your writing is, of course, important, but the essay should tell a story about you. Despite that we receive 8,000 applications and approximately 16,000 essays, your application essays allow you to demonstrate your ability to synthesize an original thought and articulate it in a meaningful and compelling way.

Cooper Union: We want to have all readers search for the student who would add to our intellectual community. I hope, in a perfect world, each reader can leave his or her personal feelings about an issue aside.

Deep Springs: Yes, that given by the college as a whole.

Macalester: No.

Olin: We are looking for people who are a good match with Olin's unique, hands-on curriculum and are energized about joining a community of people who want to build a college. [Good candidates are] willing to take risks, enjoy studying in a rigorous engineering program, and have an entrepreneurial spirit.

UNC: Admissions representatives are trained extensively; we use specific criteria to evaluate essays as well as other aspects of the application.

UVA: No.

Wake Forest: The nature and historical character of Wake Forest guides us in selection of the class. We seek students who are intellectually adept; have challenged themselves with a strenuous curriculum; enjoy academic rigor; and exhibit exemplary character, social conscience, and intellectual curiosity.

Does your office read every application it receives?

Amherst: Yes, at least twice.

Bucknell: Yes. Every complete application that we receive is read by an admissions counselor.

Cooper Union: Yes.

Deep Springs: Every application sent to us is read in its entirety by several readers.

Macalester: Yes—absolutely!

Northwestern: Yes, more than once. Every application is read twice.

Olin: Always.

UNC: Yes. Every application we receive is read by at least two readers.

UVA: We read every application.

Wake Forest: Absolutely. All applications have multiple readers.

Yale: We read all of every folder. . .every word of every essay.

How much time do you spend reading each essay/application?

Amherst: Three to 10 minutes on each essay.

Bucknell: For the Class of 2009, we received over 8,300 applications. The time required to read each application varies, depending on the content and volume of information that the applicant submits. The time devoted to reading the essay depends on its length and context. In addition, pertinent information from the essay may be highlighted and noted for consideration.

Deep Springs: As our application process consists of two parts, it is impossible to answer in general. For those who complete the entire application, each of 11 readers [will] spend approximately one-and-a-half hours on [their] application. [This] doesn't include time spent on the interviews.

Johns Hopkins: Essays can receive anything from 1 to 15 minutes of attention.

Macalester: I average 20 to 30 minutes per file.

Northwestern: We spend 10 to 15 minutes on each, with a recommended length of 500 words.

Olin: We receive nearly 600 applications. Each application is read by two members of an application reading team, which consists of an admission office staffer, a faculty member, and one or two (trained) college staff members. On average we spend about 20 to 30 minutes reading each application and then each application reading team spends an average of 10 to 15 minutes discussing each candidate.

UNC: We receive approximately 18,500 applications a year. On average, each reading of each application takes between 5 and 10 minutes.

UVA: We get about 16,000 applications for first year admission and 2,100 for transfer admission. Some applications read very quickly: valedictorian, 1600 (now 2400) SAT, top recommendations, strong involvement in school, cogent essays. At the opposite end, we can read a student who has low grades, a weak program and testing, and modest recommendations and essays very quickly too.

We spend more time on the close cases or the cases that have special issues of one kind or another (foreign transcripts for example).

Wake Forest: [It] varies with each application.

Yale: Some of them take about an hour; some of them take six minutes. I'd say a seasoned admissions officer needs to be moving through three applications an hour. We want to use our reading time where it's really valuable. And if it's clear by one reading that this is not going to be someone who's strong enough to get in, then we don't want to waste the time.

On average, how many people on your staff review applications? How many essays does a typical staff member read?

Amherst: Eleven thousand total essays [between] 13 staff members. We read regionally—i.e., an Iowa applicant is read by the Iowa admissions officer. . . . A difference of opinion results in a third or fourth read.

Bucknell: For the Class of 2009, 13 admissions counselors read applications. Each counselor reads the essay for each completed application they are reviewing. The number of applications that each counselor reads varies, but, in general, our goal is to read a minimum of 40 applications per day.

Cooper Union: Three admissions counselors and as many as 30 faculty members. The number of essays read depends on the program the student applies to—some of our programs require 15 essays. Multiply that by 800 applications and you get 12,000!

Deep Springs: Each final application is reviewed by 11 people. Each of them reads 40 to 60 applications.

Johns Hopkins: Eleven staff members. We read each essay twice. Last year we had a 9,000-student applicant pool.

Macalester: Eight staff members read applications. We require two essays from each applicant. I suppose I read about 2,500 essays during the review period, perhaps more if all committee discussion cases are included. Each application is read by a minimum of two or three readers; some are read by many more.

Northwestern: Sixteen full-time and some part-time readers [read] 1,500 to 2,000 [total applications].

Olin: Of the 100 faculty and staff members at Olin College, approximately 50 assisted with the admission process, which includes reading applications, serving on the admission application committee, meeting/interviewing students at Candidates' Weekends, and making recommendations to the admission committee.

UNC: Approximately 25 people on staff review applications. Each person reads over 1,000 essays each year.

UVA: Minimum: two. Maximum: the entire committee (16).

If we just include the longer essay question (we have short answer questions too), most read about 800.

Wake Forest: Nine [staff members each read] about 3,500 per year.

Yale: Our office has about 20 staff members. Every application will be read minimally by one person. And most applications get a second reading. And then there are some that get another one. This year we got over 15,000 applications . . . so that's about 31,000 essays.

How many applications, generally speaking, go to the committee each year?

Bucknell: At Bucknell University, the only applications that go before a "committee" of admissions officers are those that are received under the Early Decision policy. In total, this can range from 600 to 800 applications. In the Regular Decision process, applications are read by different staff members based on the student's intended major with the final approval made by the Dean of Admissions.

Cooper Union: About one-half of the initial pool.

Deep Springs: One hundred fifty to 200 (all received are read by committee).

Johns Hopkins: After the second read, it's done.

Macalester: Roughly 25 to 35 percent of our applicant pool.

Northwestern: There's no committee. We have over 14,000 applications; the third reader makes the final decision.

Olin: Approximately 200 for the 160 Candidates' Weekend slots.

UNC: Several thousand applications go to the committee each year.

UVA: A very small percentage.

If you have not already explained, what is the process that each application undergoes, from receipt to decision? How many hands does it pass through on the way?

Bucknell: The application review process is hands-on, personal, and comprehensive. Each application is placed in a folder. The application profile sheet outlining vital information about the candidate is produced to assist professional staff in the review process. The staff assigns admission rating codes to each candidate, categorizing them into either the top admit, admit, waitlist, or deny group.

Each application is reviewed by two to four staff members. It is common for some applications to be reviewed more than three times. Admission is based on competitiveness—the credentials of each applicant are compared to the overall quality of the applicant pool. The staff is interested in learning how the applicant has challenged him- or herself in high school (has he or she has taken advanced courses?). Strong performance (A and B grades) along with class rank (if available) are very important. SAT or ACT test scores are considered after the transcripts where the best possible score or combination of scores is used. After accounting for quantitative factors, potential contribution to the BU community, essay, recommendations, and other personal qualities are also considered. The staff may consider financial need as a qualifying factor in the later stages of the review process, but this process affects fewer than two percent of the applicant pool.

After a decision on an applicant is made and the decision letter has been prepared, the Dean of Admissions performs a final review prior to signing the letter.

Cooper Union: As long as the application is complete, meaning the student has submitted all of the necessary documentation—i.e., transcripts, standardized exam scores, portfolio, etc., the application is read. It can actually pass through as many as ten hands. If we're really overworked, sometimes we close our eyes and randomly pick (just kidding, of course).

Deep Springs: Each application is assigned between six and nine initial readers. We then gather around a table and deliberate over each applicant. Through successive series of deliberation, votes, and additional readers, we narrow the pool down to 40. These 40 applicants are then asked to submit four new essays and visit for an interview. All 11 members of the committee read each application. We then deliberate to come up with a final list of 13 applicants.

UNC: Applications received on-line are printed, labeled, and filed. Application materials (e.g., letters of recommendation, transcripts, etc.) are added to the application file upon receipt. Once an application is complete, the file is reviewed by multiple readers. When consensus is reached regarding the admissions decision, applications are re-filed and the decision is logged into the database. An application might pass through the hands of between three and eight people.

UVA: The application goes to a reader who makes a preliminary evaluation. It then goes on to a second reader. If it is a clear case then the decision is likely finished. After going through our applicant pool, we pull out the close cases for additional review. Usually two readers are involved with a subset of cases. In some instances, additional reads occur due to special talents (the arts), special scholars programs, or the desire to recruit under-represented minorities, students of low economic means, etc.

THE ESSAY'S INFLUENCE

Can an essay move an application from the "maybe" pile to the "probably" pile? From the "maybe" pile to the "long-shot" pile?

Bucknell: It is rare that an essay will have such an impact that it affects the application decision. However, all application essays are reviewed for both content as well as grammar. A poorly written essay can adversely affect an applicant's candidacy. However, if a student does not meet the quantitative qualifications, then the essay cannot positively affect [his or her] admission decision. There are also instances where a truly outstanding essay may push a student over the top in the final decision process.

Deep Springs: Yes, essays are essential, and the discussion of essays during committee routinely changes an applicant's standing.

Olin: If an essay is poorly written, does not address the assigned topic, or includes inappropriate content, it is unlikely the applicant will be considered for admission. Taking risks to set yourself apart from the rest of the applicant pool is fine as long as the essay is not irrelevant or erroneous. By taking applicable and calculated risks the student demonstrates their maturity and the confidence to be themselves.

UVA: A[n] essay can have significant impact on the decision.

Wake Forest: [An] essay can tip the scales in an admission or a denial. It is a very important factor in our process.

If you have an applicant with lower numbers but a great essay, what do you do?

Bucknell: If a student is not competitive in the admissions process based on the quantitative factors, a great essay [will] not affect [our] decision enough to lead to an offer of admission.

Cooper Union: If the student is in the ballpark—either talent-wise or academically speaking, then the essay can make a difference. Otherwise, an essay cannot makeup for a deficiency in an area necessary for academic survival. If an engineering student fails math throughout high school, there is no essay that can change that fact and prepare the kid for an engineering education.

Deep Springs: It is very rare for an applicant to have outstanding essays but disastrous test scores, so I can't speak to that aspect of the question. As to a low GPA, we would take it into account when deciding whether an applicant would take advantage of the intellectual atmosphere at Deep Springs. Good essays can help us with this decision by reflecting on the applicant's poor academic performance and addressing how it would affect his potential time here.

Macalester: We read the rest of the application and make a decision based on everything, not on individual parts.

Northwestern: We'd have to look at everything. Grades are most important. It's rare that a good essay would overcome bad grades.

Olin: We look for students who are able to meet a high academic standard and can provide solid teacher and counselor recommendations as well as finely written essays. If the teacher or counselor recommendation includes reasoning for poor academic performance during a particular year or semester (i.e., student illness, family problem, etc.), then a few poor grades can be "excused." However, a few poor grades must be accompanied by high test scores, a "rebound" in academic performance, and excellent recommendations and essays. We are looking to admit students who can succeed academically in a rigorous engineering program so excellent grades in math and science are a must.

UNC: An essay alone cannot make or break an admissions decision. The quality of the essay is always considered in combination with other information about the applicant.

UVA: A great essay in and of itself will not get a student in. Typically, great essays are accompanied by other evidence of success such as recommendations from English teachers.

The reality of selective admission is that most students who are offered admission are strong in most categories.

Wake Forest: If a student is unqualified academically, a great essay will not make the difference, but it certainly helps differentiate among similarly qualified students. Essays may also reveal diversity of thought, experience, or talents that are desirable in the class and may not show up elsewhere in the application.

If an essay is unimpressive but the student's grades are great, what then? Is it possible for an essay to change your mind about a candidate?

Bucknell: A strong candidate based on the quantitative factors who submits an unimpressive essay will likely still be admitted, assuming the essay was unimpressive due to content. If the essay is poorly written with some clear grammatical errors, it may cause enough concern to keep a student from being admitted.

Cooper Union: We will certainly deny admission to an applicant who has stellar grades and scores yet didn't bother to work on his or her essays.

Deep Springs: The quality of the essays most certainly outweighs test scores and GPA. It could be said that the essays initially determine what we think and SAT and test scores serve only to refine or change that initial determination.

Macalester: Then the student may not be admitted.

UVA: Yes, but there are certainly gradations of unimpressive essays. It is a holistic evaluation and not a formula.

Wake Forest: Poorly written essays submitted by academically sound students suggest a lack of interest in the University which may result in a denial of admission.

Yale: There's nothing so stellar about academic credentials that'll convince us to take [a student] without looking at the rest [of his or her application]. The transcript is certainly the single most important document. And the recommendations are very important.

You know, we admit students who write flat essays and we reject students who write great essays. At a place like Yale, there just aren't that many kids who are so powerful that we have to take them. At many other institutions, you might not have the privilege of turning down a really strong student based on the tone of an essay. Here, we can do it.

Are there essays that make you unable to turn down applicants? What are such essays like?

Amherst: [They are] real, intellectually. One particular student had the combination of a great essay and a reading list, which overcame a good but not great record; in this case the essay might outweigh other factors—these are the [top] 10 percent.

Bucknell: There are essays that are very compelling, often written about a personal hardship or family tragedy that really draws the reader into the story. Yet if the academic record suggests that the student will be unable to do the work here, that must drive the final decision.

Cooper Union: No.

Deep Springs: A single essay isn't capable of clinching acceptance. An attitude/capacity that seems to sustain itself through all of the required essays is necessary.

Johns Hopkins: There are essays that are compelling, that make the difference. So students should know that essays should be taken seriously. If a student puts effort into the essays, they should help his or her chances.

The remarkable thing about essays is that there's no ceiling on quality, unlike SAT scores or GPAs. A great essay can carry a student. A poorly done essay might do the opposite. It can certainly determine the initial path an application takes through the process.

Macalester: No.

Olin: By itself an essay will never make or break our admission decision, but a good essay can add increased validity to an "on the fence" candidate.

UNC: An essay alone cannot make or break an admissions decision. The quality of the essay is always considered in combination with other information about the applicant.

UVA: The one-in-a-thousand essay does exist but there is no formula for what it must be like. Usually, it is so jaw-droppingly original and smart that we just can't say no.

Wake Forest: The essay alone cannot guarantee admission, but it if it reveals a depth—a strength of character, or if it demonstrates a strong academic focus or diverse perspective that we seek in the class, [it] may indeed tip the scales.

GENERAL APPLICATION QUESTIONS

Is anything on the application really "optional"?

Bucknell: Most "optional" items are of a sensitive nature and, ordinarily or legally, cannot be requested of the student. Our attempt to collect such information is the result of our commitment to admitting the most diverse and talented class that we can. No student's candidacy is weakened by his or her decision to not answer an optional question, but there are instances where responses can enhance an already attractive and academically solid application. All students who are admitted to Bucknell, whether athletes, students of color, legacies, first generation, etc., must be academically qualified before other considerations are given.

Cooper Union: We don't have any "optional" sections.

Deep Springs: Yes. One possible exception is the "supplemental material" option in our second-round application. If an applicant really emphasizes an artistic ability, it is nice to have a demonstration.

Macalester: Of course—all the stuff that's labeled "optional." For Macalester, that would include SAT Subject Test results; additional submissions, such as an art portfolio; additional teacher or coach recommendations; and several questions on the application form.

Northwestern: Interviews are not required; one teacher recommendation is enough but send a second teacher recommendation.

Olin: Yes, optional means optional.

UNC: Items marked "optional" are truly optional. If a candidate chooses not to complete an optional part of the application, his or her candidacy will not be impacted.

UVA: I encourage students to take the chance to tell us about themselves outside the numbers. If we did have an optional essay I would likely encourage [them] to use it (our essays are mandatory).

If a student does not complete a part of our application we require, he or she will not be admitted.

Wake Forest: With the exception of a question concerning ethnicity, we do not have optional questions. A student would not be penalized for failing to answer that question.

How much extra material should students send? Which materials are helpful?

Bucknell: We routinely get a lot of extra material with applications—additional recommendations, writing samples, certificates of achievement, artwork, CDs of dance/music/theatrical performances and, given the pace at which we must read applications, those materials are given cursory glances at best. The admissions counselors with whom I'm most familiar are neither art nor music critics and thus are not qualified to judge or evaluate such submissions. We do seek input from faculty in Art and Music on many of the materials submitted. Their reaction can add [to] a candidate's [chances] if the rating is very strong. Additional materials to what's requested in the application that would be most meaningful in our process would be evidence of research outside of the classroom, service learning opportunities, extraordinary leadership experiences, [and the] founding of clubs or other organizations [at] school or [in the] community. An extra writing sample or recommendation would be considered, but several would be too much of a time commitment for a harried and hurried counselor.

Colgate: Some applicants provide supplementary material for review by our admission staff. If a student feels the extra submission is important enough to send, it is considered important enough for us to evaluate. While our admission process is still primarily based on a student's academic preparation, many students send supplementary information as a means to showcase a particular talent that is not already reflected in the application. A large volume of supplementary materials will not necessarily impact the admission decision (more is not necessarily better), but a carefully prepared art submission, music demo, athletic tape, creative writing example, or other submission can assist our staff as we shape our class to reflect the talents and diversity of our applicant pool. Many supplementary materials are sent to various departments on campus for evaluation. Faculty and staff in the Music, Art, and Athletics departments provide their feedback on applicants' abilities.

Cooper Union: We give guidelines regarding the submission of extra material. If a student wants us to hear them playing in the school orchestra, one or two CDs is plenty—we don't need fifty songs.

Deep Springs: There is a supplemental material option as part of the second-round application. Artwork is helpful. Anything requiring more than 15 to 20 minutes to consider is difficult to handle.

Macalester: They should send only what will reasonably tell us their story. We welcome anything that will add a new dimension and help to inform us about the applicant's values, beliefs, experiences, talents, and aspirations. But they only need to tell us once . . . we don't admit students based on the gross weight of their application files.

Northwestern: Some will go overboard on the length of an essay. We're happy to receive extra material, but not videos or CDs. We have six undergraduate schools, so students may send playbills for drama, editorial clips for the journalism school, etc. There is no need for extra essays.

Olin: Students often send artwork, CDs of their music, and other items of which they are particularly proud that are not reflected in the standard application. Coupled with the application, this helps the application reading team get a better sense of the student.

UNC: Some applicants do send extra material with their application. While we do not require or necessarily encourage them to do so, students may choose to include materials (e.g., artwork, photography, music recordings, etc.) they feel will strengthen their application.

UVA: We ask students to send CDs, tapes, DVDs, slides, etc., if they believe they have talent in the arts. They are evaluated by our arts faculty. I encourage students doing an extended essay in the IB program to send a brief summary of the topic (not the whole essay).

Certificates that extend back to kindergarten are not useful.

Wake Forest: In general, additional materials are not helpful in the process. Concentrate on completing the application properly and thoroughly, rather than adding extraneous materials.

Yale: We don't encourage students to send in other writing. But we'll read it.

Do you have a descending degree of importance that you assign the different application requirements? Is the SAT score, for example, the most important factor in your admissions decisions? Where does the essay fall?

Bucknell: Bucknell does not have a descending degree of importance for application requirements. We feel that the three main components of an application would be academic record, test scores, and personal qualities. The essay portion of the application falls under two of the three. An applicant's writing abilities are a testament to [his or her] academic abilities and the personality and style of an essay demonstrate the personal qualities of the writer.

Cooper Union: Certainly. Again, the essays become a factor which ultimately decides admission if the application is complete and the student is, academically or talent-wise, in the ballpark.

Deep Springs: There is no formal standard, but the essays are probably of first importance and the interview of second. Everything else is below these.

UNC: We do not assign a degree of importance to different admission requirements. Each requirement could play a greater or lesser role in each admissions decision, depending on the specific applicant and the combination of requirements taken as a whole.

UVA: We have no formula but SAT is absolutely not the most important factor. Performance and academic program together are the most import criteria.

Wake Forest: No. We look at the application as a total package.

Do you prefer to see students declare a major or apply undecided?

Bucknell: Bucknell's pool of applications is read according to the major to [which] a student is applying. An application is evaluated for a specific area of interest which is necessary at Bucknell due to our diverse offerings of academic pursuits; what makes an applicant a competitive electrical engineer is not always what makes an applicant a competitive musician. If a student does not have a major they wish to pursue, then they may apply undecided to the School of Arts and Science or undecided to the School of Engineering.

Cooper Union: We do not have "undecided" at Cooper Union.

Macalester: It doesn't matter. We like both undecided and committed students on the Macalester campus.

Olin: It is not necessary to declare a major when applying to Olin College. Students do not declare a major until the sophomore year.

UNC: We have no preference.

UVA: No preference, but if a student has a passion in an academic area they should prove it via activities, recommendations, and essays.

Wake Forest: All of our students spend their first two years [here] in a liberal arts curriculum before declaring a major, so neither is preferable to us in the admissions process.

Do you prefer to receive application materials online or in paper format?

Amherst: No preference.

Bucknell: We have no preference as to how we receive an application. Approximately half our applications arrive in the mail and the other half are submitted online.

Cooper Union: Either, though our support staff (data entry) certainly have an opinion here.

Deep Springs: Paper only.

Johns Hopkins: Easier to process online; however, no strong preference.

Macalester: Either is fine—no preference. As long as the handwriting is legible and we get the information we seek, there's nothing wrong with a paper application.

Northwestern: Whichever way students prefer.

Olin: We prefer to receive materials online.

UNC: We have no preference.

UVA: Online.

Wake Forest: We do not differentiate.

Yale: We probably do prefer to get applications online.

How do you feel when you find out a student will be deferring admission after acceptance?

Amherst: I think it's great, everyone should do it. . .get off the treadmill for a while and do it.

Bucknell: In one sense, it is certainly a disappointment when a student we are excited about has decided to join our community a little bit later. Many of our deferring students are pursuing interesting and engaging opportunities during this absence. Keeping this in mind, it is very exciting to hear that they are still challenging themselves and taking advantage of opportunities to develop themselves academically, socially, and personally.

Cooper Union: Indifferent; it can be interesting if the student is actually going to do something sexy like travel to Brazil to study art or live in Tibet and study meditation.

Deep Springs: Not permitted here.

Johns Hopkins: It's good—it shows a person that thinks for himself. The usual direction of the river is: senior year, during the summer go to the beach, then go to college. We welcome students who defer, who have something else in mind.

Macalester: Deferrals are approved only if the admissions committee feels the student has a good plan for spending the year off in a worthwhile way. Students must write to request deferral after being admitted. When they're approved, I'm happy for them because I know their experience will be a good one.

Northwestern: We have 30 to 40 students a year defer admission. We're happy to say yes to that.

Olin: As long as the student is doing something meaningful with their deferred year, we are happy to support their endeavors.

UNC: An applicant who has been offered admission may request a deferral for one academic year in order to work, travel, or pursue some other extraordinary opportunity. An admitted applicant may also seek a one-year deferral for military service, required religious observance, or medical reasons. Those wishing to defer admission must request permission in writing from the Director of Admissions no later than July 1 of the year for which they [were] originally admitted.

UVA: I personally wish more students would consider a gap year, but our office policy is value neutral on the issue.

Wake Forest: As a matter of policy, we do not offer automatic deferrals. A student would be required to re-apply for later admission.

What steps do you take to recognize and prevent plagiarism?

Bucknell: It is important for counselors to be aware of the many deviant opportunities for students to falsify their application and this includes plagiarism of the required essays. As professionals we have made relationships with counselors and other admissions colleagues who are a resource to discuss suspicious-looking/sounding essays. As an office, we try to retrain ourselves every season to recognize essays and topics that are questionable. By providing a thorough read of the essay, we are often able to pick out and investigate suspected instances of plagiarism. We often will evaluate these matters collectively and, if needed, call upon experts on our faculty.

Colgate: Colgate University has an honor code by which all current students are expected to abide. Students who apply to Colgate University must provide a hand-written signature (online signatures are not accepted) indicating that all of the information in their application is accurate and factual. Just as violations of the honor code are taken seriously by our campus community, students who violate the application agreement statement will normally be immediately disqualified from further consideration in the admission process. More importantly, applicants who plagiarize miss an important opportunity to give an accurate and sincere portrayal of their abilities and talents.

Cooper Union: In-house, our faculty use technology. Application-wise it's hard to predict, though we've contemplated requesting the submission of a graded paper from high school to at the very least have [a secondary] source when evaluating an application.

Deep Springs: We discuss the essays with the student in the final interview.

Northwestern: We're so specific in the questions we ask, and we change them every year, so we think plagiarism isn't really an issue. We ask our applicants to suggest questions for the following year's essays and those are used in upcoming years.

UNC: When submitting an application, students are required to sign a statement agreeing to uphold the Honor Code. The Honor Code specifically prohibits lying, cheating, stealing, [or] any conduct that impairs significantly the welfare or educational opportunities of others in the university community.

UVA: If I told you that then students would figure a way around it.

Yale: We do cruise those websites. We did find a copied essay this year and we removed that kid's application.

What kind of book would you recommend to students about to write their college essays? What would be most helpful for students in terms of preparation?

Bucknell: We think there are many valuable guides to the college admissions process and essay writing in print, but would prefer not to recommend any one item.

Cooper Union: Never forget the usefulness of the old-fashioned dictionary and thesaurus. The MLA Handbook can help as well.

Johns Hopkins: I would give them examples of good writing. Just as a composer wouldn't deny borrowing themes from predecessors, it's appropriate to learn from the work of good writers. In terms of technique for writing a good college essay, I'd look at the short story as a model.

Macalester: I don't recommend essay books for students. The end result of reading any such book is that essays all start to sound alike—i.e., they're not the only people reading those books. Students' essays should be individual works of their own creation. What works for one person doesn't necessarily work for another.

Northwestern: The best preparation for essays is writing in high school.

UVA: Students should read great writers and then write as much as they can. Reading essays by Guy Davenport, William Gass, Stephen Jay Gould, Joan Didion, Anne Carson, or Slavoj Zizek (to name just a few that I turn to for inspiration), might help.

I think the question you ask indicates what I see as the problem itself. Students are looking for a formulaic way to write well. It doesn't work that way. Someone can read books about improving any skill (skiing, bricklaying, podcasting), but it's quite a bit different when you actually have to do it. Practice never makes perfect, but it does make. Writing is a craft of making things with words.

Wake Forest: Writing, punctuation, and grammar guides such as *Strunk and White's Elements of Style.*

If you had the option of doing away with the essay requirement altogether, would you?

Amherst: No. . .the more measures you add to the way that you evaluate, the more predicted value you have.

Bucknell: No, it is important for students to be able to express themselves through an essay for various reasons. The essay allows students to disclose information not asked of them in another portion of the application [and] introduce and/or expand on interesting aspects of themselves. It allows us to see how well they can communicate through the written word.

Colgate: The application review process is highly personal; the admission staff takes the time to review each item in a student's folder, reflecting the kind of individual attention students can expect from Colgate faculty. The essay is a valuable means for our staff to gain a better understanding of the qualitative aspects of an applicant, rather than just the quantitative academic measures (GPA, curriculum, standardized testing, rank in class, etc.). As the interviews we offer are non-evaluative and not considered in the admission process, the essay also allows applicants to show us their personalities, discuss their interests and priorities, and demonstrate the quality of their writing abilities. We expect that essays will continue to be an important part of our admission process for years to come.

Cooper Union: Not at all. We need to get some insight into the kid's mind and experiences. We need to be able to find out something that is not apparent from reviewing his or her transcript, SAT and ACT scores, counselor recommendation, etc.

Deep Springs: Nope.

Johns Hopkins: No, we care very much about writing ability. We assess writing directly, through essay submissions, and indirectly, through the SAT Subject Test in Writing.

Macalester: No, absolutely not. It's the one chance an applicant has to speak directly to every reader of his or her application. What good would it do to eliminate that?

Northwestern: Writing is important. We always want to have writing samples.

Olin: No, the essay is the student's chance to shine and tell us about his or her passions. Coupled with the teacher and counselor recommendations, the essay really gives us a sense of the applicant's personality and fit for Olin College.

UNC: No. We do not interview applicants; the essay is our opportunity to get to know students better.

UVA: Absolutely not.

Wake Forest: Absolutely not. We have, in the past years, made our application more writing intensive rather than less as we become more selective and strive to differentiate among well-qualified applicants.

OFFICIAL DISCLAIMER!

Our editors aren't asleep on the job.

The following essays appear exactly as they did for admissions officers. We only changed the layout so that the essays fit on the pages of this book. Because we have not edited the essays, you may find errors in spelling, punctuation, and grammar. We assure you that we found these errors as well, but we thought it would be most helpful for you to see what the admissions officers saw—not what they could (or should) have seen. We recommend that you carefully proofread your own personal statement, but should you miss an error, take comfort in the fact that others (accepted applicants, even!) sometimes did too.

Part 3

THE APPLICANTS

AARON ANTRIM

Aaron played varsity tennis and violin in high school. A self-employed internet entrepreneur, he performed in three plays, two of which traveled overseas.

Stats
SAT: 1480 (790 Critical Reading, 690 Math)
High School GPA: 3.96 weighted
High School: Northcoast Preparatory and Performing Arts Academy, Arcata, CA
Hometown: Eureka, CA
Gender: Male
Race: Caucasian

Applied To
Amherst College
Bard College
Hampshire College
Harvard College
Humboldt State University
Reed College
Stanford University
Yale University

ESSAY

Aaron used the following essay in his applications to Bard, Harvard, Stanford, and Yale.

Evaluate a significant experience, achievement, risk you have taken, or ethical dilemma you have faced and its impact on you.

I didn't launch my first business, an origami store, when I was in second grade because I craved wealth; customers paid with worthless crayon money. I launched my origami store because I loved to play and discover.

At summer camp before second grade, a japanese woman taught me how to transform delicate red papers into cranes. Later, I learned to create origami stars, pinwheels, balloons, and boats by following instructions in manuals. When I showed my classmates these creations their eyes beamed with wonder. So I sold origami to my classmates with dazzling success. Operating my store influenced me more than any other learning experience in second-grade. As I grew I was haunted by an aspiration to become an entrepreneur.

This aspiration was intensified when I discovered the internet. The power of the internet is as obvious as the power of raw roaring waves in the Pacific Ocean. Like ocean waves that toss driftwood, fishes, and seaweed, information flows define reality; they incessantly re-sculpt parts of communities. Mainstream media reports, however, neglect to consider what I considered in ninth grade: that the internet might be useful in bays and coves. I thought the internet, like plazas, restaurants and city streets could be used as a gathering place in small communities like my home, Humboldt County.

An imaginative second-grade shop-keeper played with possibilities: a directory of Humboldt County websites, a trading place — free classified advertisements, a community calendar, and a restaurant guide with diner reviews. I dreamed Humscape.com (the name of my vision) would be polished and professional, dynamic and database-driven, like Yahoo. This dream seemed unattainable until I discovered and was astonished by the web-application software product ColdFusion. Before I understood ColdFusion code I signed away almost all the money in my bank account to buy ColdFusion-enabled webhost service.

My racing courage had won against reluctance to invest hard-earned money. I became an entrepreneur. For six months I plunged deeply into creating Humscape. com. I taught myself ColdFusion from online manuals.

When I launched Humscape.com I felt like an author who had published a book. I invited a television news team into my home. Newspaper headlines and T.V. blurbs incited hundreds of eMail requests for website hyperlinks to be included in the Humscape.com directory.

During my telephone and eMail correspondence with the operators of the local website CouponsOnWeb, I never told them I was fifteen until immediately before we met at the Humboldt Bay Coffee Company. The CouponsOnWeb team listened carefully to every word I spoke. When I strode out of the coffee shop's incandescent light and warm coffee aroma I felt like a self-confident adult.

Humscape.com was fabulously successful. This success cannot be documented on a ledger sheet — I did not earn the monetary profits I once aspired to earn. I earned experience and self-confidence, profits more difficult to earn, and more valuable than money.

See page 312 to find out where this student got in.

ADAM BERLINSKY-SCHINE

In high school, Adam created and maintained many advanced websites, including some at no charge for nonprofit organizations. He won several school and regional awards for computer science.

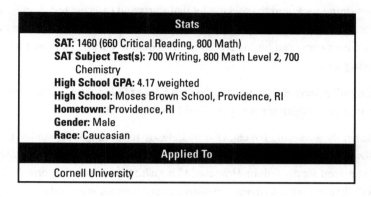

Stats
SAT: 1460 (660 Critical Reading, 800 Math)
SAT Subject Test(s): 700 Writing, 800 Math Level 2, 700 Chemistry
High School GPA: 4.17 weighted
High School: Moses Brown School, Providence, RI
Hometown: Providence, RI
Gender: Male
Race: Caucasian

Applied To
Cornell University

Please note: Adam did not disclose information about other applications.

Essay

Adam used the following essay in his application to Cornell.

> *Please write an entry from your own life journal that reports something in exquisite honesty and accuracy.*

Everyone passes that test.

Today was my long awaited driving test. I've driven the course several zillion times flawlessly in preparation for today. I was confident, but also nervous. I was already one of the last people in my class to have a driver's license; if I didn't pass today I'd have to wait another three months until I can take the test again. Worse, I'd have to be on hold at the Department of Motor Vehicles for an hour and a half like last time, when I had to reschedule my appointment because I'd be away at Cornell's summer program on the date I'd originally scheduled. But there was nothing to worry about. It would be an easy and painless ten minutes.

So there I was, sitting in the driver's seat banging my thumbs against the wheel and listening to Dad explain how the secret to success was to make sure my seatbelt was fastened *really* tightly. And red lights mean "stop."

"Sorry," was all I said, as I hit the curb leaving the parking lot where I had been awaiting the inspector. The inspector mumbled something incomprehensible, as I silently panicked. Does that mean I automatically fail? If he had said so, I would have heard it. Maybe he likes me, and is giving me a second chance. After all, he's not too scared to be in the car with me. Maybe...

All my fears were justified when we deviated from the course that I knew so well by turning back into the parking lot that starts and ends the test. Surely, he just wants me to start over and try that turn again. Fat chance. It was only then that the inspector confirmed that hitting a curb is an automatic failure, and that I had failed my driving test.

I couldn't believe it. That was the first test I'd ever failed. All I had to do was drive for ten minutes without screwing up. And I couldn't do it.

Cheerfully reentering the car, Dad was clearly relieved that he wouldn't have to share the road with me for a good three more months. The whole way home I internally yelled at myself for my failure. How could I have hit the curb on the corner that I had successfully completed so many times previously, without *ever* hitting it?

When Laura, the little brat, found out, she commenced running around the room banging into walls to demonstrate precisely how I must have crashed. I can't believe I gave her this ammunition she could use to taunt me. And so I will have to wait another three months and listen to the recording at the Department of Motor Vehicles tell me that my call is important to them and that I should please stay on the line....

See page 312 to find out where this student got in.

ALISON KAUFMANN

Alison was a National Merit Finalist and was inducted into the Cum Laude Society her junior year of high school. She spent part of the summer before her senior year in Croatia working at a camp for children who had been through the wars in the Balkans.

Stats

SAT: 1590 (800 Critical Reading, 790 Math)
SAT Subject Test(s): 680 Chemistry, 800 French
High School GPA: 4.00
High School: Marin Academy, San Rafael, CA
Hometown: Berkeley, CA
Gender: Female
Race: Caucasian

Applied To

Amherst College
Brown University
Stanford University
Swarthmore College
Wellesley College
Wesleyan University
Yale University

Essay

Alison used the following essay in each of her applications.

Evaluate a significant experience, achievement, risk you have taken, or ethical dilemma you have faced and its impact on you.

Global Children's Organization runs a camp on an island in the Adriatic for children who lived through the Bosnian civil war. Last summer I went to Croatia to be a volunteer counselor there.

The two weeks of camp were over and I was bumping along in a bus full of children en route to Sarajevo when the first glimpses of the horror that had taken place in Bosnia finally began to make the situation real. Until then, I had sympathized with a vague, history-book tragedy. Now I tried desperately to memorize the scratches on the window rather than think of my friends who lived here. I could almost smell burning. The houses crouched with mottled walls, lone chimneys stabbing skyward. This was not, could not be, someone's home.

We drove along the Sarajevo hillsides where the snipers had been and then down through the town. I kept my face toward the window as my friend Fedja pointed out the site of the first massacre, and the second, and the achingly empty hulls of brick and cement where people had once lived. Where were they now? Did they still live? Had they managed to leave or were they, like so many others who walked these streets, trapped in their city as the bombs exploded and the shells rained down?

Fedja's cousin keeps a piece of a bomb in a glass-doored cabinet, the way someone might store a china vase. It was from the time a shell fell into the dining room. When the air cleared, Fedja found his chair studded with scraps of twisted metal where he had been seated only a moment before. I would not touch the piece when they held it toward me. I did not want to touch this death, this confirmation of the horror I would have to acknowledge if I held it in my hand.

I lay in my bed that night in the reconstructed building that had been Fedja's grandmother's home, and I thought of screaming and fear and laughter and silence. I tried to remember to breathe.

At camp I had played with the children, helped them learn to swim, twirled them upside down and sat with them looking toward the sea. I had changed from an outsider who could not understand what was being said to a friend who often found no need for words. I had grown to love the feeling of being needed. I was fed by it, fed by the sense that I was making a difference and fed by the exultation that came from constantly stretching myself.

Now, in Sarajevo, I struggled to accept what had happened to this hill-cupped town. Each conversation brought another wave of denial; each added another layer to what I felt when I heard the phrase "three years under siege." As I listened to the stories, I also realized the significance of what our camp worked to achieve. It gave the children a second chance at a stolen childhood, and it gave me the opportunity to help give this gift. After seeing Sarajevo, there is nothing I would rather give.

At camp and in Sarajevo I was completely independent for the first time. I had come because I wanted to come; I wanted to feel that independence and I wanted to see a change I was helping create. I had raised the money myself. I was there without parents and without anyone I knew. The opportunities to challenge myself were everywhere — in leading activities, in forming friendships with people who knew only three words of English, in conveying to little Nino that he *still* could not swim beyond the rope . . . even though it *had* been three minutes since he last tried. I felt myself bloom in that environment, and no one else's impressions of what was possible or impossible for me could affect that.

I came back to Berkeley with photographs and memories. I have a picture from camp of 11-year-old Amra holding my guitar and pretending to play. I have memories of my three oldest boys presenting me with a seashell they found near the pier, of playing soccer in the hallways, and of singing my kids to sleep. I have the hope and the conviction that I will go back next year.

I also brought back a new level of confidence: a place within me that I have slowly been creating throughout my life and that has finally taken root. I can stand on it now, even jump, perhaps, and stretch my arms to the sky. Each day I am catching more glimpses of what I might reach.

See page 312 to find out where this student got in.

ALLISON KAY RANGEL

Allison was involved in a number of extracurricular activities, including her high school theater program, the Oregon Shakespeare Festival's Summer Seminar for High School Juniors, and an exchange trip to Japan. She was also captain of her high school's Speech and Debate team for three consecutive years and attended both the State and National Championships with her team. In addition, she completed eight AP courses, worked outside of class at a bakery and her family's farm, and was president of the Marshall Medical Junior Volunteers Association.

Stats
SAT: 1930 (750 Critical Reading, 530 Math, 650 Writing)
SAT Subject Test(s): 700 Literature, 670 U.S. History
ACT: 28
High School GPA: 3.8
High School: El Dorado High School, Placerville, CA
Hometown: Placerville, CA
Gender: Female
Race: Caucasian

Applied To
Reed College
University of California—Berkeley
University of California—Los Angeles
University of California—Santa Barbara

Essay

Allison used the following essay in her application to Reed College.

Please tell us, without word limit or subject limitation, why you want to apply to Reed College?

Why Reed?

Applications. Every single one of them seems to matter more than life itself, more than breathing and eating and my AP Statistics homework. And the stress, my God, the stress. I feel a morbid camaraderie with all those other seniors out there, all of us furiously trying to figure out *where we want to go.* It's everybody's ten million dollar question; can we really say in 500 words or less why we are qualified to attend one of the thousands of institutions that we all seem to be scrambling to get into? I'm not going to pretend that Reed is the only college I'm applying to; it is my first choice, but I'd like to think that the admissions office at Reed would be disappointed if I didn't give it a go at a few other of those afore-mentioned applications. I only say this because it is while doing those *other* applications that I had my epiphany as to why I truly want to go to Reed.

It happened in the library of my high school. I was there with several other friends, who are also seniors, and we were all doing our favorite activity….yes, that's right, working on applications. Essay after essay and question after question in the painful florescent lights of a claustrophobic facility. I tried to diligently work, but I was not as focused as I usually am. Truthfully, I was thinking about writing this essay. I was thinking of when I visited Reed, and spent the evening with a dorm host, but more specifically, I was thinking of the conversations I had participated in during dinner. I was talking to a girl named Rachel, who lived in the dorm with my host. I had asked her one of the questions I tried to ask every Reedie that I met, "What did you write your "Why Reed?" essay about?" She told me that she too had been worried about the essay when she applied (I guess I wasn't as good at masking my lurking worries as I thought). She told me stories of other students, but the one that sticks in my mind and which I thought of that day in the library was about a guy who wrote that he wanted to attend Reed because he had a passion for giraffes, and he felt that he would find others who shared his love of the animal at a school like Reed. I smiled when I thought of the story, but the ringing of the bell brought me back to that claustrophobic library, with a terribly long, boring and seemingly insurmountable application to a rather bland university blinking back at me from the face of the computer screen. I tried my best to continue, to answer the myriad questions about my social and academic life, to write answers to essay questions that only attempted to scratch the surface of who I am, of what I love. And that's when it hit me, the realization, the epiphany which showed me why I want to attend Reed so very badly. The more I tried to complete these applications with reasons why I wanted to go to one college or another, the more I didn't want to go. It's really simple when one thinks about it; while trying to convince those prestigious centers of learning that I was right for them, I was convincing myself that I wasn't. A little oxymoronic, but at least I realized it sooner rather than later. Once I finally realized this, the reasons why Reed stood above the rest quickly made themselves apparent to me.

The more time I spent on the other applications which seemed so superficially shallow in their assessment of me as a human being, the more time I spent letting my mind wander and thinking about my Reed application, which invariably led to thinking about my two visits to Reed, and the conversations and experiences I'd had as a Prospie. One of my favorite moments was when I got to sit in on a Comparative

Governments class, and just listen and watch. It is unusual for me to sit in a classroom and be freed from the responsibility of participating, and although there were a few instances when I was itching to join in the verbal fray, I found the experience rather liberating. Everyone was friendly and asked me questions about where I was from, what I was interested in, but once class began, they were all amazingly attentive. Now, you must realize that this class I visited was taking place on a Friday afternoon, and I'm sure that the coy, seductive minx we teenagers like to call the weekend was impolitely tugging on more than a few people's minds, and yet, nobody seemed bothered at all. This isn't to say they all passively listened to a stodgy professor drone on and on; to the contrary, the discussion was lively on both the student and the teacher's parts. Most striking to me at the time was that everyone seemed unmistakably interested. Not to mention *interesting*; the opinions that were fired off varied wildly, making for a much more engaging discussion. I think many people don't realize what a precious commodity discussion is; it is the fine art of exchanging opinions, without anger or resentment but certainly infused with generous amounts of passion and conviction. Sitting in Comparative Governments that day, I realized what a dying art discussion is. I, who am nearly at the age where I can vote for who runs our country, have only a few instances in my memory when I have been able to engage in a true discussion of material in the classroom. Seeing discussion alive and well that day at Reed filled me with an intense feeling I could not then define. But it got better; discussion seemed to be the coin of the realm at Reed. There were people discussing things *everywhere;* on the lawns, in the dormitories, in the dining room, on the couches (!) that were scattered here and there on the campus grounds. And the range of what they were discussing far outstripped the numerous locations for said discussions. I overheard people talking about politics, about rugby, art, technology, why they like vanilla ice cream, why the on-campus café makes the best lattes in Portland (I'd have to agree with them on that one). I was lucky enough to join in on some of these discussions, and the ones I participated in ranged in topic from Portland's jazz scene to which meal plan allows you the most ice cream. And I loved it…I adored it. I liked that the students were open, friendly. Nobody seemed stand-offish or proud, and never did I catch a whiff of condescension while talking to Reedies. This extended to the staff, from those in the admissions office to the professors of the classes I sat in on. I liked that admissions interviews were conducted by current students, and I liked that when the professor walked into Comparative Governments, I didn't realize he *was* the professor until he started writing on the board, mostly because he was dressed in jeans and a T-shirt, and he was talking, joking with the students as if he was just another Reedie. I liked all these things about Reed. The lack of pretension seemed incredibly liberating to both the students and the staff, and I certainly felt more comfortable than I had at any other university I visited. That was when I was able to define the feeling I had earlier been unable to name. I felt that I belonged at Reed.

These are the things I think of when I try to describe why I want to attend Reed. I want to go to Reed because the people there are a rarity; those who are genuinely interested in what you have to say, and do not simply wait for their turn to speak. I love that it is the kind of place where a student must be self-driven, something I have always admired and tried to discipline myself in. The students at Reed *know* that they are being given an opportunity, the opportunity to learn without restrictions and to change their minds about their lives, about themselves. The Reedies know how to focus, how to learn in class with tenacity, but more importantly, they know how to learn outside of the classroom with an equal amount of enthusiasm. The students and the staff encourage the art of discussion, a quickly disappearing discipline. In an age where, if you turn on the T.V. to one of the numerous news channels, you will see one fast-talking pundit yelling at another, it is incredibly refreshing to see such discussions being fostered instead of rejected. I want to join that tradition, to learn how to listen just as much as how to speak. All these qualities lead me back to one thing: complexity. This is what I found lacking in other universities that may have been prestigious and sought-after, but left me feeling frustrated. The questions on their applications were so skin-deep, and visiting their campuses, I had the same anti-climatic feeling. To put it simply, these places were simple. They were easily cataloged into the various roles that they not only accepted, but seemed to promote: party school, serious-minded school, school for hippies, school for yuppies. It all seemed so diluted. I have never felt this way about Reed. So as I sit here, finishing the application which opened my mind about all those *other* applications, I give you my final answer. I want to go to Reed because I am a complex person, and Reed doesn't hold that against me. Reed is a place where learning is held to the highest esteem, but where grades just don't seems to matter, a complex system if ever there was one. At Reed, professors dress in jeans, and everyone at the university seems to have a wry sense of humor, which extends to the fact that they appreciate admissions essays which focus on giraffes. At Reed, complexity isn't an impediment, it's an asset. And I appreciate that more than one essay can convey. I know I will benefit and grow both as a student and a person at Reed, not because an education at Reed will make my life and the choices within it necessarily easy, but because Reed will teach me to value that complexity which seems to be so intrinsic to who I am, and I can't imagine what more you could ask from a university.

See page 312 to find out where this student got in.

AMY BERG

Throughout high school, Amy ran varsity cross-country, varsity track, and participated in student government. During her senior year she was Commissioner of Clubs, editor of her school's literary magazine, and head coordinator of the Mr. Crescent Valley pageant, a year-long fundraiser for a local charitable organization.

Stats
SAT: 1500 (800 Critical Reading, 700 Math)
High School GPA: 3.80
High School: Crescent Valley High School, Corvallis, OR
Hometown: Corvallis, OR
Gender: Female
Race: Caucasian

Applied To
Claremont McKenna College
Colby College
Haverford College
Lewis and Clark College
Pomona College
University of Oregon—Clark Honors College
Whitman College

Essay

Amy used the following essay, which she had written for an English class, in each of her applications.

As we drove closer, I gathered my books into a neat stack. When we rounded the final corner, the redbrick façade of the library loomed, a promise of the incalculable wealth inside. We four siblings raced each other upstairs, laughing and panting. Our cloth book bags were ready in our hands, flapping against our knees as blank and lifeless as the King Tut mummy pictured on mine. As soon as we reached the first floor, the blue-green hush of the thousands of volumes was enough to quiet us even on our worst days. To run, to shout, or even to touch the regal Puss-in-Boots statue in the children's corner meant a dreaded punishment: having to sit with my mother while she perused the adult non-fiction.

On the other hand, those who behaved had the run of the library. We could never read everything those stately shelves held. My siblings and I all had our favorite haunts: mine were the "pioneer girl" stories. Among the huge wooden shelves, it was easy to imagine that I was in a magical indoor forest, dwarfed next to the stacks of knowledge.

All too soon, we found all the books we could carry, and my mother gathered us all up. I walked back to the checkout desk, my full King Tut bag bulging and banging against my legs. My arms grew heavy as I balanced my load while standing in line. Each time I gave my card to the librarian, I fervently hoped I didn't have any fines. To owe a fine was to fail the library; was I really good enough for its generosity? Once, while I was searching my pockets for quarters, an elderly gentleman behind me paid for me. When I thanked him, he said to me, "Just keep reading."

In the car on the way home, our ecstatic solitude lay undisturbed unless two of us went for the same book at once. When we stopped in our garage, those of us at a tense moment in our books would often be too captivated even to leave the car. I don't know how my mother expected us to finish any chores for the rest of the afternoon. If I was able to steal an uninterrupted half-hour, what a treasure that was! I would go into the living room and rest the book on one of our overstuffed wingback chairs. Kneeling before the book, completely devoted to every word, I leaned my body into the upholstered maroon fabric. I read the back cover, the title page, the dedication, the preface. And then, finally. . . a new adventure transcended paper and ink. I quit twentieth century Oregon for a trail across the country or a castle across the world. As I grew up, the words became bigger and the print became smaller, but the wonder at opening a book stayed the same. I may not be traveling across the prairie on a Conestoga wagon like my pioneer girls, but I know I will "just keep reading."

See page 313 to find out where this student got in.

ANDREA SALAS

In high school, Andrea was varsity tennis team captain for four years, involved in student government, on the yearbook staff, and a "peer-educator" for the AIDS Awareness Club.

Stats
SAT: 1390
SAT Subject Test(s): 730 Math Level 2, 730 Chemistry
High School GPA: 3.80
High School: Santa Monica High School, Santa Monica, CA
Hometown: Santa Monica, CA
Gender: Female
Race: Caucasian/Latina
Applied To
Amherst College
Bates College
Bowdoin College
Dartmouth College
Tufts University
University of California—Berkeley
University of California—Los Angeles
University of California—San Diego
University of California—Santa Barbara
University of California—Santa Cruz
Williams College

Essay

Andrea used the following essay in each of her applications. She combined the following two questions from the Common Application:

1. *Evaluate a significant experience, achievement, risk you have taken, or ethical dilemma you have faced and its impact on you.*

2. *Indicate a person who has had a significant influence on you, and describe that influence.*

Dear Poppy,

I realize that this letter will not actually be sent to you at Walkley Hill road in Haddam, Connecticut. In fact, it will be sent to the Admissions Office at Dartmouth College. I also know that it has been over two weeks since I received your last letter, and I apologize for not responding sooner. I always have some school-related excuse as to why it has taken me so long to reply, but the truth is, lately it has been hard to write back immediately to my dear grandfather's letters when so much else is pulling my attention away. But once I sit down with pen and paper, I know that thirty minutes later, when I seal the envelope and place it in the mailbox, I will once again be uplifted by feelings of accomplishment and renewed connection to you.

I remember that first letter I sent you ten years ago, thanking you for Christmas money and asking you to "please write back to me, and then I will write back to you, and we can keep a corespondance that way" (that was how I spelled "correspondence" at age six). Those early letters now seem so banal, inevitably beginning with "Dear Poppy, how are you? I am fine." But after a few years, they progressed to "Dear Poppy, I read the most amazing book, *The Count of Monte Cristo*. Have you read it?" I must admit to having told you many commonplace things about myself—my school schedule, the books I am reading, how my sister is doing. But I have also shared with you my most uncommon moments, special moments that seemed removed from time, when I poured out my feelings without concern for what my peers and parents would think. You became the one person with whom I could share feelings back and forth, discussing life's issues, without fear of censure.

When I write to you, I imagine you at your desk reading every word meticulously. Behind you hangs your chalkboard with those Calculus equations that always puzzled me as a child. Now I know that when I next see those equations, I will really understand them! On your desk, a photograph of me, cradled in your arms. When I write to you, I visualize these things and more. Writing to you opens up worlds past and present, yours and mine.

Once I wrote you a letter on a brown paper bag with ripped edges and pretended that I was ship-wrecked, the letter being my only communication with the outside world. In reality, it was only my communication outside my bedroom. There were also the letters written without lifting pen from paper, like the one I wrote when Grandma died. I never worried that I, an adolescent, was trying to console my far wiser grandfather about loss and death. This past August you showed me the folder where you kept all my letters. There at a glance was the Winnie-the-Pooh stationary, the crisp Florentine printed paper, the card of my favorite Alma-Tadema painting at the Getty Museum: the surfaces on which I showed you myself and the depth of my feeling. And all of the letters are addressed to you, Dear Poppy, and signed Love, Andrea, but each is from a different writer at a different moment in her life. Ever changing, yet with you always.

Love,
Andrea

See page 313 to find out where this student got in.

ANDREW COLLINS

Andrew's two most important extracurricular pursuits were his work as editor of The Exonian, a weekly school newspaper, and piano composition, for which he was selected to give a major public recital at the end of his senior year. He was a two-year letterman in track, twice served as the sports director of WPEA campus radio, and founded an adjunct student government committee his junior year, which was a forum for student interaction with Student Council representatives. In his junior year, Andrew won the Sherman W. Hoar award for excellence in American history and the Turner Exonian Award for writing and reporting for the newspaper.

Stats
SAT: 1540 (800 Critical Reading, 740 Math)
SAT Subject Test(s): 790 Literature, 720 Math Level 2, 650 Chemistry, 620 Physics, 690 French
High School GPA: 3.42
High School: Philips Exeter Academy, Exeter, NH
Hometown: Little Rock, AR
Gender: Male
Race: Caucasian

Applied To

Duke University
Georgetown University
Harvard College
Princeton University
Stanford University
University of California—Berkeley
University of Virginia
Vanderbilt University

Essay

Andrew used the following essay in his applications to Harvard, Vanderbilt, and Duke.

> *Common Application: Evaluate a significant experience, achievement, or risk that you have taken and its impact on you.*

"You'll have a great time. These elderly folks, they're so appreciative when students take the time to perform for them—and they love the music."

Over half of the audience had fallen asleep. Drowsiness had enveloped the remaining residents, who looked bleary-eyed and disoriented in their wheelchairs. One man succumbed to a grotesque yawn, and the sight of his spit-soaked, mangled gums caused me to wince. I had volunteered to play piano at Riverwoods Nursing Home along with some of my classmates, and was next in line to perform. Thinking that this audience would cheerfully applaud anything, I had elected to perform one of my original compositions. The song wasn't perfect, but I figured that an audience full of kindly old grandmothers would offer unqualified praise and perhaps a cookie or two, not criticism. Instead, dozens of eyes were staring right at me through sagging frames of flesh. I sat upright in the hard plastic chair, muscles taut, in a state of total discomfort. Someone in the audience passed gas.

When it was my turn to play, I walked over to the piano and addressed the crowd, as is customary. I said the name of my piece, and then I was interrupted—"Talk louder, boy!"—by a fierce gentleman in the front row. I apologized and tried again, but my efforts were met with jeers from the audience.

"He's just whispering!" one woman shouted with glee. Her friend nodded and whooped in approval, between coughs. No more slumber for these folks—the scene had turned rowdy, and I was stuck in the middle!

Desperate and rattled, I felt I had no choice but to shout at my maximum volume. "MY NAME IS ANDREW COLLINS," I bellowed, "AND I WILL BE PLAYING 'HIGHER GROUND!'" The audience then launched into an in-depth discussion about the origin of my name. One woman said that "Andrew" means "strong" in Hebrew, while another made the absurd claim that it means "falcon" in English. Not waiting to hear how this argument would conclude, I sat down at the piano and tried to play over their cacophonous debate.

It was even worse during the actual performance of the piece. People who heard the song in private usually complimented me heartily, and they encouraged me to play my original music in a performance setting. This crowd, however, was not impressed with the "fancy rock-and-roll" style of my composition. One woman said, loudly enough for me to hear, "I wish he'd play 'Danny Boy.'" Others drifted in and out of sleep as I continued my performance.

At one point, a skinny, pale man in the back of the room punched at the air and yelled, "Shut up!" He engaged in a brief skirmish with a member the nursing home staff, who escorted him out of the room. Finally, I finished my song and walked back to my seat, mentally and physically exhausted.

"Tough crowd," I whispered to one of my fellow performers. The rec room was in total disarray; some people were yelling and many were demanding to be wheeled back to their living quarters. It was hot and the nursing home staff seemed unable to maintain order in the frenetic atmosphere. Sweat was dripping down my face. The next week, and for many weeks afterward, I came back to play at Riverwoods.

See page 313 to find out where this student got in.

ANDREW HARRISON GIORDANO

In high school, Andrew was the treasurer of his high school theater organization, an active member of chorus with numerous solos, a participant in the "Troubadours" (an elite vocal group of approximately 20 students), a member of Mu Alpha Theta, FBLA, Mock Trial, and the Tri-M music honor society, and also performed in All-County and Area All-State vocal music festivals. During his junior year of high school, he helped to create a local not-for-profit youth theater company, The Youth Theatre Experience, that continues to put on summer shows for high school and middle school age students.

Stats
SAT: 1420 (720 Critical Reading, 700 Math)
SAT Subject Test(s): 700 Math 1C, 750 U.S.
High School GPA: 3.73
High School: Clarkstown High School South, West Nyack, NY
Hometown: West Nyack, NY
Gender: Male
Race: Caucasian

Applied To
American University
Brandeis University
Carleton College
Colorado College
The Johns Hopkins University
Muhlenberg College
Oberlin College
State University of New York—Binghamton
University of Delaware
University of Rochester

Essay

Andrew used the following essay in his applications to the schools listed above.

Topic of your choice

Smile!

Some people call it an obsessive–compulsive tendency; I call it dental hygiene.

So what if I brush my teeth for ten to fifteen minutes every night? I just like the feeling of having clean "choppers." In my opinion, having clean teeth is one of the most important aspects of one's personal hygiene. Teeth are a feature that provides others with a first impression. When you meet somebody, they smile (at least one would hope.) That smile is your first impression of them.

Truth be told, my teeth are white and straight. While one might argue that a year of braces is to thank, I also like to think of my sparkling smile as a reflection of my hardworking, meticulous, and near perfectionistic nature. This does not only apply to my teeth, but also to all of my academic and extracurricular activities, as well as to the most mundane of everyday actions. When I begin a task, whether it is a paper for school, a theatrical performance, or an act of personal hygiene, I make sure to see it through to a successful conclusion – no detail is spared. If that includes writing an outline before a paper, rehearsing lines with my mom, or even brushing my teeth for a quarter of an hour, then so be it.

One aspect of my life that has taught me the importance of first impressions is the theatre. As an actor of ten years, if I have learned nothing else, I have learned that you *do* get only one chance to make a first impression. This first impression is the audition. When an actor or actress auditions for a show, the director automatically begins to think of whether he or she has the "look" for a part. This occurs on a completely superficial level even before the director knows anything else about the performer. Then, if the auditioned passes the appearance test, he or she only gets one chance to act, sing, and dance – one chance to make a first impression.

However, the acting business is not the only place where first impressions hold a great deal of importance. For example, you, my admissions officer, are getting a first impression of me while reading this essay. We will probably never meet face to face; therefore, all you have to go on are my SAT scores, my transcript, my achievement list, and the only subjective piece of my application: this essay. As wonderful as it would be for both of us to go out to lunch to discuss politics [or] the economy, it just is not feasible. Yet again, I have only one chance to make a first impression.

So, whether you want to consider this piece my smile, my audition, or just a piece of whimsical prose, I offer you this essay as that first impression. I only hope that just like my teeth after being brushed for fifteen minutes, it too will see a sparkling and successful conclusion.

See page 314 to find out where this student got in.

ANDREW MAXWELL MANGINO

Throughout high school, Andrew's passion was his school news-paper, The Caldron. *While Andrew worked on* The Caldron, *it ex-panded from 10 to 100 staff members and won the award for top high school newspaper in New Jersey in the small schools division. Andrew taught a class on his journalism experiences at Columbia Scholastic Press Association conventions and won a national award for newspaper design. He spent his summers at journalism confer-ences and volunteering at his local newspaper. He played double bass in his high school's orchestra, jazz band, chamber group, and band, and was a North Jersey regional bassist his senior year. He was on his school's baseball and varsity cross-country teams, and was president of the National Honor Society.*

Stats
SAT: 1510 (750 Critical Reading, 760 Math)
SAT Subject Test(s): 760 U.S. History, 760 Math IIC
High School GPA: 99.5 (out of 100) weighted
High School: James Caldwell High School, West Caldwell, NJ
Hometown: West Caldwell, NJ
Gender: Male
Race: Caucasian

Essay

Andrew used similar versions of following essay in his applications to Brown, Chicago, Columbia, Harvard, NYU, Penn, Princeton, Syracuse, Tufts, Washington, and Yale.

> *Common Application: Indicate a person who has had a significant influence on you, and describe that influence.*

His arms flew through the hot summer air. There was a deafening delay. Someone shouted, "We love you John!" Had he read my mind? Snapping open my camera, I focused intently on his expression. Suddenly, the blistering B-flat chord thundered from the platform and applause spread through the crowd like an electrical current. The musical rush of Star Wars was contagious. For two minutes and fifty five seconds, the Blossom Musical Festival audience was mesmerized, and I realized why I had convinced my family to drive eight hours for the moment. His music, in its grandeur and consonance, was perfect. *I want to tell him how it makes me feel!*

One year later and miles from Cleveland, I waited anxiously in Tanglewood, Massachusetts amongst fellow diehards. With my Star Wars score in one hand and Greatest Hits piano book in the other, I wondered what I would tell him. *Should I explain where my passion began?* For more than a decade, I had listened to an array of music that included everything from Jewish chants, Christmas classics, and traditional Afghani hymns to, Bob Dylan, Gustav Holst, and Blink 182. But over time, dramatic movie themes began to stand out most. As I got older, I turned from dancing around the house with my mom to Whitney Houston's *I'm Every Woman* to conducting the 1984 Olympic Theme in front of my cat, cuing imaginary trumpets with pretzel rods. During school presentations and in my film projects, I blasted his music, determined to share his genius with others. *Should I tell him about my own experience playing the double bass?* After all, that instrument had sparked my interest in orchestral music. But that night, I learned that it did not matter what I was planning to say after all. An usher appeared to apologize. The maestro had left.

Two evenings later, I returned to Tanglewood without a ticket. A thunderous storm accompanied the evening performance, leaving the field a muddy mess. But it was my last chance. Begging a guard to let me in, I sprinted across the grass with the Star Wars score clutched to my chest. Tchaikovsky's 1812 Overture blasted and canons exploded behind me. Then, in a rush of mud and water, I found myself at the stage exit for the second time that week. As I panted, a lady emerged. I could not hear what she said, but I clearly saw her signal for me to join her. Nervously, I stepped forward and peered at the stage door.

In the next moment, a dapper, white-haired man in a tuxedo appeared. John Towner Williams seemed to glow as he reached out with his conducting arm to shake my hand. For a second, I could not think. "Mr. Williams! I admire your music so much," I managed to say. "E.T., Star Wars, Indiana Jones, Harry Potter, The Cowboys, the NBC News Theme, the Olympic themes, Superman…the way you use the instruments to create such strong emotions is amazing. How do you create so many perfect pieces?" He chuckled and I handed him the score. "Oh! Look at this," he said, smiling. "It's one of my favorites." I told him I agreed and asked him to sign it and make it out to my high school orchestra. "I've convinced them to perform your Jurassic Park suite next year," I said. "We really think it will revitalize our group!" The words rolled off my tongue faster than the bass section's ominous low notes in the JAWS end credits. But he responded calmly. "Thank you, Andrew. Please do send me a recording." And then, before walking away, he turned. "We *will* meet again."

He was right. Months later, as my arms sweep through James Caldwell High School's air-conditioned symphony room, I shut my eyes and imagine that our group is recording on the floor of Lincoln Center. I look to the brass section. Seeing the focus in their eyes inspires me to conduct with even more emotion. I turn to my left. The violins are playing in unison. I look up to my bass teacher for approval, but he is too engaged to notice. Then, one minute and thirty eight seconds into Jurassic Park, with my arms dramatically flailing, a cymbal crashes, intensifying the moment. Then it hits. I *have* met him again: the first time in person, this time through his work. Before, I did not share the moment with anyone. Now, I am surrounded by others whose passion for John Williams matches mine.

See page 314 to find out where this student got in.

AUDREY NATH

Audrey won first place in the Texas Music Teachers Association's High School Division Piano Concerto Contest her senior year and placed at the state level the three previous years; she also performed with numerous orchestras. She was captain of her high school's Academic Challenge B Team, salutatorian of her graduating class, and a National AP Scholar. She conducted scientific research the summer following her junior year of high school on the gold-labeling of the nicotinic acetylcholine receptor and cervical cancer detection using fluorescence spectroscopy.

Stats
SAT: 1550 (760 Critical Reading, 790 Math)
SAT Subject Test(s): 800 Math Level 2, 730 Biology, 750 Chemistry
High School GPA: 6.62/6.00
High School: Memorial High School, Houston, TX
Hometown: Houston, TX
Gender: Female
Race: Asian American

Applied To
Harvard College
Massachusetts Institute of Technology
Rice University

Essay

Audrey used the following essay in her application to Rice.

The quality of Rice's academic life and the residential college system is heavily influenced by the unique life experiences and cultural traditions each student brings. What perspective do you feel that you will be able to share with others as a result of your own life experiences and background? Cite a personal experience to illustrate this. Most applicants are able to respond successfully in two to three pages.

I've noticed that if I stare at something and really concentrate on it, I can still see its outline after it is gone; the same goes for focusing on one sound or one word until it lingers in my mind. Four summers ago, as I felt inundated with knowledge and ideas, I centered my mind on my surroundings of art in order to comprehend the volume of artistic concepts. Such was the enrichment I gleaned from studying composition at the American Festival for the Arts during the summer before the 8th grade. The results of this experience are ingrained both in the way I view music and life itself.

On the first day of the music program, I carried myself with a shy and self-conscious demeanor into the composition room where I was initially intimidated by a roomful of people who appeared to be bigger, older, and smarter than I was; little did I know that they would later become a family of mentors to me. Within the first day, Chris, our instructor and sage leader, introduced us to the work of late 20th century composers with a discussion and analysis of pieces by John Corigliano and Tan Dun; before then, I thought classical music ended with Aaron Copland.

Over the course of eight weeks, we would write two pieces to be later performed by faculty, study theory, and analyze orchestral and chamber works. As respite from this arduous study, we would listen to whatever music we deemed "interesting." These pieces would range from Beethoven's last string quartets to Chris' own soundtrack to a Civil War documentary; the dulcet sounds would both inspire us and fill the room for hours. To me, our assignments appeared impossible at the time as I had studied piano seriously for only four years; that training did not give me a fraction of the composition, theory, and literature knowledge that everyone else possessed. However, instead of allowing me to remain a confused spectator during theory lessons and discussions, Chris and the other students would explain the concepts in question. With this guidance and my fears assuaged, I eventually became comfortable enough to complete a complicated voice leading problem on my own or sight-sing in front of this group of encouraging supporters. By the end of the summer, I completed two original pieces and experienced the joy of having my own thoughts played back to me. Overall, I was exposed to a world of art that had previously seemed foreign and intimidating to me.

Even after the summer was over, Chris continued as our mentor and helped us explore our surroundings. We would take trips around town to the living art that is our city. From art festivals and museums to parks and Chris' own neighborhood, our excursions were as enjoyable as they were intriguing. Once, when we visited a special exhibit of photography at the Fine Arts Museum, my friend and I posed as siblings as we proceeded to call Chris "Dad" in order to obtain a family discount. Even though Chris was visibly not more than ten years older than me, and the three of us had about as much ethnic diversity as the Democratic National Convention, our ploy worked swimmingly. Within the museum, our curiosity was piqued by paintings that mimicked picture frames and photographs of doorways. When Chris took us downtown to analyze the architecture of structures and buildings, the city that we thought we knew so well transformed into a forest of sculpted monoliths as the streets we wandered were an odd, one-way maze.

Following my study of composition and our adventures with Chris, the world around me became a different place. Whereas my love for music started as a means for me to grasp onto clarity of thought, it had transformed into a structured passion. No longer was music just a series of soothing sounds. Instead, music became the counterpoint of two dogs barking or the rhythm of lights blinking; music became the movement of life. I realized that there was beauty in every bit of life, from the order within chaos to the chaos itself; it was the relationship between the constantly evolving patterns that grew out of living that was beautiful. Individual relationships and events, as complicated and inexplicable as they may seem, embody beauty when put in perspective of the larger order of life. This idea is modeled by abstract musical concepts that usually seem incomprehensible until they are interpreted in the context of an underlying pattern.

Since the summer when a family of musicians took me in to learn about the world of art and life itself, my perspectives headed in a new direction. I began to see life not as rigid layers within black and white lines; rather, I could relate the complexities of relationships with my surroundings, other people, and myself to a chromatic brushstroke of sound in a Debussy string quartet or an intricate orchestration within a symphony by Berlioz. Similarly, people were no longer simply right or wrong, intelligent or dull, talented or inept; the psychology behind their actions was just as complicated as the thoughts and events that made them. As of this very moment, four years after I studied composition at the American Festival for the Arts, I can still hear the faint resonance of comrades toying with ideas on the piano and singing a tune heard from an orchestra rehearsal; such is the shadow of an experience that filled my mind so long ago.

See page 314 to find out where this student got in.

BRANDON MOLINA

Brandon was a four-year letterman in football, wrestling (best finish: third in state), and weightlifting. He was class president his junior and senior years and worked as a student coordinator for the Special Olympics. He was also a student representative on his high school's Serious Discipline Committee, which recommends actions for the administration to take with students who commit serious discipline or honor infractions.

Stats
SAT: 1420 (690 Critical Reading, 730 Math)
SAT Subject Test(s): 710 Math Level 1, 800 Biology
High School GPA: 3.67
High School: Berkeley Preparatory School, Tampa, FL
Hometown: Lutz, FL
Gender: Male
Race: Caucasian

Applied To
Columbia University
Elon University
Harvard College (early action)
Stanford University
Tulane University
University of Pennsylvania
United States Military Academy

Essay

Any topic you would like to discuss in 250 words or less.

The Real Thing

As a seven-year-old, I wrote a personal letter to the president of Coca-Cola, begging for his assistance. Having just returned from a ski trip to Stratton Mountain Vermont, I found my self unable to locate a specific product. At a convenience store on the mountain called "Bear Necessities", my mom bought Coke in eight ounce glass bottles that were reminiscent of those she would buy when she was young (although thicker glass only allowed 6 1/2 oz. of beverage). Whether it was the novelty of the bottles or the nostalgia I knew my mom felt, something made the Coke taste better out of the little glass bottles. I saved the empty container and upon my return home (to Pleasantville, NY at the time), I realized that my local grocery store did not stock these bottles. Neither did the local pharmacy. Neither did the local 7-Eleven nor the one in near-by Chappaqua. In fact, after a day in the White Pages, I realized that the item of my desire was nowhere to be found.

That night at dinner, after telling my parents the story of my day, they suggested that I get some information about the bottles. My mom was a recruiter at the time and furnished me with a telephone number for Coca-Cola. The following day I got a mailing address for the President and CEO, and wrote him a letter. I suppose that not too many seven-year-olds voice their concerns to this man, for I promptly received a response. To my dismay, the letter was an apology. "Unfortunately," it read, "we are unable to provide this product in your region." It began to explain, in very simple terms, that it was not cost effective for Coca-Cola to distribute the product in my densely populated area. His only recourse was to offer me coupons for other Coca-Cola products. For the next two years, I got to sample the bottles on infrequent occasion, whenever we hit the slopes.

My interest in the Coca-Cola Company grew and I began collecting Coke memorabilia, starting with a bank in the shape of a glass Coke bottle, which helped afford later pieces. In sixth grade I was plotting a graph of Coke stock on my America Online account. Also in sixth grade, something great happened: My family moved to our current hometown of Tampa, FL. Here, the eight ounce glass bottles were available in many grocery stores, pharmacies, etcetera. By this time my Coke collection was overtaking my room, and the access to these bottles did not ameliorate the situation. I collected bottles of all ages and editions, some full and some empty.

My collection has meaning that is two-fold. Certainly, a relatively large portion of a seventeen-year life has been devoted to searching, saving, and organizing. However, at a young age, the love that I knew for Coca-Cola taught me lessons about initiative and perseverance that I did not know. Fortunately I learned about these two qualities through a personal interest rather than having to complete an assignment. Of all my Coke products, my Coke-labeled furniture, and my Coke Christmas ornaments, my favorite item is a circa 1920 Coca-Cola glass bottle that was given to me by a friend whose brother found the bottle in a riverbed near Jacksonville, FL. Whenever I look at it, I am reminded of the time when I first began my collection on Stratton Mountain, Vermont.

See page 315 to find out where this student got in.

BRIAN TRACY

Brian was a four-year letterman in golf and qualified for the district championship his senior year. He also received a national award for piano auditions and an altar server award from the Knights of Columbus.

Stats
SAT: 1380 **High School GPA:** 4.00/4.00 **High School:** James M. Coughlin High School, Wilkes-Barre, PA **Hometown:** Plains, PA **Gender:** Male **Race:** Caucasian
Applied To
University of Notre Dame (early decision)

Essay

The following essay is Brian's personal statement.

"Nowhere else but Notre Dame." These words appear on the front cover of the viewbook, and they immediately bring to mind many images pertaining to the university. This phrase can also be the answer to a myriad of questions about great universities, outstanding athletic programs, and long standing, revered traditions. However, the question that comes to mind when I hear those words is, "Which college do I hope to be attending next year?" I often ask this question of myself whenever I wonder about my future. Friends and family ask me about my dreams for the future as well, because they are eager to know my plans. I believe that it would be a great honor and accomplishment to be able to tell both them and myself, "Nowhere else but Notre Dame."

I consider myself to be an honest, friendly, dedicated, and hardworking person with strong religious beliefs who is eager to help others and to always do what is right. I give great attention to everything I do, and I constantly try to challenge myself. For example, taking college courses during my junior year challenged me and provided an idea of what I would face in college. I also believe that I am a team player. My participation in sports and in groups in school has helped to build and reinforce this characteristic. Besides my commitment to school, I also try to help my community and to be a leader. My experiences in Junior Leadership Wilkes-Barre gave me great opportunities to meet with today's leaders and to become a leader of tomorrow. Junior Leadership also helped me to give back to the community through our service project, a community mural.

I also consider myself to be an enormous Notre Dame fan, not just of the football team, but of the college, too. I'll admit it: I cried the first time I saw *Rudy*. I fell in love with the campus when I visited there a few years ago. There just seemed to be a friendly, warm feeling around campus and on the faces of students I saw. It was during that trip that I first became interested in going to Notre Dame. However, I am not applying simply because I like the university. I did research on the nation's best colleges, and Notre Dame's name kept appearing. I have talked with several alumni, all of whom agree that attending Notre Dame was one of the best things they ever did. In addition, I was greatly impressed with the impressive graduation and employment rates. Finally, because Notre Dame has such strict admission standards, I know that if I am accepted, I will be surrounded by only the best and brightest students in the nation.

I thank Notre Dame for including Section 8 on the application. It does provide a chance to go beyond the transcript and to introduce myself and the kind of person I am. Hopefully, I will be given the chance to become part of a special tradition, one that includes Touchdown Jesus, the Golden Dome, the Grotto, and much more. Where is all of this possible? Nowhere else but Notre Dame.

See page 315 to find out where this student got in.

CANDACE SEU

Candace was involved in a wide variety of activities in high school, including 4-H, student government, Math Club, and a writers' collective.

Stats
SAT: 1560 (760 Critical Reading, 800 Math)
High School GPA: 4.00
High School: Waiakea High School, Hilo HI
Hometown: Hilo,
Gender: Female
Race: Asian American
Applied To
California Institute of Technology
Harvey Mudd College
Illinois Institute of Technology
Pomona College
University of Southern California

Essay 1

Candace used the following essay as the personal statement in her Caltech application.

When I was five, my father told me to become a doctor. Doctors make a lot of money, so I readily agreed. Everyone had decided that it would be befitting for me to become a doctor. I had decided that it would be befitting to become rich.

For seven years, this was the established plan of action. It was inevitable that I would become a rich yuppie, commute to work in my luxury car, and come home in the evenings to my 2.5 kids and their dog. Thankfully, this future was forever postponed when, in intermediate school, I realized that I neither cared about money nor medicine. What I wanted to do, I realized, was science.

Like all of the other seventh graders that year, I was forced to do a science fair project – and like most, I prepared to hate it. As far as I could tell, Mr. Ahmadia was making attempts on my life again. The fact that this was not the case came to me only in retrospect, when, surveying the results of my finished project, I realized that the torture had actually been fun. Although I complained when I was forced to do two more projects within the next four years, it was only half-heartedly so.

My interest in science was further developed when I traveled to New York for a three-week course in neurobiology during my sophomore summer. There, I developed a genuine interest for the neurosciences, and began wondering about the possibilities of becoming a research scientist. The next summer, I had the chance to try out that career path when I was selected to participate in the Roswell Park Cancer Institute Summer Student program. Those seven weeks were the best summer of my life – because even when I contaminated the cell cultures, even when my tests didn't work, and even when my results came back inconclusive —I knew that this was what I wanted to be doing for the rest of my life.

At the moment, my passion for knowledge draws me towards the neurosciences, a world where there is still much to be discovered. More specifically, I would like to focus my studies on neurodegenerative diseases, with a possible hope of developing a therapy or cure for such afflictions as Alzheimer's disease.

I don't expect to achieve anything that the world will remember and thank me for – I know that this seems self-defeating, but it only stems from my desire to reject any idealistic heroism in my motivations. I *would* be completely joyful to be able to have a part in something that would favorably impact many people's lives – but I will be equally joyful if I can do the same for only one person. If I can prevent one person from developing Alzheimer's, or give one family a little more time to enjoy life with a person they love, I will be satisfied with my work.

Essay 2

Candace used the following picture book as the supplemental essay in her Caltech application. According to Candace, the prompt was as follows:

> *The vibrant and diverse undergraduate student body at Caltech is considered by many of its members to be one of the best things about the school. What talents or qualities can you contribute to this and to your fellow students? We want to know what you are like outside of academics.*

A Candace lived on a very small island.

The Candace was worried.

Her Caltech application was due in four days, and she still didn't know what to write for the second topic. "Three essays? Someone in the admissions office is a sadist," she grumbled.

She tried to think very, very hard.

"How about if I tell them that I can sing all the "Pokemon" names in Japanese?" she mulled.

Just then, Candace heard some knocking.

"Eh?" she wondered.

A little squirrel climbed out of her head.

"Well...I can make Pokemon figures out of kneadable eraser. I made five of them in Physics last week."
"What?" The squirrel appeared flustered.
Candace looked at him worriedly.
"I also draw pictures on my calculator," she offered.

The squirrel looked angry.
"I make crafts out of duct tape?" Candace suggested meekly.

"Don't you have any...normal, useful interests?" The squirrel was beginning to have a black look on his face.

The two pages listing the applicant's dubious interests and "talents" have been lost to posterity due to youthful self-effacement, or maybe prudence.

We apologize for the inconvenience.

Candace thought for a moment.
She frowned.

"Maybe not," she said slowly. "But that is what I am.
And that is what I am happy to be."

She nodded.

"Thank you, but I don't need your help anymore."

And with that, Candace hopped off to the mailbox.

See page 315 to find out where this student got in.

CAROLINE ANG

In high school, Caroline competed on the speech and debate team for three years (winning the state tournament her senior year), the field hockey team for two seasons, and the softball and track teams for one season each. She was editor-in-chief of the school yearbook her senior year, held various leadership positions in the Choir Club and Christian Club, and worked part-time in a coffee shop.

Stats
SAT: 1500
SAT Subject Test(s): 800 Literature, 780 Math Level 2
ACT: 34
High School GPA: 3.96
High School: Leland High School, San Jose, CA
Hometown: San Jose, CA
Gender: Female
Race: Asian American

Applied To
Brown University
University of California—Berkeley
University of California—Los Angeles
University of California—San Diego

Please note: Caroline did not disclose information about other applications.

Essay

Caroline used the following essay in her applications to the schools listed above.

The personal statement is your opportunity to introduce us to you and to educate us about those personal aspects that you determine are vital for us to know. We ask only that whatever you write be honestly written and in your own handwriting.

Personal Statement

I am:

A dreamer who trembles in delight and terror as she considers what happiness and heartache the future may hold.

A humorist who continually expands her repertoire in pursuit of the perfect joke. (Two pretzels walk down the street. One of them was a-salted.)

An athlete who makes up in spirit and hard work what she lacks in talent.

A bookworm who, at 3 a.m., firmly promises that she will read "just one more page" before she sleeps...

A writer who strives to capture on paper the essence of life as she sees it, and who loves to pen short stories and reflective essays.

A daughter who is entering the last stage of the parent-child relationship- friend-ship with Mom and Dad.

A romantic who tries on her prom dress late at night and waltzes around her bedroom to music unheard by the rest of the world.

A conservative who supports the time honored values on which our forefathers founded this country.

A teacher who carefully plans her Sunday school lesson, but isn't afraid to scrap it last minute to fit the kids' needs at that particular moment.

An aesthete who waits outside her house for that instant when the lavender, fuchsia, orange, gold rays of the descending sun shoot across the sky and man has a glimpse of heaven on earth.

A student who loves learning for learning's sake, not just to pad a college tran-script.

A Christian who is continually striving and struggling to follow Jesus' ex-ample.

A guitarist who strums and plucks out songs and instrumentals, some that she's written herself.

A connoisseur who celebrates the beauty and diversity of the snack food aisle in supermarkets.

A leader who accepts being a role model with mixed pride and trepidation.

An optimist who can't wait to seize her future and make her dreams of knowledge, writing and love come true.

A sleeper who escapes pressure and reality through a wonderful invention called the snooze button.

A worrier who compensates for general unluckiness through careful planning and anticipation.

A seeker who wants to get to the crux of the purpose of humanity- why we're here and where we're going.

A conversationalist who explores the heavy issues of life in depth, and chats about the lighter ones.

An economist who knows the value of money, now that she's had to work for it.

A skeptic who wants to believe in the innate goodness of man but cannot gloss over the mess he's made of the world thus far.

A sister who inundates her little brother with advice- how to pick outfits, deal with teachers and melt girls' hearts.

A crusader who enthusiastically sets out to conquer the world but gets her cape stuck in the doorway.

A maniac who rides shopping carts at amazing speeds with her best friend in empty parking lots after hours- drunk not on liquor, but on *life*.

An idealist who believes with all her heart that indifference is the worst crime of all… that having passion for what one does makes all the difference…

A complete paradox who is one thing, then another, one extreme, then the total opposite… a bundle of earnest contradictions.

I am:

Caroline Chiu-Ying Ang.

See page 315 to find out where this student got in.

CAROLINE HABBERT

Caroline held many leadership positions in high school, including Student Senate President. She was on the yearbook staff and the varsity softball team for four years, and head both operations her senior year as editor and captain, respectively. She was also involved in the Ohio Math League, the Service Club, and her school's Cum Laude and French Honor Societies. Outside of school, she taught and attended religious school for four years, volunteered at a nursing home weekly, and spent her summers bicycling. The summer before her senior year, Caroline cycled across the United States.

Stats
SAT: 1510 (770 Critical Reading, 740 Math)
SAT Subject Test(s): 750 Math Level 2, 750 Biology
ACT: 34
High School GPA: 3.98
High School: Seven Hills Upper School, Cincinnati, OH
Hometown: Cincinnati, OH
Gender: Female
Race: Caucasian
Applied To
Brown University
Stanford University
University of Michigan
Washington University in St. Louis
Yale University

Please note: Caroline did not disclose information about other applications.

Essay

Caroline used the following essay in her application to Brown, and modified it for her other applications. There was no formal essay question.

This summer I pushed myself to the limit time and time again. Many times when I thought that I could not go any further, I had to rely on all of my inner strength to pull myself through. This summer I spent eight weeks on a bicycle that carried not only me, but all of my worldly possessions for those eight weeks, from Seattle, Washington to Sea Bright, New Jersey. I moved my legs around in constant circles for seven or eight hours a day, every day, all the way from the Pacific to the Atlantic. And at the end of each day, when I was more tired than I could possibly imagine, I set up my tent, rolled out my sleeping bag, and slept until a "mornin' folks" forced its way into my consciousness and told me that it was time to begin the process anew. We encountered crosswinds so strong that we exerted more effort trying to move in a straight line than trying to move forward; swarms of mosquitoes so thick that standing still for more than ten seconds and maintaining enough blood to function were mutually exclusive; huge trucks heading towards us while passing cars on their side of the road, forcing us to abandon the little strip of shoulder we occupied; and, of course, uphill roads than seemed to take forever to crest at the top of the mountain. Despite all of the setbacks and adverse conditions, I made it across the country under my own power. I will probably never again experience anything so amazing as the feeling I had when we first saw water in New Jersey. Getting there had required me to utilize both emotional and physical elements of myself that had never before been tested. I had never before sat on a bicycle seat for 55 days in a row, nor had I ever faced something I wasn't confident I could do. But I did do it. I called upon all of the tenacity, persistence, and strength that I have, and I made it.

This is not the first physical challenge I have conquered; my photo albums display mementoes from three other long-distance bike trips. Nor is this the first emotional challenge I have faced. Every week, in fact, I am tested in new ways as a volunteer at a nursing home. During my six years there I have worked with countless residents, but one woman has been a constant. Each time I go, I make it a point to stop by Sarah's room to spend some time alone with her. The first I met her, Sarah was the feisty old lady playing Bingo who explained to me that some of the other women occasionally had a hard time finding the right square. Unfortunately, her spunk did not last much longer. Already 90 when I met her, her health began a slow decline soon after I met her. Most upsetting to me was the fact that her mental facilities were slowly deteriorating. When I first began visiting her, she would challenge my presence on any day other than Sunday. Then, as the days started to blend together, she would realize that it was Sunday when I arrived. Finally, she quit commenting on the days at all. She lost the sparkle that crept into her voice when she talked about her daughter, she stopped telling me about the additions to her photo gallery, and she didn't seem to care about what was going on outside of her room. But she still had enough spirit left to smile every week when I stopped by and ask how I'd been, to listen to me talk about school and my family, the weather and how nice she looked. Until this Sunday, when she didn't recognize me. After I had watched her sleep for a minute, I rubbed her arm and said her name. She slowly opened her eyes and lifted her head off her chest. I waited for the smile and the "Caroline." They didn't come. She closed her eyes and lowered her head again, leaving me squatting by her chair. . .

Watching this transformation has given me my first lesson in the realities of life. Although I am invincible now, I won't always be. Aging is a fatal disease everyone gets if she lives long enough. The nurse I talked to said that she could "go at any time." Time: it is such a relative thing. When I was on my bike this summer, the hour that it took to go twelve miles sometimes seemed like it would never end. The two months that I was gone seemed to last forever. But I can still remember the day that I met Sarah six years ago as vividly as if it were yesterday. And it doesn't seem fair that Sarah's life, long in terms of human time but short in relation to the world, will soon be a memory too.

See page 315 to find out where this student got in.

CAROLINE MELLOR

Caroline ran varsity cross country all four years of high school (she was captain during her junior and senior years), and varsity track and field for three years. Caroline also took an interest in child development and earned her 90-hour clock certification for pre-school teachers, which allowed her to work half-days at a Montessori preschool during her senior year. In addition, she interned at the Education Directorate of the American Psychological Association, co-edited her high school's psychology journal, presented research at the Eastern Psychological Association's Convention, and was selected from among her high school peers for the county social science award.

Stats
SAT: 1180 (610 Critical Reading, 570 Math)
SAT Subject Test(s): 590 Math, 610 World History
High School GPA: 3.6
High School: Walt Whitman High School, Bethesda, MD
Hometown: Bethesda, MD/Washington D.C.
Gender: Female
Race: Caucasian

Applied To
Bard College (early decision)
Reed College (early action)

Essay

Caroline used the following essay in his applications to the schools listed above.

Describe a personal struggle

Balancing the See-Saw

"Beat her up," one of them shrieked; referring to me, while the four of them pounded their fists into their hands on the sidewalk corner. I had merely suggested that we run faster, but my cross country teammates' response demonstrated that they didn't agree. Although they were entirely kidding about the violence, such a strong statement was quite frustrating.

For me, running isn't just a stress reliever; it has become a way of life. I look forward to escaping into the looming trees of the Capital Crescent Trail, for this place has more worth to me than just being able to escape into it. Deemed the cross country team's "den mother," I'm always ready to take someone home, help them stretch, listen to her trials and tribulations during a long run, and even organize our annual running camp trip to Vermont. But in this instance, they wanted to do less than what was required to accomplish our best and my not allowing the weaker choice to me made, just didn't settle well with them.

After an awkward silence, we began our daily run with the temporary resolution to decide on the eventual pace as we went. We darted past the middle school and across the neighborhoods, with only casual comments, such as announcing when one spotted a yellow car as we made our way into downtown Bethesda. The first red light we came to changed too fast, leaving us with no time to move to a solution on our work ethic conflict. We continued past the commercial glitter at every store, and came to the intersection of Green Twig Road and Wisconsin Avenue. Then my twinkle of laughter at a street name turned into an explosion of giggles at our absurd conflict. I then exclaimed, "girls, where are we going?" Laura, Rachel, and Kate looked at me as if I belonged in the "abnormal" section of my Psychology textbook, while the only action Becca could muster was to raise her hands to her ears and hiss at me. Then I added, "ah, no, not our route... I meant the point of being here, are you guys... feeling okay - enough for a smudge more?" As the concern echoed through my stern voice, I received understanding nods from my fellow runners as we pressed on through the buzz of traffic to finish our run at the harder pace I had requested.

We did make out daily water stop at a local coffee shop, where they always seem to feel sorry for us, as when we come struggling in, they respond quickly with out cups of water. When we returned from our run, we may all have been on "runner's highs," but the discontented sentiments seemed to have disappeared on their own. We had completed a sweltering nine mile run, and now as we strode to the same sidewalk corner, words of "thanks, the run felt amazing," came from my teammates.

I knew that tomorrow I would be able to physically and mentally take myself farther, while today I had compromised just enough to keep the team bonded. Even though I may have sacrificed a portion of my own success for the team, that part will be returned in the form of the team's success and happiness. That afternoon I felt marvelous myself and almost enjoyed being the "bad guy." It is important to listen to those around you, but only while eavesdropping on what you are thinking yourself.

See page 316 to find out where this student got in.

CAROLINE LUCY MORGAN

Caroline held a number of leadership positions, including: Student Government President, Key Club President, Mock Trial Team Captain, and Varsity Tennis Captain. She was also Class Secretary her junior and senior years.

Stats
SAT: 1420 (700 Critical Reading, 720 Math) **High School GPA:** 4.12 weighted **High School:** Decatur High School, Decatur, GA **Hometown:** Decatur, GA **Gender:** Female **Race:** Caucasian
Applied To
Davidson College (early decision)

Essay

Write on a topic of your choice.

"Since we are justified by faith, we have peace with God through our Lord Jesus Christ, through which we have gained access to this grace in which we stand; and we boast in our hope of sharing the glory of God. And not only that, but we also boast in our sufferings, knowing that suffering produces endurance, and endurance produces character, and character produces hope, and hope does not disappoint us, because God's love has been poured into our hearts through the Holy Spirit that has been given to us." Romans 5: 1-6

For seven months I have clung to this scripture, hoping that these verses, which accurately depict the nature of my faith, will sustain me during this time that questions it. Last spring, I anticipated my significant worries to be prom and AP tests. Yet seven months ago they did not take precedence in my life. As a scared sixteen year old, I stood in awe of life while in fear of death, specifically my friend Sarah's death, which was so irrational and threatened my faith.

My life is better because Sarah Woolf was in it. She acted as an example and a guide: when she dressed up as a table for Halloween, I costumed myself as her chair; when she could have won our three day Monopoly game, she gave me the Boardwalk as a present; when I craved the Indigo Girls, we would cruise in the Woolfinator II, her '92 Honda Accord, and sing to passing cars. Words are inadequate to say how amazing she was, and how deeply she enriched my life. Now I *have* to believe there is a loving and caring God.

What is not explainable, comprehensible, nor rational is that this person whom God loved, and whom we all loved, could suffer from a disease as agonizing as bone cancer. Though her pain was unjustifiable, I must now come to terms with the faith I so desperately need but do not quite understand.

First, I remember that faith has held me this far, and I must establish that faith will be the guiding light in my future.

Second, I must look at Sarah's life as a gift of God's incessant grace. Rather than being distraught over God's place in this inexplicable situation, I must understand that the last word is not death but the grace of God.

Finally, I must not be consumed by my own grief but use what I have learned from Sarah to move forward through it. Rare maturity emerged as Sarah responded to her cancer: she maintained straight A's in her full load of AP courses, despite a demanding and grueling chemotherapy regimen; she asked to be cremated so that the funds saved could be donated to the Humane Society; the Monday before she passed away, Sarah beckoned her friends to her side to placate our agony while, with dignity and poise, Sarah embraced her own. As Sarah modeled, what distinguishes people from one another is not what happens to us, but how we respond to what happens to us.

Today I have seventeen years behind me, and I know, by the amount of grief I have observed and experienced, that through Sarah's death, life is affirmed. I know, by how much I mourn the loss of one, an amazing one, that life is good, and people are good, and above all that God, who is present during sorrow and suffering, is, in fact, good.

See page 316 to find out where this student got in.

CHELSEA R. STITT

Chelsea served as president and secretary of her high school's Student Council, secretary and treasurer for a local youth group, student representative to the school board, and a member of Future Business Leaders of America (FBLA), the French studies club, the ski club, Applebee Pond/SADD, and Big Brothers/Big Sisters Tutoring. In addition, she was on the Girl's Varsity Basketball Team, and was captain of the Varsity Tennis Team and junior captain of The Sugar Busters Walk Team for Diabetes Research. Chelsea has also spoken in Harrisburg for the National Character Education Foundation and volunteered with local programs such as Camp Sunshine, KT Summer Library, Sunday School, Relay for Life, and Vacation Bible School.

Stats
SAT: 1730 (510 Critical Reading, 670 Math, 550 Writing) **High School GPA:** 3.8 **High School:** Elderton High School, Elderton, PA **Hometown:** Kittanning, PA **Gender:** Female **Race:** Caucasian
Applied To
Duquesne University University of Pittsburgh Villanova University

Essay

Chelsea submitted the following essay to Duquesne University and Villanova University (changing the school name for each)

How the school would affect my life and help me in my career

When I was a child, I frequently spent nights at my grandparent's home. While I was there, I would watch the television program, "Law and Order" with them. It absolutely fascinated me. I admired the lawyers and their clever tactics and approaches to the interpretation of the law. I have known from the time that I was ten years old, that I was meant to be an attorney. Over the years, I have become increasingly interested in the political world and our country's government as well. As I searched for a university that could enrich and prepare me for both of those fields, I discovered that Duquesne University is distinguished in these areas and that they could greatly assist me in achieving my goals in life.

If a person wants to get far in this world, they have to have goals. Mine are clear and I feel that I can reach them. I hope to attend a notable post-secondary school for Political Science and then continue on to graduate school for law. Upon graduation, I hope to start out at a legal firm and eventually advance and own my own firm or become involved in a partnership. I have attended several mock trials and I truly enjoyed each and every one. Throughout my educational career, we have discussed thousands of court cases and it amazes me how one small trial can affect the entire world. I hope to use my learned skills and creativity to win cases and become a great lawyer. After I have gained a solid reputation and a strong base, I then wish to get involved in my true passion, Politics.

I have chosen political science as my intended major because I want to make a difference for the citizens of our great nation. I hope to run for state representative and help to improve Pennsylvania. My greatest goal in life is to become a senator. I understand that this is incredibly difficult, and out of three hundred million citizens, only one hundred are senators, but I feel that if you can dream it, you can achieve it. After intense research between accredited universities, I have come to the conclusion that Duquesne has the most prestigious and beneficial program to enhance my skills and to make me into one of the best attorneys in our nation. I feel they will give me character and help to improve my speaking and political approaches. I personally feel that Duquesne University will help me to become the person that I want and need to be. They will be the difference between a mediocre lawyer and an outstanding United States Senator.

See page 316 to find out where this student got in.

CLAUDIA GOLD

Claudia played piano for eleven years and taught private piano lessons to children. She helped teach an autistic child to speak, read, and write under the guidance of a psychologist. She was president of her high school's math club her senior year and its treasurer her sophomore year. She was active in theatre and drama and took ballet classes for ten years. She attended the Young Scholars Program at Florida State University, where she worked on a research project involving gamma emissions from fused rubidium. She also participated in an exchange program in Spain, which included classes at the University of Salamanca.

Stats
SAT: 1520 (740 Critical Reading, 780 Math)
SAT Subject Test(s): 780 Math IIC, 670 Biology
ACT: 33
High School GPA: 4.20 weighted
High School: Spanish River Community High School, Boca Raton, FL
Hometown: Boca Raton, FL
Gender: Female
Race: Caucasian

Applied To
Brown University
Cornell University
Massachusetts Institute of Technology
New York University
Rice University
University of Chicago
Yale University

Essay

Claudia used the following essay in each of her applications.

Please write something that will help us get to know you better.

It is a statistical fact that about three percent of babies are born breech. It has not been determined, however, whether prenatal upside-downness affects spatial orientation during the rest of the baby's life. But in my case, reversed entry into the world appears responsible for at least one significant subsequent event.

During my twelfth year of life, while attending a performing arts summer camp in New York, talent scouts from Nickelodeon Studios in Orlando arrived on campus to search for kids possessing unusual and entertaining talents. I didn't give it much thought until a bunkmate reminded me of my unique skill: I had developed, after considerable practice, an ability to play piano upside-down. To do so, I would position my back and shoulders on the piano bench and reach up to the keys with crossed forearms. Along with 350 other hopeful campers, I stood in line to show off my talent, aspiring to become the next Nickelodeon television star.

Foolishly, I was ecstatic when I received a phone call from casting agents three months later inviting me to participate in the pilot episode of Figure It Out, a show in which kids with unique talents appear before a panel of so-called celebrities who try to guess the hidden talent through a series of yes/no questions.

Despite dreams of a stylish arrival via Nickelodeon's private jet, my parents packed up the family minivan, and we arrived three hours later in Orlando, Florida.

Upon arriving at the sound stage, I was whisked down a corridor. As I neared a room labeled "Hair and Makeup," what sounded like the tantrum of a spoiled child became louder. When the door opened, I was surprised to see the back of the bleached-blond head of a grown woman, obviously infuriated, surrounded by hair stylists and makeup artists. When she heard me enter, she stopped arguing abruptly and swiveled her chair to greet me with a huge, collagen-enhanced smile.

"Hello, I'm your host Summer Sanders!" she announced a little too cheerfully. "You must be our special guest! I hear you have a special talent. But don't tell anyone. It's a . . . shhhhhhh. . . secret." With that, she grabbed a vat of Vaseline, smeared it across her front teeth, and walked out the door.

With my "specialness" confirmed, I was subjected to a complete makeover. The stylists repeatedly complemented my features yet painted over each of them until they were no longer recognizable as my own. (I still don't understand why I needed a pedicure when I would be wearing sneakers.)

Later, in the coffee room, while searching for any reading material besides Nickelodeon Magazine, I stumbled upon something that solidified the experience as one that would forever change my conception of the world: there, lying next to the sink, was the script for my show! The show, whose essence was spontaneity and suspense, was entirely a sham. Although to the viewers the celebrities' comments appeared cleverly improvised, each word had been carefully crafted, and even the destiny of the player, pre-determined. To my simultaneous horror and glee, amongst the final words of the script were "Claudia wins!"

I learned a lesson that proved to be a guiding principle for my life. My realization that Figure It Out, a seemingly innocent children's show, was nothing more than a derivative, commercialized, and manipulative institution, was the equivalent of many children's realization that the tooth fairy is a myth. As children, we look up to those older than us for the paradigm of how we ought to live our lives. As each facade was unveiled, my perception of the adult world was transformed. Figure It Out has become, for me, a metaphor that has helped me to identify the kind of person I strive not to become — one who is deceptive, hypocritical, and superficial. Thus, it has helped me understand the kind of person I hope to be. It helped me to "figure it out."

See page 316 to find out where this student got in.

CLAYTON KENNEDY

Clayton was valedictorian of his class and honored as one of the top 100 graduating high school seniors in Missouri. He was active in his school's theater department and excelled at soccer and cross country. Vice president of the National Honor Society, he devoted time to art, Spanish, and public service organizations at his school. Volunteer work included: Big Brothers/Big Sisters, Women's Survival House, and Easter Seals, for whom he worked as a camp counselor for intellectually, physically, and emotionally disabled youth and adults. Clayton traveled abroad several times and taught English for three months in Parral, Mexico.

Stats

SAT: 1460 (690 Critical Reading, 770 Math)
ACT: 33
High School GPA: 11.1 (out of 11.0) weighted
High School: Warrensburg High School, Warrensburg, MO
Hometown: Warrensburg, MO
Gender: Male
Race: Caucasian

Applied To

Bard College
Colorado College
Goucher College
Hampshire College
Lewis and Clark College
New College of Florida
Pitzer College
Truman State University
University of Puget Sound

Essay 1

Clayton sent the following essay to every school to which he applied.

Describe a significant experience in your life.

The license plate of New Hampshire reads *Live Free or Die*. Undoubtedly, this refers to the revolutionary cry for liberation from repressive outside forces. A more befitting interpretation for me, though, would imply a deliverance from the abusively restrictive nature of *myself*.

The downward spiral was fast and fierce. It was the spring of my eighth grade year and with each passing day I drew increasingly within. My peers were waging a battle for sameness, and I stood confused, an all-too-conscientious objector. My intrinsic, subconscious need to fit in actively conflicted with my disgust of the "ideal" person I seemingly had to become to do that. Analytically, I was far advanced; emotionally, I was the runt. My world felt out of my control and I groped for something that was not. Jarring months passed, my parents dragged me to the doctor, and the words were finally spoken aloud: anorexia nervosa.

In the midst of one of the most rapid growth periods of my life, I was shutting my body down. My parents were terrified but were determined to help me trounce the disorder. In a plea for magic, my mother and I trekked down to rural, central Mexico where, for three months, we lived with a family and taught daily classes of English to local children. The hope was that the sudden and succulent change of scenery would snap me out of it. The scheme faltered and I returned not as a healthy, actualized young man, but a wasted, frantically weak sack of bones whose emotional fragility embarrassed even the little bit of himself that remained. My body had surrendered a third of its original (and never excessive) weight, and my psyche had relinquished even more. Without fear of over-exaggeration, my state was horrific—I could not even cognize what it would be like to be better. Doctors insisted I be hospitalized ("or else he might not wake up some morning…"), and there I stayed for over a month.

With parachutes open and uplifting drafts finally blowing through, the real journey began. The hospital gave me a calm reflection period, and in time, rational thought became less fleeting. Upon my release, I returned to my freshman year of high school, just over four months tardy. To say that the following period was plagued with failures is an understatement. I do not know if I will ever engage in a more difficult or perverted battle in my life. To actively fight oneself is insidious business. At all times I betrayed part of myself, causing emotional endurance to be nearly impossible to regain. I had to quadruple any willpower I had used in starving myself to now replenish my "masterpiece."

From where did this willpower come? Having seen the grueling depths, the splendor of the crisp air above began to sink in. This world is full of harmony and I realized that *I* could be a player of it. I began to develop my worldly, aesthetic values. I found peace in everything from the sparkle of one's eye to the hue in a stretching sunset to the innocence in a kitten's face. In essence, these became my religion. I now live for that beauty. I strive to create that beauty.

I am that beauty.

I am Maya Angelou, spinning tragedy into harmony. I am Roberto Benigni, leaping across seat tops. I am the invincible boy who dreams to go to Mars. I am the wise and weathered grandma who cherishes her loved ones. I frolic in the gales, like the resplendent autumn leaves. I soften sharp edges, like the buoyant, babbling creek. My compassion is thrilling, my creativity transcending. I love unabashedly, sing uncontrollably. I am far too enthralled by the euphony of the world to experience anything less than adulation and a fierce desire to explore and help better it. Yes, I will be shot down, *time and time again*, but wounds heal stronger than before. Darkness is an essential step in true enlightenment.

In eighth and ninth grade, I was bloodied. I was bloodied by my peers and I was bloodied by myself. From the grotesque depths of helplessness, though, I have soared to individually unprecedented heights. I have opened myself up and found that I have the ability to be the very person I dream of being. Yes, I am still a teenage boy who goofs up all the time, but I am where I want to be in my mental, emotional, and (not to be forgotten) physical development.

More than any other achievement in my life, I am proud of this one. The chemical deficiency that led to this devastating, psychological disease was absolutely out of my control; the warm power that was used to beat it was not. What underlying, overriding lesson has enlightened me, then? Simplistically speaking, I suppose the expression *Live Free or Die* fits. A more personally appropriate way of stating it, though, is this:

If I live free, I fly.

Essay 2

Clayton used the following essay in his application to Bard, revising it for other schools.

Why are you applying to Bard?

I am a hungry, greedy little boy. I want it all, and have no shame in saying this. Though the bran of my life helped me build a powerful system, my body is aching for something new, something tastier, something richer, something *better*.

I am tired of airy snacks and refreshments; I long for more sustaining meals that will challenge and excite me.

I am tired of waiters and cooks who care little about their customers or commodity; I dream about gourmets who will not only personalize my feast, but will actually take me back into the kitchen and enlighten me the on process of making it.

I am tired of obnoxious atmospheres with rude or apathetic people; I desire a more intimate setting where my peers have both the aspiration and ability to recognize the fresh herbs we so giddily savor.

I am tired of monotonous, conventional meals; I drool for liberally seasoned cuisines to match myself.

I am tired of being the only one who actively enjoys and contemplates his food; I am ready for a place that demands it of everybody.

I want these things. I crave these things. In many ways, I *need* these things if I am to continue to develop in the ways true to my rhythm. Should I undergo a mundane, conventional education, I will make the most of it. I will feel, however, that it is an unfortunate waste of a fervent and fiery mind. Should I be able to attain a harmonious education from an engaging school such as Bard, I have no doubts that I will flourish in ways I cannot possibly imagine. It may be greasy, I may get messy, but I will end the experience a richer, "fuller" person.

See page 316 to find out where this student got in.

DANIEL FREEMAN

Dan participated in numerous activities in high school, and spent all four years in student council and class leadership positions. He was very active in the arts through theater productions, bands, and choir. He also served as captain of the regional office of his youth group. Dan was recognized his senior year as a Presidential Scholar, National Merit Scholar, All-State Academic Scholar, and Project Imagine Arts Scholar.

Stats
SAT: 1590 (790 Critical Reading, 800 Math)
SAT Subject Test(s): 800 Math Level 2, 790 Biology
ACT: 35
High School GPA: 4.00
High School: North Farmington High School, Farmington Hills, MI
Hometown: Farmington Hills, MI
Gender: Male
Race: Caucasian
Applied To
Yale University (early decision)

Essay

Dan does not recall the exact wording of Yale's essay question, but it basically asked applicants to write about an activity that was important to them.

The Conquest

It was a crisp, clear June day in Rocky Mountain National Park, a few miles outside of Estes Park, Colorado. Before me stood an imposing sight: Estes Cone. With a peak at twelve thousand feet above sea level and a base at eight thousand, this mountain would be a challenge for any hiker. I was no hiker; I was an unathletic, awkward 15-year-old boy. Nonetheless, I loaded my pack with salami, pita, and water and set forth.

At first the going was easy. I knew we had to ascend four thousand feet before reaching the peak, and as we passed the fourth of five mile-markers, I questioned whether we had gained more than fifteen hundred. After lunch my trip's supervisor explained the situation. The next mile included almost three thousand feet of vertical gain. We would split into two groups: one would go quickly, the other would be allowed breaks. The fast group would see the top and the slow one would be forced to turn back when they met the others coming down. I decided then that no chunk of rock could conquer me, and so I set forth with the fast group.

The pace was grueling. My muscles screamed out for rest, and I began to regret that I had chosen to audition for the musical instead of trying out for the tennis team. As we pushed forward, the angle of elevation increased from twenty degrees, to thirty, to nearly forty. I fell further and further behind until I was told that I should simply wait for the slow group to catch up and continue with them. I curtly responded that I would be fine and proceeded onward. Pain tore through my legs as I pulled my body weight over each rock. The back of the group flittered in and out of my view, pulling me forward with only dim hopes of success.

Time wore on, and pain faded into numbness. Each foot followed the other in a grim succession. The trees thinned with the increasing altitude, and the peak grew nearer. Suddenly I heard my friend Dan holler down, "Hurry up man, you've just about made it, and we're sick of waiting for you!" My vigor restored, I pushed on quicker than before until I broke through the tree line. A bald, craggy expanse of rock surrounded me. The others were waiting, cameras in a pile, in preparation for a group shot at the summit. In one final act of endurance, I pulled myself over the top to join the others in triumph. My climb was complete.

As I looked down from that peak upon the miniaturized ranger station and the surrounding vistas, I received two things. One would shape my leisure time for the remainder of high school – a love of hiking. Whenever I get the chance, I escape from suburbia and enter the wilds. Since that fateful summer I have hiked in three countries: through the heat of Israel's Judean Desert, over the rocky cliffs of Canada's Lake Superior Provincial Park, and throughout the forests of my native Michigan's many state parks. I now am a hiker. Even more importantly, I was given confidence.

Physical limitations and the limitations that others place on me no longer deter me from setting and reaching my goals. Life is my mountain, and no rock-strewn face will keep me from reaching the summit.

See page 317 to find out where this student got in.

DANIEL MEJIA

Daniel was valedictorian of his high school and president of its largest club, Operation Smile. While managing more than 150 students in Operation Smile, he helped raise more than $20,000 to provide free reconstructive surgery for children and young adults. A Boy Scout for six years, Daniel won his rotary club's Service-Above-Self Award for service to the community. He played varsity tennis and winter track, as well as soccer on the freshman team. He was also a paperboy for five years. A scholar in the National Hispanic Recognition Program, Daniel was selected for the New Jersey Governor's School of International Studies. He was in the National Honor Society and the Spanish Honor Society.

Stats
SAT: 1390 (680 Critical Reading, 710 Math)
High School GPA: 4.51 weighted
High School: Lawrence High School, Lawrenceville, NJ
Hometown: Lawrenceville, NJ
Gender: Male
Race: Latino

Applied To
Amherst College
Georgetown University
Harvard College
Princeton University
Rutgers University—New Brunswick
Tufts University

Essay

Daniel submitted the following essay to Amherst, Georgetown, Harvard, and Tufts.

Beep, beep, beep. My alarm goes off at 5:30 AM. I dart outside in my oversized t-shirt and pajama pants to bring in the newspapers as the rain pours out of the sky onto the freshly printed papers. The daily morning pressure has begun – I must deliver the papers by 6:30! Why did it have to rain today? I get onto my bicycle and prepare to enter the dark, misty, morning . . . Whoa, I almost rammed into a stray trashcan in the road. I swerve to the left to avoid a giant puddle. Okay, my first house is a porch customer. I get off my bike and run through the grass up to my customer's porch twenty feet away, but on the way I step in dog poop. I'm just going to have to move on – a paper boy's got to do what a paper boy's got to do! I begin to shiver with mud on my clothes and water leaking into my old sneakers. There are only five papers left. After another grueling ten minutes I'm finally done! I begin to walk inside the house to dry off, and of course it stops raining at that moment.

Why do I keep this job, a job that requires getting up in the wee hours of the morning to deliver newspapers to demanding and unsympathetic customers? There are the obvious reasons, such as for making money, gaining responsibility, learning how to run a business, and meeting many new people. But, well, there's another reason that I don't like to admit to the "guys;" I also do it for a girl. Not just any girl, but rather a girl whose very presence has changed my outlook on the world and allowed me to escape the typical high school goal of popularity.

Fast forward six months, and I have finally saved up enough money to buy a used 1996 Nissan Maxima and to take this girl, Megan, to New York City's Tavern on the Green, the restaurant of her dreams. (Trust me, it's a restaurant that has very "undreamy" prices.) Megan is bursting with excitement as we walk through Central Park to get to Tavern. It's her sweet sixteen birthday. I put my arm around her and point out the "bright stars in the sky"; she giggles, but gives me those sarcastic eyes. She knows I'm overdoing it. Finally we go in and have a great time despite my reminder that she does not need to order the most expensive entrée. The night is followed by my surprising her with ice-skating under the Christmas tree at Rockefeller Center. Personally I do not get too many thrills from the night's activities. Nonetheless, her ecstatic smiling eyes at the end of the night prove that at least this morning's paper delivery was worth it. I secretly get my own joy driving us off in my new used Maxima.

See page 317 to find out where this student got in.

DAVID AUERBACH

David was competitive in many areas and competed at the state level in speech and debate, youth legislature, and mock trial. He was also active within his high school as editor of the school newspaper, National Honor Society president, a mathematics tutor, and a member of the track and cross-country teams. Outside of school, he did independent genetics research and worked on preserving the ecosystem of a local river.

Stats
SAT: 1560
ACT: 35
High School GPA: 4.00
High School: Sprague High School, Salem, Oregon
Hometown: Salem, OR
Gender: Male
Race: Caucasian
Applied To
Carleton College
Dartmouth College
Macalaster College
Willamette University

Essay

David used the following essay in each of his applications. He explains, "I picked the 'anything you want' option because I felt the other questions were too confining."

Cleaning Your Room Can Change Your Life

Recently, during a futile attempt at cleaning my eternally messy room, I tripped over the leg of a chair and fell sprawling to the floor. As I lifted my head, I found that I was at eye level with the very bottom shelf of my bookcase. One book on it caught my eye—a book I had last read in eighth grade. I pulled the book out and began to read....

I read of a world where the written word is forbidden, where books and other printed material have been banned for decades. Without the printed word, intellectual life withers and debate dies. In the absence of debate there are no disagreements. In this dystopia, all are equal because no one excels and mediocrity rules. All are therefore happy. On the surface, the system seems to work.

Enter Guy Montag. Guy is a fireman; that is, his job is burning books. He enjoys his job, for he knows he is making the world a safer and happier place. He is a perfect product of the system...until he meets Clarisse.

Clarisse and her family are misfits. In Guy's hyperaccelerated world, they still enjoy walking. In his world, questions are discouraged, because asking questions is part of the process of discovery. Clarisse is expelled from school for asking questions. She has a natural curiosity about others; in her words, "I just want to figure out who [people] are and what they want and where they're going." Perhaps the most profound question in the book is Clarisse's simple query to Guy: "Are you happy?"

As he ponders this question, Guy realizes the fallacy behind the "equality" he fosters. By destroying books, he forces people (including himself) to give up their individuality and ability for independent thought. They become dependent on the system, expecting everything to be handed to them on a plate.

What did I learn from this book? I learned from the frenetic pace of Guy's world to slow down and take time to enjoy life. I learned from Clarisse's curiosity that there is nothing wrong with asking questions. I have always been an inquisitive person, but since first reading this book, I have become even more inquisitive about the world around me. Finally, I learned the incredible power of knowledge. Knowledge bestows the power to create or destroy. It enables us to judge and to choose. The ability to make decisions is what makes each of us so different and interesting.

For me, reading this book was a life-changing experience. I often pause and ask myself: "What knowledge have you gained today? What power has that knowledge given you? How has it made you different?" One additional difference reading that book made to me was the realization that books and especially their contents need to be protected in order to avoid mediocrity. And thanks to Ray Bradbury, I now know that *Fahrenheit 451* is the temperature at which book paper burns.

See page 317 to find out where this student got in.

DAVID GIBBS

David served as captain of his high school basketball and baseball teams.

Stats
SAT: 2060 (610 Critical Reading, 760 Math, 690 Writing) **High School GPA:** Did not have a GPA **High School:** Riverdale Country School, Bronx, NY **Hometown:** Harrison, NY **Gender:** Male **Race:** Caucasian
Applied To
Tufts University (applied early decision) Tulane University (applied early decision)

Essay

David submitted the following essay to the schools listed above.

Topic of your choice.

Danny Almonte and Me

Tuesday, July 27th, 2001. We've had a great run up to this point. Because we lost the second game of the district tournament, we had to win seven in a row in order to win the championship. Now, after winning our first two games of the Section tournament, we are in the finals. A win today would put us in the State tournament with a chance to go to the Regionals.

I step off the bus and see players from the other team, Rolando Paulino, getting out of their cars in the parking lot. These kids are humongous. They're twelve?

"Danny, me da algunas semillas girasoles," one of them says. I don't understand Spanish. If they speak Spanish during the game, we'll have no chance of figuring out their strategies.

"Play ball!" says the umpire as Rolando Paulino takes the field. We're at bat, and before I know it we already have runners on second and third. How did that happen? Rolando Paulino is supposed to be amazing. Maybe we do have a chance to – but there's our third out.

I take the mound for the bottom of the first. Curve ball, high. Bad decision. OK, here is a fastball. Wow, he hit that a long way. I guess this team really is as good as it looks.

Here's their Number Three batter, a tall, skinny kid with some facial hair, the one everyone has been talking about. Danny Almonte. I tell myself to relax, but I don't take my own advice: I throw a fastball down the middle. Danny wastes no time in crushing it to the fence. Suddenly, I'm pretty sure I know how this game is going to play out.

The rest is a complete blur. All I remember is Rolando Paulino hitting a lot of balls hard and me doing a lot of second guessing.

Afterwards, even though I am upset that this great run we've had is over, I accept that Paulino is better than us. Now it is time to concentrate on winning our league championship.

That night at dinner my dad and I discuss the game. He brings up some points that hadn't occurred to me: that Danny Almonte threw the ball nearly 80mph, at least 8 mph faster than any other Little League pitcher; that kids who have facial hair are probably fourteen and fifteen; that the thirteen members of Rolando Paulino attended eight different schools – a difficult feat considering that all the players must live in the same neighborhood. "David," he says, "there's a strong possibility that this team was cheating."

Almonte's team forfeits LLWS victories

Sports Illustrated: Friday August 31, 2001

SANTO DOMINGO, Dominican Republic (AP)–Little League pitcher Danny Almonte is no longer perfect–because he's no longer 12.

The boy who dominated the Little League World Series with his 70mph fastballs was ruled ineligible Friday after government records experts determined he actually is 14, and that birth certificates showing he was two years younger were false

There it was in black and white. Danny Almonte ruined my chance of playing in the Little League World Series.

It's now five years later, and the name Danny Almonte still upsets me. It has taken me that long to articulate the effect this episode has had on me, both as an athlete and as a person. Under the influence of a crooked coach, Danny's team ruined the integrity of Little League Baseball. They weren't able to distinguish right and wrong. They lacked the discipline to resist temptation. Every time a person or a team taints a sport, the accomplishments of honest athletes go unnoticed. Competition itself depends on the honesty of the players: cheaters not only ruin the significance of victory and defeat for everyone else, but also undermines the sport they claim to love. Because I have seen cheating up close and have been directly affected by it, I can't take cheating lightly in any realm of life, whether it be sports, school, or business. I would never want to make someone feel the way I felt after I found out that all my hard work – my dream – was ruined by cheaters.

Today, Danny Almonte and I still aspire to play baseball at the highest levels. He appears on television and in the newspaper occasionally, and he is a more talented ballplayer than I am, but I would never want to trade places with him. I'd rather be an honest loser than a dishonest winner.

See page 317 to find out where this student got in.

DIANA SCHOFIELD

In high school, Diana was a four-year letterman and captain of the varsity swim team. While on the swim team, she achieved several state honors, and was voted MVP twice in a row. She also was concertmistress of her high school's faculty/student orchestra, attended Governor's School for violin, and participated in the Spoleto Study Abroad program for orchestra. She was a member of the National Honor Society and was nominated for the Morehead Scholarship.

Stats
SAT: 1380 (700 Critical Reading, 680 Math)
SAT Subject Test(s): 660 U.S. History, 680 Spanish
ACT: 31
High School GPA: 4.23
High School: Ravenscroft, Raleigh, NC
Hometown: Raleigh, NC
Gender: Female
Race: Caucasian

Applied To
Boston College
Cornell University
Emory University
Georgetown University
Harvard College
Northwestern University
University of North Carolina—Chapel Hill
University of Pennsylvania
Washington University in St. Louis

Essay

Diana used the following essay in each of her applications, with the exception of Georgetown.

Cite a meaningful first experience and explain its impact on you.

I greatly appreciate the concept of taking a *siesta* in the afternoon. I love the fact that the salad comes after the main course, and the cars are all the size of Volkswagen beetles. Olive oil really can accompany any meal. You can't go anywhere without seeing a duomo or a fresco. Punctuality is not a necessity of life. No one in Italy ever seems to be in a rush, because there is no time.

E.M. Forster wrote, "The traveler who has gone to Italy to study the tactile values of Giotto, or the corruption of the Papacy, may return remembering nothing but the blue sky and the men and women who live under it." Such was my experience as I, a student of music, spent a month in Spoleto, Italy this past summer. I originally applied for a spot in the Spoleto Study Abroad program in order to play the violin, study opera, history, and learn Italian. But what I came away with was the influence of the Italian culture, which will follow me wherever I go.

As I lugged my overweight, eighty-pound suitcase (nicknamed "The Big Mama") down a narrow cobblestone alley, I wiped the sweat-smeared makeup from my forehead and worried about what the lack of air conditioning and overwhelming humidity was going to do to me. And no email? Nevertheless, I couldn't wait to start classes, begin rehearsals, and get out into the city. I couldn't seem to get over my American ways of rushing from one activity to another; "exhausted" became my only response to the typical Italian greeting "Come stai?" As I wearily walked to class one morning, I noticed this incredible view overlooking most of Spoleto. I stopped dead in my tracks and studied the fog settling over the tiled roofs of modest stone houses. Laundry lines hung from window to window like vines. This was not the Italy of the Olive Garden and Parmesan cheese commercials. This *was Italy*. Why had I not noticed this magnificent site before? I took a picture, and every time I passed that spot, I paused to study the amazing world below me. My American schedules and routines were discarded, along with my makeup and hairdryer. I slowed down, took many scenic routes, began sampling new flavors of gelato, and trying out my nascent Italian skills on vendors in the piazzas. I could spend literally hours sitting in cafes chatting with friends, and in a very "Lost Generation" style, writing in my journal. Living in Italy for a month is more than eating the food, purchasing postcards, and attempting to decipher the language, it is living the life and the culture. In that month I became an inhabitant of the country, an Italian by my lifestyle and mindset. When I physically returned to the States, my thoughts were in Spoleto, Florence, Siena and in other beautiful cities. As I readjusted to life in Raleigh, North Carolina, I never lost my Italian flair. I discovered that Italy is not only a place, but also a state of mind.

See page 317 to find out where this student got in.

ELIZABETH JEFFERS ORR

*Along with participating in the International Baccalaureate pro-
gram in high school, Elizabeth was also a cheerleader, lacrosse
player, and member of student council and National Honor Society.
She spent the summer before her senior year living with a family
of eight in Costa Rica and helped rebuild their town's community
center while also teaching English classes. Throughout high school
she volunteered for a Denver-based organization that put on the
annual televised holiday parade in downtown Denver.*

Stats
SAT: 1330 (680 Critical Reading, 650 Math)
ACT: 29
ACT Writing: 11
High School GPA: 4.2
High School: Littleton High School, Littleton, CO
Hometown: Denver, CO
Gender: Female
Race: Caucasian

Applied To
Bates College
Colby College
Kalamazoo College
Kenyon College
Lewis & Clark College
Macalester College
Oberlin College
University of Denver
University of Puget Sound

Essay

Elizabeth submitted the following essay to the schools listed above.

Topic of your choice

Beaches are meant to be rocky and gray. The ocean is meant to be deep blue
and frigidly cold. You have to jump in because getting in step by step is intolerable.
Everyone else's white sand and turquoise blue fantasies mean nothing to me. I know
only the whitecaps and fog, along with the trees and cliffs, that surround the beach
of my memories. Every recollection I have, of any summer, involves Skillings, my

family's summer home on the coast of Maine. The wooden walls of that one-hundred year old house contain remnants of not only my childhood, but also the echoes of three generations of my family, who all vacationed there.

It is easy to forget that I am part of this extended family. I am at least ten years younger then the rest of my generation; all of my cousins already have kids, some of them approaching middle age. I live in Denver, approximately fifteen states away from any other family member. Out of the myriad of genetic possibilities, I inherited my mother's hair, skin, and eye colors, making me a dark-skinned brunette, a rarity in this family of pale, blue-eyed red heads. Age, location, and appearance all loosen the obvious ties to my family.

Sometimes I question what we have in common, but there is a connection. My dad and uncles used to swim in this ocean when they spent their childhood summers at Skillings. Their names are carved into the sixty-year-old furniture. Here I share toys and books with my cousins, who have already moved on to adulthood, and with my father, who doesn't remember leaving them behind. They slept in the room I sleep in now, just as my cousin Becky did before me. She left a pair of sandals here seven years ago. I borrow them sometimes, just as I borrow the raincoat my aunt Louise used to wear. Everyone who comes to stay at Skillings leaves something behind; Becky's shoes, Louise's coat, my dad's copy of Just So Stories. I can picture some future niece or nephew of mine wearing the same goggles I've worn, diving head first into tidal pools to stare at the same starfish with which I've been transfixed.

At the end of every vacation, as our car pulls out of the driveway, I get my last glimpse of the deep blue water, and I cry. Only at Skillings do I feel like part of my extended family. Although most of them are older and far away, I know that, just as I do, they revisit their history here. Skillings encases the memories and belong-ings of my family, pieces of our lives, saving them for later, for others. Unlike me, the older members of my family no longer cry when they leave, but I know they did once. Maybe some day, once I'm older, I will stop, too. Until then, I will leave the remains of tears behind to mingle with those of my family, who all are at home amongst the rocks and fog.

See page 318 to find out where this student got in.

ELLISON WARD

In high school, Ellison was a Peer Leader and a member of the Cultural Awareness group, as well as a member of the soccer, basketball, and lacrosse teams. She was also extremely interested in Spanish language and culture and a studied abroad the summer after her sophomore year.

Stats

SAT: 1570 (780 Critical Reading, 790 Math)
SAT Subject Test(s): 770 Math Level 2, 740 Physics
High School GPA: Ellison's high school did not calculate GPA, but she had about an A-minus average.
High School: The Nightingale-Bamford School, New York, NY
Hometown: New York, NY
Gender: Female
Race: Caucasian

Applied To

Brown University
College of William & Mary
Connecticut College
Duke University
Johns Hopkins University
Harvard College
Princeton University
Yale University

Essay 1

Ellison used the following essay in her application to Princeton and modified it slightly for each of her other applications.

Common Application: Evaluate a significant experience, achievement, or risk that you have taken and its impact on you.

So I'm sitting on my couch, wrapped in a blanket that I have somehow wrestled from my sister, enthralled by the electrifying activities taking place before me. The movie is *Outbreak*, and our star, Dustin Hoffman, is in the middle of a standoff with his superior officer, Donald Sutherland. Their argument centers on a certain town in California, contaminated with a certain deadly yet suddenly curable virus, and a plane carrying a chemical agent that will wipe out the entire population of the afore-mentioned town. "No!" my sister shrieks. "Don't drop the bomb!" As the plane veers out over the ocean, the missile flies into the crystal clear waters and creates an immense, mushroom-shaped wave. "All right!" shouts my family, as out of the jubilee rises my tearful cry, "Wait! What about the marine life?!"

All right, so this is an overly dramatic version of the actual events, but the gist is the same. My bizarre attachment to the fictional fish is largely a product of my summer; I worked for eight weeks in the Coral Lab of the New York Aquarium on Coney Island. I'll admit that my interest in the Natural Sciences was pretty general; I thought corals were beautiful, and I had fond memories of childhood trips to the Aquarium every time I visited my aunt and uncle in Virginia. I was thrilled to be working at the lab, but when you came right down to it, one truth remained: I had no idea what I was doing. No amount of ninth grade biology (or tenth grade chemistry or eleventh grade physics, for that matter) could have prepared me for the intrica-cies of the filtration system in a room full of corals being used for research projects or the manual dexterity required by the micropipeting process. But by the time August rolled around, not only had I mastered the fine art of maintaining a number of different filters and the rather painstaking procedure of micropipeting, but I had figured out what it is that has always drawn me to the sciences. Everyone I met, no matter how grating, overbearing, or bossy he might have been, could be reduced by the mere sight of a tank to an awed silence. And most that I met were not in any way grating, overbearing, or bossy. In fact, they were enthusiastic, dedicated, and friendly to anyone interested in their field to the point of annoyance. And they are just who I want to be.

The funny thing about this whole essay is that I don't even want to be a marine biologist. What I really want to study are the Earth Sciences, but the specifics are not important. I learned this summer what it is to be passionate about what you are doing, to have an unchecked enthusiasm for even the dirtiest aspects of your work. To spend your life in the quest for knowledge that could make the world a better place may sound like a lofty goal, but when it's a real possibility, it's utterly amazing. Like any profession there are twists and turns, opportunities for frustration, disap-pointment, and conflict, but everyone in that lab knows he is doing something he can be proud of and that might help the world better understand how we can save our planet. Now that I have seen the kind of passion and love with which these people work at their jobs, I would never settle for anything less.

Essay 2

Ellison used the following essay in her application to Princeton. The prompt below is an approximation.

What book has had the most effect on you and why? It can be a book you read on your own, in class, or anywhere.

Of all the books that I have read, the one that has affected me the most is <u>Native Son</u> by Richard Wright, which I read for my Harlem Renaissance English elective junior year. Never have I read a book in which the protagonist has such a wildly different sense of the world than the expected norm. Suddenly I was exposed to a way of thinking that was extraordinarily different than my own, and Wright's compelling portrait made it easy for me to understand this startling point of view. Before reading this novel, I had always closed my mind to those who did not agree with my liberal yet stringent morality; I could not (or would not) allow myself to explore a mindset that would allow someone to commit a crime so egregious as murder. <u>Native Son</u> has allowed me to face the fear that comes with venturing into the unknown, and to explore a variety of opinions before settling on one of my own, rather than automatically following that which I feel best fits my profile of convictions. Open-mindedness and the ability to withhold judgement are extremely important qualities in a world where so many cultures and ideals mix, and Richard Wright's novel has helped me to work towards gaining both of these qualities.

Essay 3

Ellison used the following essay in her application to Princeton. The prompt below is an approximation.

Name one thing that you wish you understood better. Explain.

Of the many things that I wish I understood better, the one that I am faced with the most often is my sister. I see her everyday; we attend the same school, share a room, and share our parents. I feel as though I should understand her feelings and be able to identify her moods with ease after thirteen years of living with her, but she remains one of the biggest mysteries in my life. She's talented, intelligent, and undoubtedly the wittiest person I know. Yet she is also picky, stubborn, and prone to outbreaks that I am powerless to stop. Not that I think these outbursts are a sign of some underlying psychological problem; they are hardly that serious. But when I am coming closer and closer to moving out of our room and thus putting a hole in our relationship that may not be refilled, I can't bear to watch our days together wasted on her bad moods.

Maybe it is because I am too close to her that I can't see the way my own actions affect her, but I simply do not know how to behave so that I won't set her off. My parents seem to have some idea; they often think that I am trying to aggravate her on purpose. But I want nothing more than to have the harmony (and that truly is how I would describe the situation) that we often live in be permanent. I'm just not sure how to make that happen.

Essay 4

Ellison used the following essay in her application to Princeton. The prompt below is an approximation.

> *If you could hold any position in government, what would it be, and why?*

If I could hold any position in the government, I would be the President. Opportunities such as this do not present themselves very often; it seems only natural to choose the position in which I could effect the most change. Although I have nothing but respect for the principles of our government, there are many aspects of the actual governing of our country that have room for improvement. The corruption, partisan hostility, and sordid scandals that have come to characterize our government are an embarrassment. The most effective way to increase the esteem in which the world and our own people hold the administration is to place in the most visible position someone clearly dedicated to the upkeep of the noble ideals upon which our country was founded. This is where I come in. Although the actual fulfillment of the duties of this office would be by necessity far less idealistic than my diatribe on the Founding Fathers, the government is in dire need of someone who has at least some small sense of the merits of such antiquated conceptions as liberty, freedom, and limited power. If I could, in my stint as President, represent citizens of the United States as the open-minded, intelligent, respectful, and more-interested-in-foreign-affairs-than-the-private-life-of-our-president people that many are convinced we are not, than I would have succeeded in fulfilling one of the most important goals our Presidential candidates should have.

Essay 5

Ellison used the following essay in her application to Princeton. The prompt below is an approximation.

Name one thing that you would do to improve race relations in this country.

The problem of race is one that has plagued our country since its inception, and it is virtually impossible to come up with one or two simple steps to that would lead to its repair. It seems that virtually every solution opens a Pandora's box of new problems, and it is difficult to sort through the insanely numerous opinions, stereotypes, prejudices and points of view that constitute our population. This being said, no real progress can be made without small strides, as controversial and tiny as they may be. The best solution would be a spontaneous dissolution of prejudice and the opening of people's minds; a slightly more realistic solution might be to rearrange the zoning of public schools, and to then promote diversity within those schools. Arranging school districts by neighborhood in many cases results in an uneven balance between different ethnicities, which in turn results in increased hostility and divisiveness. By instead creating magnet schools that draw from a variety of neighborhoods, diversity of race, as well as socioeconomic class, religion, sexuality, and all the other characteristics that make people different, would be increased. Forcing the truly complete integration of the nation's schools may be one of the only ways remaining to break down the barriers separating the vast groups that populate the United States. Although it may create resentment, disagreement, or discomfort at first, it seems a somewhat feasible way of promoting the harmony to which we aspire.

See page 318 to find out where this student got in.

EMILY ALLEN

A National Merit Scholar, Emily was active in her church's youth group and lead worship services. At her high school, she acted in school plays, played in the school band and flute club, and took six Advanced Placement courses. She went to Bolivia for a summer with Amigos de las Americas, and attended the National Young Leaders Conference. A Girl Scout for eight years, she earned the Silver Award.

Stats
SAT: 1600 (800 Critical Reading, 800 Math)
High School GPA: NA—Emily was in the top 10 percent of her class
High School: Henry M. Gunn High School, Palo Alto, CA
Hometown: Palo Alto, CA
Gender: Female
Race: Caucasian

Applied To
Georgetown University
Harvard College
University of California—Berkeley
University of California—Los Angeles
University of California—San Diego
University of Pennsylvania
University of Southern California
Yale University

Essay

Emily submitted the following essay, in response to various generic prompts, to every school to which she applied. The version she sent to UC schools, however, was slightly longer than the following version.

My summer partner and I stood, watching the truck rattle away, leaving us alone by a rural Bolivian farm. We turned to each other, matching expressions clear on our faces: What have I gotten myself into? Did I ever think volunteering for eight weeks in a Spanish-speaking community would build my language fluency and sense of responsibility? *Claro que sí.*

Last summer I participated in *Amigos de las Américas.* In *Amigos*, two teens stay with host families in a Latin American country and work on projects chosen by the local community. Eight months of training sessions led up to the summer experience; I attended fifteen evening meetings, five Saturday workshops, and three retreats. At the same time I raised over $4000 by selling grapefruit, oranges, and poinsettias and by writing letters asking friends and family to sponsor me. I also engineered an additional $2000 grant from my dad's company to help with scholarships in my chapter of *Amigos*. I enjoyed preparing and giving presentations to parents and fellow trainees, especially because I got to improvise a cohesive talk out of a bare outline of information.

I put Bolivia as my first choice, so I was pleased that I got to go there. My Bolivian community chose two projects for my partner and me: facilitate the completion of the community building—a doorless, windowless, two-room project abandoned several years earlier—and hold English classes for local kids at the school. The latter project succeeded because the students showed an eagerness to learn. With classes held for an hour, six days a week, we soon discovered the difficulty of creating new lessons and activities. In addition, the lessons had to be adaptable for an age range of six to sixteen and a group size range of three to forty-three. When we had enough high school students to make a separate class, I would take them into another classroom to help them with their English homework and questions. When I had difficulty eliciting requests for what they wanted to learn, I would spontaneously use my background in drama to create a lesson such as touching each body part as I named them or creating family trees to remember the words for various relations. The younger students especially enjoyed the games we taught them, and I occasionally overheard a spirited game of Perrito (my loose translation of Red Rover) being played during school recess. One time, before class, the school gatekeeper (who never complained about having to come back in the evenings to re-open the school after-hours for our classes) brought a set of dominoes to me and asked me to translate the English playing instructions. I felt thrilled that I could provide that small service for him.

Our other project, the community building, took longer to show progress. We had a hard time getting workers to come to the building site to use the materials we had bought. We would visit one town leader's home, and after making polite conversation we would finally ask for and receive a promise to send workers the next day. When no one showed up to work with us, we would look for the man we had talked to, only to discover he had left for the day and wouldn't be back until dark. This happened several times with different leaders, so we finally held a town meeting, with our field supervisor present, to explain the urgency of finishing the construction before we left in three weeks. Apparently the meeting worked, because three to six workers started showing up every day at the site. When we left, the doors and windows were installed and the interior walls were painted.

I expected that my summer with Amigos would be more fulfilling than, for example, a week-long "mission trip" to Mexico with a youth group because the personal accomplishment would be clear. I would wake myself up, set my own schedule, and take care of the details of completing projects. I saw myself taking on a comparable level of responsibility for projects at college and in a future business setting. As it turned out, I found no such clarity about who was responsible for events. Perhaps, if I had pushed harder, the community would have worked on the building faster. However, that might have led to a lack of community responsibility and sustainable interest in and maintenance of the building after my partner and I left. The community played such a large role in the work that I soon realized I could take care of my end of things, but only encourage them to work on their parts. Once they got going, it was exciting to see their growing enthusiasm extend to new plans to add on a kitchen, bathroom, and patio to the existing building. When I left, workers had already dug the hole for the bathroom, bought the supplies for the kitchen, and arranged to continue the shifts of workers. When I look back at my summer, I can admit that I didn't do everything single-handedly. Nonetheless, I still take pride in my participation in the whole community effort. Even without the expected results, my experience will help me when I work on projects in the future. I also have come away with more confidence in my adaptability: if a truck dropped me off in a rural village today, I know I could move past any initial uncertainties to explore new ways of understanding my world.

See page 318 to find out where this student got in.

EMMA FRICKE

Emma played field hockey for four years and was captain of her school's JV team for two. She was active in student government and was class secretary for two years. She actively participated in volunteer activities with her church and school. She also worked at day-care centers and baby-sat.

Stats
SAT: 1220 (640 Critical Reading, 580 Math)
SAT Subject Test(s): 580 Biology, 550 Chemistry, 600 Math Level 1
High School GPA: 3.35/4.00
High School: Belmont High School, Belmont, MA
Hometown: Belmont, MA
Gender: Female
Race: Caucasian

Applied To
Mount Holyoke College
Smith College
Sweet Briar College
Vanderbilt University
Wellesley College

Essay

Emma used the following essay in each of her applications.

Choose a significant occurrence in your life and discuss why it has impacted you.

What first comes to mind when the words sing-a-longs, radio shows and art projects are listed together? For my brother and I, these words have a special meaning. For us, they mean to load up our suitcases with every single "important clothing item" and fill our back-packs with tapes, art materials and any other fun items that we deem "necessary" for yet another Road Trip.

For as long as I can remember, my family has been throwing gear into the car and heading off on adventures. My brother and I have always been in charge of packing our own bags and bringing things to keep us entertained. Usually, we don't need many material items. We pool our imaginations to invent games, sing songs, and play bingo. We also do back scratching, head massaging, and feet fighting. The two of us always bond no matter how feisty we have been during the weeks before. Together, we fall into our "road trip mode" of cooperation the second we hit the highways.

I am by no means saying that every road trip we have taken has been perfectly pleasant. Once, my brother, who was three months old at the time, screamed all the way from Texas to Missouri. When I was two and my brother was not yet one we moved from Texas to Massachusetts. On the last leg of the journey in Connecticut, my father came down with the chicken pox. I am told that when I was four on a trip to Alabama, I sang the same song over and over for an hour. At that point I calmly announced, "Let's turn the record over!" And for the next hour I sang a new song. Another time, when I was in eighth grade and I thought hard rock was the coolest. I made my family listen to it all the way from Boston to Florida. My brother and I have also gone through "creative" stages. On our annual road trip to Missouri, we decorated all the windows of our car with beeswax clay. "Hey Mom," we exclaimed, "when it melts on the windows it looks just like stained glass!" Another time we made glitter paintings. We called the glitter "magic dragon dust." When we arrived at our campsite for the night, the mystical "dragon dust" covered our entire bodies, our seats and the floor, (and about 1% of it was on its actual designated spot, the paper.) The dragon dust lingered for years in the car. On a road trip, mechanical difficulties are bound to happen. En-route to Minnesota, our alternator belt fell off along the highway. We exited quickly but couldn't find a gas station anywhere. Luckily, straight-ahead was K-Mart. Rejuvenated with hope, my brother, my best friend and I ran in, asking every sales clerk around if they could find us a new alternator belt for the car. "No" was the answer. Picture us: a family (plus one) sitting on the curb eating carrots at K-Mart next to a smoking and smelly car. We didn't give up, though. Eventually, my dad found a tow-truck service to take him to a gas station so he could buy a new belt. Pretty soon, we were back on the road again singing our hearts out.

As the years have progressed, our Road Trips have changed significantly. Now we have three drivers instead of two and we all can agree on music (well, sort of). My brother has become a professional backseat driver and we can go for longer than one exit without having to stop for a bathroom break. Lately though, my family has begun taking road trips with my father's brother and his family. They have four children ages two, four, seven and nine. Now my brother and I are the designated babysitters instead of the babysittees. They have a van and so my brother and I sit with kids piled on each lap and entertain. Last year, while driving from Alabama to Florida to visit our grandparents, we successively rapped every child's song that we could think of; rap, apparently, is now the cool music of choice, (not hard rock, like I used to think). We also have refined our talent of making up stories "No, I want a scary bunny story, not a funny alligator story," and have learned the gift of patience.

This gift of patience is invaluable. In order to succeed in what I love to do, working with young children; patience is something that I have to draw upon often. When I am ready to throw up my hands in desperation while babysitting or working in the church nursery, I remember how my parents dealt with my brother and me throughout the years of Road Trips. Smiling from this, I roll up my sleeves and whip out some glitter and paper or begin to sing the songs that I remember from my childhood. My parents have taught me that children are a gift and their creativity and outlook on life is something that should never be suppressed or overlooked. Now that I am a senior in high school, I am sad to think that my road trip days with my family are almost finished. Hopefully, college will be one big Road Trip where I will use the important aspects of creativity, compromise and overcoming obstacles. I will always know how to enjoy life even though what is presented to me may not be "magic dragon dust."

See page 318 to find out where this student got in.

ERIC OSBORNE

In high school, Eric was actively involved in many areas of student life. He was assistant editor of his school's yearbook, a columnist for its student paper, and a member of its civic-service organization. During his senior year, he was president of Government Club, through which he served as lieutenant governor at his state's model legislature. He lettered in track for three years, in yell-leading for two, and won his school's Spirit Award senior year for his dedication and inspiration to the track team.

Stats

SAT: 1460 (750 Critical Reading, 710 Math)
SAT Subject Test(s): 800 U.S. History, 800 World History
ACT: 32
High School GPA: 4.10 weighted
High School: Memphis University School, Memphis, TN
Hometown: Memphis, TN
Gender: Male
Race: Caucasian

Applied To

Amherst College (early decision)

Essay

Evaluate a significant experience, achievement, risk you have taken, or ethical dilemma you have faced and its impact on you.

From a Dunce to Demosthenes

ERX, the word rings clearly in my ears today. In 6th grade some of my peers decided it would be funny to make fun of the lisp that Eric Osborne had. They took my first name and added a lisp sound to the end of it, finally arriving with a new nickname for me, Erx.

As a little kid I had somehow learned to say "S's" incorrectly. Rather than the smooth hissing sound most people make, my "S's" were a saliva-filled slur that lisped sideways from my mouth. In my earliest years my teachers, parents, and friends would try to correct me. Wanting to please them, I would swallow all the saliva in my mouth and speak slowly, enunciating as clearly as possible. But it never made a difference.

As I grew older the other kids started to make fun of my speech. Every time I opened my mouth, some sneering comment was sure to follow. I was embarrassed by all this and soon preferred keeping quite to being made fun of. I became something of a recluse. Eric Osborne was the shy kid who, for fear of being made fun of, hardly ever spoke. Mute, I became a virtually friendless wanderer.

My parents had opposing views of the situation. My mother was worried about me: she was worried that I never brought friends home, that I never went out to spend the night, that I always seemed sad and depressed. My father had a different view: he was upset that I could never "enunciate clearly." My speech impediment irked my father greatly. For years he corrected me to no avail, and he became more upset with each passing day.

By third grade I had gone through speech therapy, but things had not improved. Afterward I had always looked upon speech therapy as something only young children went through; I did not consider repeating it myself. But by eighth grade things were changing. Although I now had more friends, the teasing was continuing, and I was more aware of my personal image. In addition my father had decided that enough was enough and it was now time to put an end to my impediment. Speech therapy seemed the best course of action. With my guidance counselor's help we found a speech pathologist, and I went back to speech therapy.

It took the pathologist less than ten minutes to diagnose my problem. She told me to move my tongue to the level of my teeth and blow out air. I did, and a correct-sounding "S" reverberated through the room. It was the smoothest feeling that had ever come out of my mouth. A new world of possibility seemed in front of me. For the next year I worked on consciously placing my tongue. I would stand in front of the mirror and practice, pushing against my jaw, moving my tongue, and blowing air. I progressed slowly from the ABC's, to short sentences, and finally to conversation. When talking with my friends I tried to speak correctly, and if I messed up I would correct myself. My friends were amazed at the transformation, but nobody was happier than I when the pathologist pronounced me cured. Fixing my speech problem was an amazing accomplishment that I had never truly expected to achieve, but what amazes me the most is how far I have come since. In ninth grade I joined our school's Government Club and became actively involved in Model UN and the Youth Legislature, conferences involving public speaking and debate. The kid who just a few years before would not talk with anyone, was now giving speeches before groups of a hundred people. Time and again my advisors and my peers would commend me for my speaking (once a fellow delegate even compared my speaking to that of the great orator Cicero). Junior year I won great praise for a campaign speech I had given: dozens of people told me the speech, citing the importance of friendship, had moved them. The speech got me elected Lt. Governor for next year's conference. A month later I was elected President of the Government Club. I had come all the way from being a recluse to being a gifted orator and the leader of our school's largest and most speech-oriented organization.

I consider overcoming my speech impediment to be one of my greatest achievements ever. No longer am I a friendless wanderer, now I am more extroverted and enjoy having many friends. I speak up in class without hesitation and converse freely with strangers. I am even scheduled to give a twenty-minute speech in assembly, something rare for students. Anyone who knew me as a child and could see my outspoken self today would be amazed at my transformation. Correcting my speech impediment was a great achievement that has changed my life...no one calls me ERX anymore.

See page 319 to find out where this student got in.

FAITH NANCY LIN

Faith was co-captain of her high school's Envirothon team and participated in Tierra, its four-year biotechnology program. She was also School Site Council chairperson, National Honor Society vice president, and a California Scholarship Federation officer. Faith's honors and awards include: National AP Scholar, National Merit Commended Student, University of California—Riverside and The Press-Enterprise Scholars' Award, and salutatorian of her high school. She was also active in her local community as core leader/ coordinator of her church's youth group; a piano accompanist for Sunday church services; a volunteer for La Sierra Public Library, Parkview Community Hospital, and the Riverside-Corona Resource Conservation District; and a research assistant at the University of California—Riverside.

Stats

SAT: 1520 (760 Critical Reading, 760 Math)
SAT Subject Test(s): 800 Math Level 2, 780 Biology
High School GPA: 4.63 weighted
High School: Arlington High School, Riverside, CA
Hometown: Riverside, CA
Gender: Female
Race: Asian American

Applied To

University of California—Berkeley
University of California—Los Angeles
University of California—San Diego
Yale University

Essay

Faith used the following essay in her application to Yale.

Write on a topic of your choice.

I hope that Yale University has a large supply of water. When I say this I am not referring to a love for the nearby Atlantic Ocean or for the aquatic sciences. My infatuation with water springs from a different source. The water that I am most concerned with is that which washes over me when I take a shower. I am the type of person who spends much time in the bathroom, and while some individuals may find showering to be a trivial and even unnecessary part of their routines, I believe that my hygiene habits have played a role in developing many of my personal characteristics.

I refuse to go to bed without taking a shower. Though showering can be time-consuming, I am unable to forsake this beloved activity. Over the years it has trained me in the area of commitment, equipping me to excel in my academic studies. My high school record attests to the fact that I devote a wholehearted effort to whatever I do. Past trials have taught me that if I neglect either my daily shower or my scholastic studies, I will only experience a feeling of uncleanliness.

I am not the only person in the house who showers. Thus, I have been required to learn how to work around my family's schedules, sharpening my skills of time-management in the process. These skills benefit many areas of my life. Last year Arlington High School was able to take home the Envirothon state championship because of the team members' abilities to manage their time. As a team co-captain, it was especially important that I learn to arrange my schedule. I have always been able to allot time for showering, no matter how busy I may be, and in the same way, I managed to attend Envirothon practices while remaining involved in church activities and focused on my academic studies.

Oftentimes I must be the last one to shower to ensure that everyone in my family receives hot water. Showering teaches me the ways of self-sacrifice so that I put others' needs before my own. It has encouraged me to make other sacrifices. Volunteering at the hospital means that I am unable to spend my Saturday afternoons with friends. Playing piano for Sunday service means that I must spend hours practicing. My hectic schedule sometimes leaves me little time for myself.

Showering is important to me because it sets apart a time for relaxation and reflection. The bathroom provides the perfect atmosphere for pondering since there is little chance that I will be interrupted, and the rushing water has the ability to stimulate my thoughts with its gentle sound. Within the tiled walls I am able to draw life lessons from the commonplace events of each day. In numerous ways, showering connects to the life I lead outside of the bathroom. Showering allows me to take time to simply contemplate, and I would like to think that I finish each shower a more thoughtful and self-aware individual.

See page 319 to find out where this student got in.

FATIMAH KAUSAR ASGHAR

Fatimah was a member of varsity crew during her junior and senior year of high school, and was part of junior varsity crew when she was a sophomore and freshman. She also spent time volunteering with such organizations as The Harvard Square Homeless Shelter, Woman to Woman, and the National Honors Society, of which she was treasurer. In addition, she interned at the Summerbridge Cambridge division of Breakthrough Collaborative, a non-profit program designed to aid students academically by having college and high school students design and teach classes that will appeal to their interests. She was also involved with the Youth Involvement Subcommitte, a program that advocated lowering the voting age in local elections to 17.

Stats

SAT: 2020 (680 Critical Reading, 620 Math, 720 Writing)
SAT Subject Test(s): 760 Literature, 630 Math I, 660 Spanish, 690 U.S. History
High School GPA: 93 (out of 100)
High School: Cambridge Rindge & Latin School, Cambridge, MA
Hometown: Cambridge, MA
Gender: Female
Race: South Asian

Applied To

Brown University (early decision)

Essay

Fatimah used the following essay in her application to Brown University.

Describe a person who has influenced you.

My eyes immediately rested on the second seat in the first row, where a twelve-year-old boy reclined backwards in his chair. They remained fixed on his nonchalant figure as the welcoming introduction to my middle school literature class flowed smoothly from my mouth. The white shirt that hung loosely off his frail body seemed like enough clothing to drape a small town and the complacent smirk across his face foreshadowed that he would be my "trouble maker," the type of student that I had been warned would be intolerable in my class. On that day it did not occur to me what an impact one twelve-year-old could have.

Weeks later, his head hung low as the discussion turned to stereotypes, a theme in our story. The confident smirk that he wore faded as it was his turn to speak. "They think I'm stupid. Because of what I look like," he answered dully, trying to shrug it off as though he did not care. The other students in the class nodded placidly, and my stomach twisted into a knot. Vainly I tried to argue with them, but it was clear that my students had made up their minds. As a fifteen year old Pakistani girl who grew up in a liberal urban environment, I always considered myself to be non-judgmental. Naively I thought that my conditioning had raised me to be fully accepting of everyone around me. However, upon labeling Jose as a problem child, I violated the commandments of good teaching. Suppressing him by confining him to a stereotype would limit his progress. The effect of what I had deemed to be a harmless stereotype hit me hard. Like his other teachers, I had lowered his academic confidence by doubting his ability when I first met him.

The wounds inflicted by his insecurity ran deep. The frustration was prevalent around him as he told me multiple times that he was too stupid to write anything down. Ignoring the excuse that I had previously accepted, I began to push him harder than I had intended, refusing to settle for failure. Using what I knew about his background and upbringing, I began to alter my teaching style, making it more accessible to him. Through my persistence, he grudgingly accepted that he would not be able to worm his way out of assignments. For endless hours I sat with him, trying to tackle literature from different sides as I tried to help him find the beauty in the meanings and ideas that were buried in the pages of the story. The hidden potential that was previously clouded by self-doubt trickled through, and within weeks Jose became one of the best writers in my class. I realized that understanding a student's background was the key to helping him academically. Without being aware of it, Jose had introduced me to educational anthropology, something that I am interested in pursuing in the future.

A year later I saw him again, registering for camp. Enthusiastically, he told me that his grades in literature went from a C to an A. Entering my first teaching internship at the age of fifteen, I was not expecting to have a life-altering experience; I simply wanted to alleviate summer boredom. However, watching him grow from rolling his eyes in class to getting out of his chair and arguing his point enthusiastically before a panel of other teachers convinced me otherwise. For the first time, I felt truly rewarded for helping another person. I realized that I had succeeded in making a change in at least one student's life. In witnessing the successes of someone else, I discovered how much potential I have to create change.

See page 319 to find out where this student got in.

GAURAV P. PATEL

Gaurav graduated summa cum laude as salutatorian of his high school and received several local and national awards, including the Atlanta Journal Cup Award, American Academy of Achievement Honor Student (the top 400 seniors in the nation are chosen annually), Marietta's Teen of the Year, Young Leader of Tomorrow, Furman Scholar, the Outstanding Junior Award, and several academic awards in school. Many of his achievements focused on the French language; he was selected to attend the Georgia Governor's Honors Program, received the Oxbridge Academics French Scholarship to attend the Academie de Paris, received the American Association of Teachers of French Travel Award, and placed first in the state and fifth in the nation on the National French Exam.

Stats
SAT: 1500 (760 Critical Reading, 740 Math)
SAT Subject Test(s): 740 Math Level 2, 750 Chemistry, 740 French with Listening
High School GPA: 4.40 weighted
High School: The Walker School, Marietta, GA
Hometown: Smyrna, GA
Gender: Male
Race: Asian American
Applied To
Dartmouth College
Harvard College
Princeton University
University of Pennsylvania
Yale University

Essay 1

Gaurav used the following essay in his applications to Dartmouth, Penn, and Princeton.

First experiences can be defining. Cite a first experience that you have had and explain its impact on you.

Here I was in Hemingway's "moveable feast," yet unfortunately I was without a feast of my liking in Paris during OxBridge Academic's L'Académie de Paris on the program's French Language Scholarship and the National French Honor Society's Travel Award. In the world's culinary capital, I, a true francophile who cannot get enough of the French culture, could not find anything to eat. Surely, the croque monsieur or even les escargots tempted the taste buds of the over one-hundred other participants in the program; but my taste buds seemed to cringe at the sight, god forbid the smells, of such foods. However, I somehow survived on les sandwich and by my fascination of France and what else she had to offer.

My classes Littérature française and Medicine at L'Académie unmasked the educational merits that often lie hidden behind façades for the 'traditional' visitors of Paris. Classes began at 9:00 a.m. after a French breakfast and ended at 12:00 p.m., when students traversed the Parisian streets to grab a sandwich and enjoy lunch in the Luxembourg Gardens or in the gardens of the Rodin Museum. Minor classes began at 2:00 p.m., but the city became a teacher's aide, a type of three-dimensional video. Studying literature and fashioning my own poems in a café where Hemingway used to frequent or creating my own literary "salon" at la Mosquée became reality during class. The beauty and the scintillation of the French language came to life even more so for me. I never ceased to be enthralled, for I was finally immersed in the culture, the language, and the tradition of my academic passion in life: French.

The whole city transformed into a massive university; there was always something to learn outside of classes. Attempting to speak French with a native or ordering lunch in French became a unique type of erudition. While studying abroad, I not only received a stable background with lively teachers in my classes, I also began to experience French life — I was a Parisian for one full month (or at least I tried to be).

In Paris, I never had a dull moment. Whether it was a walk to the Eiffel Tower or a short journey to the nearby Versailles or a candle-light stroll in and around Vaux-le-Vicomte, I never tired. Having a cappuccino with my newfound friends at a café as we watched others briskly walking by on the Champs-Elysées or travelling on the Métro became adventures. The French culture offers a city and a country where the joy of life is present all around.

Nevertheless, I had to leave my utopia. On my last stroll around Paris and in the Luxembourg Gardens on the morning of my departure, I came to realize that I had had an extraordinary experience that many will never savor. Learning French amongst les français was a dream that I had finally fulfilled, and it is a something that I crave yet again — without the food if possible.

Essay 2

Gaurav used the following essay in his applications to Harvard and Yale.

For Harvard he responded to the Common Application question: Evaluate a significant experience, achievement, or risk that you have taken and its impact on you.

Yale provides a blank page and asks applicants to write about themselves.

Every taste of life brings some new knowledge to each person, and thus, experiences are the way we grow, the way we live, and the way we survive in an all too changing world. Each and every unique bite of life fills the human body with suffering, achievement, or satisfaction. Personally, I feel that experiences which content the soul are the most worthwhile. Of my many personal adventures in life, I feel that my experience tutoring a young eighth grader in my sophomore year of high school has given me the feeling of greatest satisfaction.

This young man was of Middle-Eastern origin and was having trouble organizing his thoughts in English; he lacked the motivation necessary to succeed in his class and was, therefore, about to fail. He became overly frustrated and discouraged with himself. His English teacher, my teacher in eighth grade, felt that this student did not believe in himself because English was his second language; his teacher thought that because of my patience, maturity, and agility in working with others I could truly help him. His teacher, moreover, knew that I have the ability to interact in language, for I speak English, French, and Gujarati. And so I began tutoring him. I spent about three hours a week working with his vocabulary and his thought processes in English; I discovered that he had amazing, sophisticated ideas and concepts, but the reason he consistently failed exams and essays was that he could not express his thoughts coherently in English. Nevertheless, after about two months, he not only began to show some improvements, he also gained confidence and enhanced his self-esteem. Furthermore, I feel that he actually started to grasp a larger concept of the English language and its often complicated structure.

Helping others has been a way of life taught to me by my parents ever since I was young. By example, my parents taught me that giving to charity, speaking with one who may be distressed, reading to a youngster, or talking to an aged person enhance the value of the soul, and each awakens a sense of euphoria. Tutoring Parham has truly been one of the greatest experiences in my life, for not only did I aid this intelligent young man in receiving better grades, I feel that I taught him something that he will always remember. Speaking and writing correctly and effectively in English is a necessity in not only the United States and England but in the entire world; furthermore, I feel that I brought out a new confidence in himself. I realize that this experience may seem somewhat minute to those of others — I could have written about my other awards, but this tutoring taught me something about myself. Helping Parham to learn and to grow buttressed the already strong moral values planted by my parents, and it made a difference in the life of another — the main objective.

See page 319 to find out where this student got in.

GIANNA MARZILLI

Gianna was awarded several Scholastic Art Awards in high school, including a Fine Arts Portfolio award. She was photography editor of her high school newspaper and very involved in the music department as a pianist, singer, and brass player.

Stats
SAT: 1460 (770 Critical Reading, 690 Math)
SAT Subject Test(s): 770 Literature, 750 Math Level 1, 650 Math Level 2
High School GPA: 4.44
High School: South Kingstown High School, Wakefield, RI
Gender: Female
Race: Caucasian

Applied To
Amherst College
Brown University
Carleton College
Colby College
Macalester College
Skidmore College
Smith College
Tufts University
Washington University in St. Louis
Wellesley College
Williams College

Essay

Gianna used the following essay in each of her applications.

Common Application: Indicate a person who has had a significant influence on you, and describe that influence.

Within the prison of room 216B, I curled up under a flimsy hospital blanket, flanked by my teary eyed mother and an ever-present nurse. Clenched teeth prevented puddles in my eyes from moistening parched cheeks. How could a body that I'd taken such good care of turn against me so suddenly?

"A classic presentation of insulin dependent diabetes." My soul flung itself against the bars of the bed, attempting to escape the doctor's words. Blood boiled through sugar soaked veins as I envisioned a life dominated by injections, schedules, and restrictions. What right did she have to assign a biological label to something that encompassed so much more than a malfunctioning organ? I resisted the urge to rip out my IV and throw it at her. Instead, I threw myself into the daily struggle of maintaining a quasi-normal metabolic state. Despite my efforts, it became increasingly clear that the human brain was never meant to play pancreas. I became convinced that it was no longer a question of "if" I would succumb such diabetic complications as blindness, kidney failure, and limb amputations, but "when."

Enter Delaine. She had gotten my number through a friend of my mother's, and suggested that I consider an insulin pump, a device that delivers insulin 24 hours a day through a tiny infusion line. I returned her call intending to disregard the advice. I didn't want a constant reminder of my disease clipped to my waistband; I wanted people to leave me alone to contemplate my miserable future.

Fortunately, Delaine ignored my wishes. A diabetic for 16 years and a pump user herself, she had nothing but praise for the little machine. No more schedules, shots, or "diabetic diet." Best of all, the improved control meant a reduced risk for complications. It wasn't a cure, but I was convinced. Delaine was living proof that my diagnosis wasn't a death sentence, and for the first time in months I felt hopeful. A week after I began pumping, we met in person over ice cream sundaes.

"How many carbohydrates are in this creation?" she asked, gesturing grandly toward her dish. I paused, wanting desperately to thank her for everything she'd done for me, to explain that the matted fur of my old teddy bear had finally recovered from the endless nights I'd spent sobbing into his stomach.

I wanted her to know that she had transformed my perception of diabetes so much that I would no longer give it up. I've watched her use her illness to connect with people and offer them encouragement, and I want to help others the same way. Last week, I overheard a woman mention her newly diagnosed husband. I've never been an extrovert; words don't have a particular flair when escaping from my mouth into the ears of strangers. Yet there I stood, offering support and advice to a person in need. She's taught me to enjoy every moment because there are no guarantees; I refuse to have any regrets if this illness becomes stronger than I am. She is a master weaver, creating a blanket of kindness that will warm me forever.

Perhaps I should give her this essay, because I still haven't figured out how to tell her that. How do you make someone understand that she is responsible for turning your life around? As I was about to make an attempt, the waitress approached.

"Is everything. . .all right?"

I tried to recollect my thoughts, but they had conveniently escaped me. Our server must have wondered what was so intriguing about the ice cream that it warranted such intense scrutiny. As I looked down to program 9.3 units of insulin, I laughed. Another thing that I couldn't explain! Only the owner of a translucent blue, back lit, beeping pancreas would analyze the carb content of a double fudge sundae before diving in spoon-first.

See page 319 to find out where this student got in.

HALEY A. CONNOR

Haley was managing editor of her high school's yearbook her junior and senior years. After playing piano for six years, she began playing the harp her senior year. She also attended the High School Summer Scholars Program at Washington University in St. Louis between her junior and senior years.

Stats
SAT: 1300 (620 Critical Reading, 680 Math)
High School GPA: 3.04
High School: Regents School of Austin, Austin, TX
Hometown: Austin, TX
Gender: Female
Race: Caucasian
Applied To
Washington University in St. Louis (early decision)

Essay

Washington University in St. Louis asked each applicant to make up a question and answer it. Haley posed the question:

Who or what has influenced you as a person the most up until now?

From the time I was a small child I loved to draw but never had formal instruction on how to draw realistically. Then one summer, while still in my elementary school years, I met a kind-hearted elderly wildlife artist at an art school day camp.

Mr. Hal Irby, an experienced and well-known local artist and teacher, helped me to develop my passion for art. At Laguna Gloria, the art studio where he taught, he was a revered instructor. The art studio requested him to return to teach his beginner's drawing class, long after he had retired and moved to the peace and quiet of the country. Mr. Irby had a unique style of drawing that looked realistic yet he drew only with small dots, no lines at all, even to create shading.

He changed my perspective on art. He made art more enjoyable and interesting. Art has become more than just a pastime for me. Mr. Irby taught me how to draw what I see, something for which I yearned. For me he made art more than just being creative.

Mr. Irby brought books, magazines and his own drawings to class. He asked the students to copy the pictures exactly as we saw them. We were taught to draw what the eye sees, not the image we might have in our mind. He encouraged me and helped me to draw the picture I had in front of me by showing which parts needed improvement and which parts were correctly rendered.

I went back to attend Mr. Irby's class for two additional years after that first camp to get the basics of drawing ingrained fully into my mind. After that first class, I felt more confident and pleased with my own talent and my learned skills. A desire was ignited in me to pursue realistic expression in my art. I intend to improve my skills in the coming years. I may decide in the course of my studies to have my hobby of art become my career because of the fulfillment it gives to me.

See page 320 to find out where this student got in.

HANNAH REBECCA STERN

In high school, Hannah helped others develop their writing skills by working as a tutor. She received many awards for her high grades and also for her participation in the Girl Scouts. For her Gold Award Project, she wrote a 58-page handbook dealing with survival in the real world, and then organized and ran the accompanying workshop. The guide so well received it was added to the school library. In her spare time, Hannah worked as a cashier at Target to help fund her internship at the Visual Photography studio.

Stats
SAT: 1930 (730 Critical Reading, 660 Math, 740 Writing)
SAT Subject Test(s): 770 Literature, 770 French
ACT: 33
High School GPA: 4.08
High School: Rancho Bernardo High School, Poway, CA
Hometown: Poway, CA
Gender: Female
Race: Caucasian

Applied To
California State University—San Francisco
University of California—Davis
University of California—Irvine
University of California—Los Angeles
University of California—Santa Barbara

Essay

Tell us about a talent, experience, contribution, or personal quality you will bring to the University of California.

My zeal for writing compels me to pursue its study any time I can. Whether for assigned work in class or an idea lit by flashlight late at night, I take up my pen whenever possible. I hope to write for a living in the future, and would love to use my skills to contribute to the community of the University of California. The resolve I have shown in the past shows my dedication to achieving this goal. Throughout my high school career, I have led the discussions in my English classes, adding insight of my own while I pondered the ideas of my classmates. I have participated in clubs and held office in one, and continue to tutor struggling English students, but afterward I always find time to write. After completing my schoolwork and performing my daily duties, I use my time to do what I love to do. Writing has always been my focus. Even during my extracurricular activities, I remain attentive to the English language. Tutoring students in English gives others a chance to enjoy reading and writing and keeps my basic knowledge sharp - I will take any practice I can get.

My passion for the written word will carry into my studies at the University of California, where I will continue to devote myself to the advancement of my craft. This devotion has shown itself in the past through my determination to find an outlet for my writing. On July 21, 2006, I found such an outlet at Visual Photography, where I was having my senior pictures taken. In conversation with the photographer, I mentioned that I hoped to find an internship opportunity with a local newspaper. The photographer brought up the student recognition program called F.A.C.E that the studio was conducting in partnership with the Poway Chieftain, one of those newspapers. The task of copy-editing the biographies of student participants seemed overwhelming to the Visual Photography staff. As copy-editing is the final polishing step in the writing process, I knew this would be the perfect chance for me to hone my skills in this practical aspect of writing. This would let me see the work of others in the way that publishing companies might view my work later. After speaking with the studio's manager about helping with this task, I walked out of Visual Photography overjoyed. My 23+-hour internship at Visual Photography began in August of 2006, and my supervisor thought my editing work impressive enough to merit my addition to the studio's payroll in September.

My service at the Visual Photography studio as a copy-editor has given me the entry-level experience necessary to continue to climb toward my goals. Working in its office environment has been good practice for my future interactions with the corporate publishing world. I was also able to watch its interactions with local newspapers such as the North County Times and the Chieftain. When my supervisor took me on an introductory visit to the Chieftain, I spoke with its Editor-in-Chief, and arranged a winter internship. At Visual Photography, I created my own job opening and also opened the door to my journalistic career. This gateway is far from the last I will find: Where writing opportunities do not exist, I will create them.

I look forward to sharing my enthusiasm for the English language working with the published professors in the English Department of a University of California campus. I am eager to add my thoughts to the university's melting pot of ideas and inspiration.

See page 320 to find out where this student got in.

HEATHER FIREMAN

In high school, Heather helped found a chapter of the B'nai B'rith Youth Organization and served as chapter president and regional historian. Her freshman year, she competed in the International Olympiyeda Science Competition and won a summer trip to Israel to compete in the finals.

Stats
SAT: 1600
SAT Subject Test(s): 800 Math Level 2, 790 Chemistry
High School GPA: 4.00
High School: Stratford High School, Houston, TX
Hometown: Houston, TX
Gender: Female
Race: Caucasian

Applied To
California Institute of Technology
Massachusetts Institute of Technology
Stanford University
University of California—Berkeley

Essay

Heather used the following essay in her applications to Caltech and MIT.

The prompt was to make up a question that is personally relevant, state it clearly, and answer it. Heather posed the question: What areas are you particularly interested in studying and why? How did your interests develop?

Everybody is curious. Some people are more than others. They aren't satisfied with a simple explanation. They must know how and why. They are scientists.

Some people think it's irrelevant how or why the world works just so long as it does. Content not to think too hard, they miss out on the sheer wonder that is the world around them. Scientists, on the other hand, learn something amazing every day.

I first began to think about a future in natural science as a seventh-grader when I started a book called Hyperspace, by physicist Michio Kaku. I was somewhat familiar with science fiction staples like black holes, time travel, parallel universes, and higher dimensions, but only as plot devices on Star Trek. A lot of it was beyond my grasp, since I had never taken a physics class, but I had always been interested in the concepts. To think that real scientists seriously theorized about any of it inspired me to read on.

I turned to The Physics of Star Trek, which considered the possibility (or not) of the many novelties of the show (like the holodeck, warp drive, and matter transporter) actually existing within the confines of the physical world. Physics seemed a wonderful adventure, so naturally I couldn't wait for my first physics course in high school.

I had to survive chemistry first. At my school, chemistry was considered the most difficult subject around. I didn't have much trouble with it, so I enrolled for a second year to prepare for the AP exam. Concurrently, I took physics and a required semester of biochemistry. I wondered at times if I was nuts to do so, but I braved the elements and was fascinated by what chemistry had to offer: a background for interpreting natural happenings and a means to advance scientific understanding in general, a worthwhile pursuit.

The AP in chemistry required not only a wealth of knowledge, but also an abundance of lab work. I grew confident working with the techniques and equipment and always looked forward to working in the lab. Concepts were one thing, but demonstrating them in the lab provided a whole new insight into what made things work and introduced us to many lab techniques and approaches. Investigations into enzyme performance revealed the effects of various influences; countless titrations of solutions perfected our methods; gel electrophoresis and qualitative analysis tested our nerves and concentration. That year, chemistry was my most challenging subject, and it took up a significant portion of my time. But it was also the most rewarding. Suddenly, it seemed like chemistry could be part of my future. Now, it seems a more and more possible path. In the meantime, I am a school science lab assistant. I want to explore chemistry and chemical engineering, physics, and biochemistry before narrowing my choices. I want to work in the laboratory, either on the pure or applied side of science.

In any case, I will never stop being curious. I'm a scientist.

See page 320 to find out where this student got in.

JAMES GREGORY

James was student body treasurer his senior year, a two-year letterman in basketball, and basketball team captain. He was a National Merit Scholarship winner and named to the basketball Academic All-State Team his senior year.

Stats
SAT: 1540
SAT Subject Test(s): 800 Math Level 2, 780 Spanish
High School GPA: 5.13 (out of 6.00)
High School: Walter Hines Page High School, Greensboro, NC
Hometown: Greensboro, NC
Gender: Male
Race: Caucasian

Applied To
Duke University
Harvard College (early action)
Princeton University
University of North Carolina
Yale University

Essay

James used the following essay in his applications to Duke and Harvard, and modified it for Princeton. He also used it in his National Merit Scholarship application.

Write about a matter of importance to you. If you have written a personal essay for another purpose—even an essay for another college—that you believe represents you, your writing, and your thinking particularly well, feel free to submit it.

To really understand who I am, remember your childhood. Remember the pleasure that eating a great big peanut butter and jelly sandwich delivered? How it seemed to just slide down your throat and ease into your stomach? That sandwich is the result of the perfect combination of ingredients, all working together to create a satisfying experience. If any one ingredient were missing, the whole sandwich would fall apart. In fact, I would argue that the world is very much like one large PB&J, filled with many different ingredients. People can be classified according to their personality and similarity to these ingredients. I am like the chunky peanut butter. Although I may not be as showy as the jelly or as visible as the bread, I am the heart of the sandwich. I am essential to the sandwich's success. I work behind the scenes, holding it all together, keeping all the ingredients organized and focused on their task. I lead through example, but I am flexible. I am able to work with any kind of jelly. I am slightly shy, so I do not need to be the center of attention; I am content in leading without recognition. However, you always know I am there. You taste all my chunks, all the little quirks that set me apart from the rest. Whether it is my dry sense of humor, my volunteer work at a summer day camp for my kids, or my fervent school spirit, each unique piece guarantees that your experience will not be mundane and bland. With every bite you take, you taste more of me: my excellent grades, my size 15 feet, and my dedication to Student Council. I am more fun than creamy peanut butter; you never know what to expect, but you know that it is going to be good. However, my most important attribute is my willingness to sacrifice to help others. I have unselfishly stepped aside on the basketball court to let the team as a whole shine, and I enthusiastically devote time to service projects through Junior Civitans that help the community. This desire to help is ingrained in my personality, and drives my plan to become a physician and continue my service to others. I refuse to give up before I attain this dream; I have the persistence of the little glob of peanut butter that sticks to the roof of your mouth. No matter how many times you smack you mouth, I will not go away. This drive has enabled me achieve academic success, success that I will continue into my higher education, and into my life. I am fun, I am good for you, and I am more than the sum of my pieces. I am the chunky peanut butter.

See page 320 to find out where this student got in.

JAMIE BUSHELL

*In high school, Jamie was awarded both the Scholar Athlete and
Junior Excellence in Writing Awards. She was also the president of
Letter Club, captain of the Varsity tennis and lacrosse teams, and a
member of Mu Alpha Theta Society, the Foreign Language Society,
and the high honor roll.*

Stats
SAT: 1240 (600 Critical Reading, 640 Math)
High School GPA: 4.46 (out of 5.0)
High School: Paul D. Schreiber High School, Port Washington, NY
Hometown: Port Washington, NY
Gender: Female
Race: Caucasian
Applied To
Reed College
University of California—Berkeley
University of California—Los Angeles
University of California—Santa Barbara

Essay

Allison used the following essay in her application to Reed College.

Please tell us about a risk you've taken.

A Risk I've Taken

I had never considered myself a daredevil or major risk-taker, nor had I experienced the fear and trembling that risk generates. All of that changed when I registered at Princeton University's Girls' Elite Lacrosse camp last summer. All alone, with only my duffel bag at my side, my eyes stared straight ahead, espying callous and unfriendly girls linked arm – in –arm, shouting happily together. I kept my head down as I walked a solitary mile to my dorm room, only to discover I didn't have a roommate. Tears swelled in my eyes as I looked away from my parents when they left. For the first time in my life, I wasn't excited about playing lacrosse.

I knew I had to self-administer some powerful, emotional first aid, so I began by reminding myself that the true reason I was at camp was to improve my skills, and increase my passion. I told myself, "It's just four days, Jamie; you can do it."

For the next hour, I rested on the hard mattress, with my head buried in my pillow, listening to music. I began to recall how I felt, at age eight, walking out of the school bus on my first day of summer camp, when again, I knew no one. My nerves were shaking incredibly, but as I walked into the bunk and saw ten other girls sitting by themselves, I ventured over. That small act of bravery initiated relationships that still exist. Thus, I resolved that despite an initially undesirable situation, I was determined to make the best of this experience too.

The first night, I prepared myself to eat dinner alone. As I closed my dorm room behind me, I took a deep breath and walked to the cafeteria. After getting my food, the real test began. Would I find any people to sit with? Would they talk to me? Would they like me? As I approached random tables, I head a voice from behind me: "Do you want to sit with us?"

"Sure!" I said with a huge sigh of relief. As I sat down, the awkward silence was palpable. In an attempt to break it, I asked the three other girls where they were from. "St. Mary's," one girl said. "Garden City," another replied. Coincidentally, they lived in towns close to my own. In fact, our lacrosse teams played against one another during the school year. Moreover, to my great delight, two of the other girls had also come to the camp by themselves. A sense of comfort was developing, and for the rest of camp, as much as a friendly wave was enough for me to know I wasn't really there by myself.

On the last night of camp, as ten of us sat outside chatting, it struck me that every one of us had arrived by ourselves. As the non-stop conversations flowed from school to social activities, it hardly seemed that I had known these girls for only three nights.

At that moment, I realized I had been narrow-minded and hasty in judging people. I had become friends with the girls I presumed to be callous. I have discovered that situations that I might not appreciate at first, can turn out to provide some of my best memories. In this situation, I allowed my anxiety to shape my opinions about the girls, rather than allowing myself the freedom to experience and find out.

Not only did I discover my capability to overcome an adverse situation, but I learned that taking risks, with its potential rewards, such as obtaining new friends, compensate for any fear of failure.

Since then, I realize that taking a risk does not have to be as exotic as skydiving or bungee jumping, for the greatest, most gratifying risks come when one takes a step out of her comfort zone. The greatest risk of my life resonates with part of my favorite quotation from M.A. Hershey: "risk shook my spirit, confirmed my courage and reinstated my daring." I can now officially call myself a daredevil.

See page 320 to find out where this student got in.

JAMIE MANOS

Jamie was a very active, well-rounded student in high school. She played soccer and ran track for four years and actively pursued her passion for music by performing in a number of ensembles, which earned her national recognition and allowed her to travel cross-country.

Stats
SAT: 1280
SAT Subject Test(s): 680 Math Level 1, 660 Biology
High School GPA: 95.7 (out of 100)
High School: Old Town High School, Old Town, ME
Hometown: Old Town, ME
Gender: Female
Race: Caucasian

Applied To
Cornell University (early decision)

Essay

Write about three objects that will give the admissions office insight to who you are.

The Jigsaw

Jigsaw puzzles are challenges that test one's ingenuity. They are composed of a number of pieces, each piece separated from and unique to the others. It is the job of the puzzle solver to examine the many pieces of the puzzle and find correlation between them, using these relationships to mold the seemingly unrelated mass into a finite object, a beautiful picture. I have always enjoyed assuming the role of a puzzle solver. Even as early as the age of three, I would spend my spare moments piecing together puzzles, always eager to see the diverse, colorful masterpieces they formed. As I grew older, I was able to apply my puzzle solving skills to life and began to view the world I lived in as a collage of puzzles. It became apparent to me that the people in this world are each a separate puzzle in the collage of life; they look similar when viewed from afar, but upon close examination it is apparent that each puzzle is unique; each is composed of separate sets of experiences and personality traits. I, too, am a puzzle in life's collage. My experiences have molded me into who I am. The many facets of my life and personality can be portrayed by the three types of pieces that compose a jigsaw puzzle: the rounded, filling pieces, the corner pieces, and the edge pieces.

The edge portions of a jigsaw puzzle are generally the first pieces that the puzzle solver tries to work. Once the solver has connected the edges, he has a strong foundation from which to build. This foundation leads the puzzle solver to the puzzle's solution as I lead others. The foundation of a puzzle is rigid, strong, and unwaveringly straight in much the same way as I am disciplined, strong, and honest. These qualities allow us both to be effective in leading others to success.

Success is not always easy to come by, however. The foundation of a puzzle would not be complete without one very important type of piece, the corner piece. The corner piece, which is not always easy to find, is a key piece to the jigsaw. It shapes the puzzle, bends a straight line. Like the jigsaw puzzle I have been shaped by many turning points. One corner piece of my life occurred during my sixth grade year when my band director saw much talent in a very young flautist. He recognized my alacrity in learning and started me out on the trombone, the basics of which I had mastered in a few weeks. Within a month I had been placed in the top jazz band and was introduced to the art of jazz, a form which has offered me a variety of opportunities and experiences.

The most important source of variety in the jigsaw is provided by the middle, filling pieces. Each piece is different in size, shape, and color, but fits together with all of the others to fill the framework, to portray an image with essence, to solve the mystery of the unfinished puzzle. My mind is like a collection of fillers; it is able to analyze situations and provide solutions from a variety of different angles, depending on which pieces are put together. It is only by viewing the problem from all angles simultaneously that I am able to generate the final picture, portray the puzzle in its entirety.

Solving the jigsaw is not an easy task. It takes much hard work and dedication on the solver's behalf, even when he is getting to know himself, deciphering his own puzzle. I, as the middle piece, the corner piece, and the edge piece, provide many representative components of my whole puzzle. The many facets of my personality and my life experiences converge to make the puzzle that is me. However, mine is a puzzle that is not yet complete. As I grow and undergo new experiences, I discover new facets to my personality. My life is a unique, unfinished puzzle to which all of the pieces have yet to be found.

See page 320 to find out where this student got in.

JANE SHA

In high school, Jane interned at a biotechnology company and participated in various community service organizations such as the Jenny Lin Foundation, Asian Student Union, and Key Club International, of which she was treasurer and newsletter editor. She served as co-captain of her high school tennis team for two out of the four years she was a member, and received various awards such as the AP Scholar Award, Varsity Scholar Award, Key Club Award, and Academic All-CTF Selection Award.

Stats
SAT: 1920 (610 Critical Reading, 730 Math, 580 Writing)
SAT Subject Tests: 730 Ecological Biology, 750 Math Level II, 730 Chinese with Listening
High School GPA: 4.34
High School: Castro Valley High, Castro Valley, CA
Hometown: Castro Valley, CA
Gender: Female
Race: Asian American

Applied To
New York University
Stanford University
University of California, Berkeley
University of California, Davis
University of California, Irvine
University of California, Los Angeles
University of California, Riverside
University of California, San Diego
University of Pennsylvania
University of Southern California

Essay

Jane submitted the following essay to the schools listed above.

> *How have you taken advantage of the educational opportunities*
> *you have had to prepare for college?*

From fifth-grade science competitions to high school experiments, science has been a driving force in my life. Ever since I was little, I wanted to learn not only through textbooks, but also in a professional lab. This past summer, I had the opportunity to work as a volunteer intern at Nanoplex Technologies Inc. Because very few high school students get to experience this, I didn't want it to slip away from me and accepted the challenge with full enthusiasm. I felt prepared to expand my knowledge and confidently put my best foot forward onto a whole new level.

For the first few weeks, I was exposed to different proteins, buffers, and high-tech equipment. My research project was to detect anthrax spores in air samples. Due to anthrax's toxicity, I simulated the model by using a protein called thrombin. I tested to see if a substance called aptamer would be able to detect it. By using a fluorescent microscope, any sign of fluorescence indicated that the thrombin was detectable. With the help of many other scientists perfecting this method, we can rapidly detect anthrax spores in the near future to combat terrorism.

On my last day there, I worked with three proteins, each in a group of ten test tubes. Each group was diluted with a liquid buffer until I was left with three test tubes. I noticed the first tube was a murky brown, the second a lighter shade, and the third, when held up to the light was the clearest of them all. In past experiments, I had failed to obtain significant results, but I didn't allow a few errors discourage me. This time, I meticulously used a pipette to draw up the liquids, and then released them into an imaging well. Carefully cradling it like a newborn, I gently laid it to rest on a fluorescent microscope. The computer connected to the microscope asked me, "Would you like to FOCUS…" and without a hint of hesitation, I clicked "Yes". My feet dangled from the twirling white chair while I watched the images brightly flash before me on the computer screen. Sweat beads began to form on my forehead as my heart raced. Before I knew it, and after half an hour of anticipation, the third test tube gave me the most promising results. Since this tube lacked cluttered proteins after the dilution, fluorescence occurred, which was what I had hoped for. This was a personal victory, and a chance to positively impact the science community. With the urge to further my science career, I have submitted my research project to get it published, patented, and entered in the Intel Science Talent Search, a prestigious nationwide pre-college science competition.

From this experience, I have learned that my intellectual curiosity led me to a hands-on experience of science in the real world. After getting the seemingly unobtainable results, I now know that nothing is out of my grasp when I have the motivation, passion for exploration, and thirst for success. For me, learning is like protecting the flame of a torch because no matter what difficulties I have to overcome, the torch I hold will never extinguish. Even though some moments in my learning experience have been murky, I have faith and perseverance to pull through. I still have mountains to climb, torches to hold, and opportunities to pursue, but one thing is for sure: my future, like that test tube, when held up to the light, looks clearest of all.

See page 321 to find out where this student got in.

JESSICA LAU

In high school, Jessica was elected class president, Student Council vice president and secretary, and National Honor Society president. She won four varsity letters on the soccer and track and field teams, and played JV softball. Jessica wrote for the school paper, competed on the Quiz Bowl team and in the Science League, appeared in four school musicals, and was an active Key Club, Volunteer Club, and FBLA member. Outside of school, she volunteered at her church, Lions Eye Bank of New Jersey, SAGE eldercare agency, and local hospital. Jessica also was selected for the New Jersey Governor's School in the Sciences, the U.S. Senate Youth Program (as a New Jersey delegate), and the Rensselaer Polytechnic Medal for Math and Science.

Stats
SAT: 1580 (790 Critical Reading, 790 Math)
SAT Subject Test(s): 770 Math Level 1, 780 Math Level 2, 760 Chemistry
High School GPA: 4.38 (out of 4.50)
High School: Jonathan Dayton High School, Springfield, NJ
Hometown: Springfield, NJ
Gender: Female
Race: Asian American

Essay

Jessica used the following essay in her applications to Dartmouth, Harvard, Tufts, and UVA, and shortened it for Princeton.

Common Application: Indicate a person who has had a significant influence on you, and describe that influence.

I had the best seat in the classroom. Second row from the front, fifth seat back — not the most facilitating position for a slightly near-sighted freshman to learn world history from. No matter. In my mind, the Bantu and the Bushmen played second fiddle to a boy named Brian.

To me, Brian was the paragon of human existence. I, on the other hand, remained quietly, passively, and uninterestingly in the background, stifled by shyness, and getting out of high school not much more than good test scores and As on my report cards. I was part of the furniture, and "Unobtrusive" was my middle name. Brian was the oil to my vinegar. His strength of character (combined with his extremely good looks) lit up any room he entered and touched all those lucky enough to be graced by his presence. His self-confidence, persuasive abilities, unending capabilities, and almost childlike enthusiasm for everything literally put me in awe. I recognized in him not only qualities I desired in my potential boyfriend, but also everything I'd always wanted for myself.

My excessive adoration drove me to ridiculous lengths. I went about meeting my goal of becoming his girlfriend strategically. The closer to him I got, I figured, the easier the catch. Therefore, when soccer season started, and Brian joined the team, I decided to give the sport a try myself. Brian chose computer science as his elective, so I did as well. When he auditioned for the school play, I followed suit. Like a lemming, I blindly trailed his footsteps, wherever they led.

Alas, my efforts failed, and my beloved soon found a love of his own. It was a sad day in my life. However, all was not lost. I was left with all the new activities, the residue of my unsuccessful pursuit. To my surprise, I realized that they were more than meaningless, leftover obligations; they had acquired personal significance and importance to me. Before soccer, I had never played on a sports team, and my eyes were opened to the benefits of the comradery and cohesiveness of a team, and even to the physical benefits of aerobic activity. I discovered my hidden talent in computer programming, and I proceeded to take all of the classes my school offered. I loved the thrill of becoming a new person (even if only a townsperson or chorus member) on the stage, and I fed my interest by making play auditions an annual event.

From there, I started taking my own initiatives. I had forgotten my timidity; I gained the confidence to go out and do things by myself and for myself. I joined the softball team and volunteered for the Key Club. I raised my hand in class and took an active role at school. I fearlessly and enthusiastically tackled everything in my path. This change in me benefited not only my school career, but everything I did, from the first impressions I make on new friends to my mood in general.

One late spring day in history class, our teacher, Miss Duke, opened the class for student council nominations. Sure, I was now involved in the school, but I was no leader. I promptly shut my ears and diverted my attention. A few minutes later, in the midst of my daydream, I heard my name. Its source? None other than He Himself; Brian. Did I accept the nomination? I forgot my hesitancy, delivered a somewhat shocked and disbelieving nod, wrote a speech, and before I knew it, became class president.

This single event completed the transformation in me. My role as a participant developed into that of a leader. I learned the thrill of spearheading a project. I realized the excitement of making things happen. Best of all, I discovered the reward of inspiring other people, showing them what was shown to me.

Following a boy around was not the proudest moment of my life, but in doing so, I grew a lot as a person. As my eyes were opened to the benefits of simple school activities, I gained self-confidence, an open mind, and an ambition that has defined who I am and where I am going.

See page 321 to find out where this student got in.

JESSIE SEYMOUR

In high school, Jessie was a four-year letter winner and senior captain in field hockey, a four-year academic letter winner, and senior captain of the track and field team. She was president of the National Honor Society, a four-year member and senior president of the chorus, a National Merit Scholarship Program Commended Student, and the recepient of various academic awards.

Stats
SAT: 1370 (730 Critical Reading, 640 Math)
SAT Subject Test(s): 710 Literature, 620 Math Level 1
High School GPA: 95.0 (out of 100)
High School: Central High School, Corinth, ME
Hometown: Kenduskeag, ME
Gender: Female
Race: Caucasian
Applied To
Cornell University
Dartmouth College
Middlebury College
University of Maine

Essay

Jessie used the following essay in each of her applications.

Common Application: Topic of your choice.

To say that my summer at Gould Academy was an eye-opening experience would be the understatement of a lifetime. It's more like for four whole weeks I didn't even blink. I signed up for a summer of intense learning, intense play, and the chance to get away from my flat, eastern Maine home and live in my beloved Western Maine lakes and mountains. At least this is what I told my friends at home, who couldn't begin to comprehend why someone would WANT to go to Summer School for FUN. Summer and school are two words that clash in the ears of the average 14-year-old, but to me it was the opportunity of a lifetime. To quiet my friends' disapproval, I told them it was kind of like summer camp with classes and went happily on my way.

I arrived with big expectations. Meeting my dormmates on the first night there was the first indication that my expectations weren't big enough. My roommate was a girl from Eastern Maine with a background similar to mine, so we understood each other. The rest of our floor, however, we met with awe and appreciation. Maine is not a state noted for its racial or cultural diversity, yet here we were surrounded by several girls from the Dominican Republic, a girl from Spain, one from France who was of Asian descent with an American name (she alone was diverse enough for several people), and lots of girls from Western Maine, New Hampshire, and the rest of the U.S., all of different social classes and carrying with them their fascinating life stories. We were all incredibly different, but we all had one thing in common: we were nuts enough to want to go to school during the summer.

The novelty of the situation didn't end with the many faces of different colors. The class I took was an immersion in Creative Writing, which also included interpretation of literature and cultural analysis. Eight students sat around one enormous table and we read, wrote about, discussed, and interpreted literature and the world around us on a level that none of us had ever been on before. On my first paper I got a B on what would have been a definite A+ at my home school. The class was drastically different from anything I'd ever experienced. Like taking up a new sport, it hurt at first. Gradually, though, the playing field became familiar territory and I got grades like any I had ever achieved. In every English class I'd ever had, teachers were too concerned about where kids put their commas to worry about seeking deeper meaning. At first I was skeptical about what I was supposed to be learning. I didn't think that E.B. White's "Once More to the Lake" was about something other than a man who takes his son to the spot where he spent his summers as a kid, or understand the truth behind pop culture. It took awhile, but my young, sparkly-eyed teacher finally convinced me that there was meaning behind the words. It was quite a revelation.

The teachers, the students, and the energy at Summer School forced my mind to contort itself into new positions that it had never been in before. I was used to ef-fortless A's. While that fueled my self-esteem, it wasn't satisfying. If I could get A's with no effort, what could I do *with* effort? At summer school, I learned more about my potential than anything else. At my regular school, I was a big fish in a small pond, but by doing well at summer school, I realized that I could be a big fish in a big pond too. After summer school, my whole outlook on life was different. Like in "Once More to the Lake," there was *meaning* behind everything. I saw the world and my future in a broader perspective. Suddenly I saw that there *are* people who care about learning, and they *are* interesting. It *is* possible to bask in the pleasures of life and challenge yourself intellectually *at the same time*. That is what I learned in Summer School. This is also what I seek in college.

See page 321 to find out where this student got in.

JING YI HON

In high school, Jing Yi was an active member of the Drama Society, leading her to later be elected vice-president of the group. She also was a member of the Student Council and Prefectorial Board, and for her efforts was awarded the Edusave Award for Achievement, Good Leadership, and Service by the Singapore Ministry of Education. Outside of school, she spent a good deal of her vacation-time as a journalist at both a local Chinese and English newspaper.

Stats
SAT: 2130 (710 Critical Reading, 740 Math, 680 Writing)
SAT Subject Test(s): 750 Math I, 730 Literature
High School GPA: n/a
High School: Hwa Chong Institution, Singapore
Hometown: Singapore
Gender: Female
Race: Chinese
Applied To
Brown University
Columbia University
Northwestern University

Essay

Jing Yi submitted the following essay to Brown University and Columbia University.

In reading your application, we want to get to know you as well as we can. We ask that you use this opportunity to tell us something more about yourself that would help us toward a sense of who you are, how you think, and what issues and ideas interest you most.

The Very Secret Diary of Hon Jing Yi

January 1, 2037

Resolutions for the year 2037

I MUST shed ten pounds.

I will learn Japanese.

I will keep spirits high at ST!

WOW!! It's 2037!! And I'm turning 49!

Oh dear, 49 does sound like a huge number. I have almost forgotten what it's like to be eighteen! Life as the new Chief Editor of The Straits' Times (ST) has been taxing, but it fills me with pride knowing that I work for the most prominent newspaper in Singapore.

But what's more exciting is I have finally realized my childhood dream!! I remember vividly when I set my goal to be Chief Editor –during my internship as a journalist at a major Chinese newspaper. I loved everything about the job, including the writing, the reading and of course my favorite part– the interviewing. And I decided if I was going to do something, I was going to do it well.

Even as a little girl I'd always been very clear about what I wanted. I knew, for instance, that Literature was what I sincerely enjoyed. Nothing was (and still is) more satisfying than reading good pieces, and the works of my favorite authors like Sylvia Plath continue to enthrall me even till this day. I suppose only my true love and determination to explore Literature at a deeper level could have motivated me to choose the unconventional subject combination of reading Literature in English and Chinese, which of course almost no one does in practical Singapore where the Sciences are given more focus. In fact all my friends thought I was insane when I chose to read Literature at college! "NO ONE IN SINGAPORE MAJORS IN LIT," they declared. But I'm glad that I followed my heart, no matter how atypical that decision was.

Speaking of school, I cannot believe it has been thirty years since I left junior college! The best lesson I had ever learnt from school was the importance of spirit. Till this day, I have never forgotten what the power of enthusiasm and true passion can achieve. I remember how, as a prefect, I took the lead in preparing my class for a song-writing competition. Though our song was silly and the dance ridiculous (some of us actually dressed up as a huge caterpillar!), we impressed with our zesty class spirit, and eventually bagged the top prize. In fact my teachers were so blown away by our performance, they mimicked our dance steps all through my school life!

In fact, I think my vivacious personality has been a great help at work. I do everything I can to keep spirits high at the ST, to ensure that every single one of us is still full of with enthusiasm about our work!

Oh wow it's three in the morning! I can't believe I spent the first three hours of 2037 reminiscing about my schooldays. Such sweet memories I have!

Goodnight!

NB: What I have written here is factual and truly what I feel, with the sole exception of my becoming the Chief Editor (which at least has not yet come true).

See page 321 to find out where this student got in.

JOANN REBECCA GAGE

JoAnn was on the varsity basketball team and volunteered as a middle school basketball and softball coach for four years. She was also a tour guide at her school and a member of the Cum Laude Society.

Stats
SAT: 1440 (700 Critical Reading, 740 Math)
ACT: 31
High School GPA: 3.98
High School: Cranbrook Kingswood Upper School, Bloomfield Hills, MI
Hometown: Dearborn, MI
Gender: Female
Race: Caucasian
Applied To
Bryn Mawr College (early decision)

Essay

Common Application: Describe a meaningful experience that contributed to your personal growth.

Early in my sophomore year, during a basketball game, I injured my right knee. I later found out that I tore my acl; one of the most devastating injuries for a basketball player. I was faced with two options: undergoing reconstructive surgery and months of physical therapy, or forego surgery and accept the end of my basketball career. Since I had already played for six years, and because I was not going to quit without trying to recover, I elected to have the surgery. I was extremely upset and nervous, but I saw this challenge as a test of my commitment and determination.

The surgery seemed like a success, three weeks later I was far ahead of the recovery schedule. Then, without warning, the patellar tendon in my left knee tore. Now I needed a second, more invasive, surgery that was not optional. In seconds I saw my recovery time go from four months to complete uncertainty. The second surgery forced me to wear a knee immobilizing brace and use crutches for over four months. My entire summer from May to September was spent on crutches.

I was always very independent, but I felt like I had entirely lost control in my life. Everything I did was dictated by my crutches and therapy schedules. At therapy I made many friends with the other patients, but during my year and a half recovery, I saw so many people come and go, yet it seemed like I never made any progress. I was completely frustrated. My situation seemed hopeless, and I was desperate to see any sign of healing.

During my recovery I felt so alone and isolated. I ached for anyone to talk with who could understand what I was going through. However, no one could help. I constantly felt confused and angry. Everything was so painful that I was scared that I might never be able to play basketball again, but I still believed that I could comeback, even if it was years away. Most of my recovery I felt that it was me against the world; it was a constant uphill battle with no end in sight. Everyday was more of the same feelings of frustration, helplessness, and desperation. I cried and wished that it would all go away, but it remained.

Now, nearly two years later, I am playing basketball again. I achieved my goal. When I look back on everything I went through I am truly proud of myself. I know that I can overcome any obstacle. I have learned so much about myself, I know that I have the determination and endurance to successfully defeat the most insurmountable challenges. This is the hardest thing I have ever done, but it has strengthened me like nothing else could. Honestly, it has all been worth it, and I do not regret anything. If asked again, I would absolutely make the same decision.

See page 322 to find out where this student got in.

JOSEPH A. RAGO

In high school, Joe was an editor of his high school newspaper and president of the Honor Society; he was also involved in independent scientific research.

Stats
SAT: 1470 (780 Critical Reading, 690 Math)
SAT Subject Test(s): 680 Math Level 1, 690 Math Level 2, 700 Chemistry
High School GPA: 3.90
High School: Falmouth High School, Falmouth, MA
Hometown: Falmouth, MA
Gender: Male
Race: Caucasian

Applied To
Brown University (early action)
Dartmouth College
Princeton University
Yale University

Essay

Joseph used the following essay in each of his applications.

Write on a topic of your choice.

At the last minute, I was snatched from the clutches a southern upbringing.

When I was quite young, my family moved from a small town in Northern Virginia to Falmouth, Massachusetts, a small town on Cape Cod. While it is impossible to empirically test my hypothesis, I have come to believe that this relocation has been one of the major influences in my life. College-bound students often write of the significant people or the important events in their life that have been formative in their intellectual development. In the same vein as these other factors, the flinty character of Cape Cod has shaped my personal growth and evolution.

Jutting thirty-five miles into the Atlantic, many parts of Cape Cod were isolated for years from mainland America. But this rustic area is the same one where some of the first Americans persevered in an uncertain world for the sake of principle. And though their Puritan faith is no longer the Cape's dominant religion, its ethic of common sense and hard work, its demands for a life of independence and clarity, and its aesthetic of simplicity and harmony have genuinely affected the character of Cape Codders.

These attributes have sustained the region both through times of confidence and times of urgency. At the beginning of the eighteenth century, the golden whaling industry, the foundation for success, began to falter and decline. The Cape surrendered the easy reliability of prosperity and lapsed into a recession. But within a few years, a Cape Cod resident developed a method for extracting salt from seawater on a massive scale. By mid-century, the region was exporting 35,000 bushels of salt annually, and the economy rebounded. The Cape is a land where necessity is met by resourcefulness. Whether it is harvesting cranberries or netting cod, people have always ably used their intellect and ingenuity to earn their livelihood.

Now, things have changed. The Cape does not depend on whaling or salt, but largely on tourism. Sightseers, like the barbarian horde descending on the Roman empire, overrun Cape Cod each summer. The popular image of the place, nursed by a bustling vacation industry, is the one found by these wayfarers: catered, served, and enjoyed. But the Cape less traveled is where the deeper truths, with an explorer's inspiration, can be discovered. It is where the scotch pines murmur and the soil unfurls a chorale linking residents to all things past and present. It is where the thundering ocean communicates possibility and optimism. It is where lonely, crumbling stone walls, denoting a faded hierarchy, stretch off into the woods obscured beyond sight. In the isolation, the qualities of reverence and veneration for community and continuity are conveyed. The Cape has rooted residents to the past, advocating a respect for history and an admiration for natural beauty.

Cape Cod is rapidly succumbing to the incessant pounding of the Atlantic Ocean. One foot of ephemeral coastline is washed away each year; on the outermost shore, the sacrifice is three times that. Although these changes are swift in geological time, they pale in comparison to the changes induced by human development. We look at a world that has taken far longer than a single lifetime to create, an environment whose fragile and ineffable beauty is swiftly evaporating. The pace of geologic changes, measurable in human time scales, reminds us that all life is fleeting. Yet if this realization is elegiac, it is also rousing. The Cape tells us to live life fully - to let no moment pass by unappreciated, to enjoy what we have, and to find the august world delightful to live in.

There is a fine line between ego and egotism. And all areas of the country can find some kind of pride in their distinctive cultural flavors and tales of history. But I am thankful that the lessons I have culled from my community have come from Cape Cod. The wisdom found there will stay with me throughout the course of my life.

See page 322 to find out where this student got in.

JOSEPH I. MALCHOW

Joseph started a small company that produced software and was featured in The New York Times. He also did voiceovers for television and radio, establishing what he describes as "a relatively well-respected brand name in the audio production field." At his high school, he managed Stage Crew for two years.

Stats
SAT: 1520 (790 Critical Reading, 730 Math)
High School GPA: 4.50 weighted
High School: Scotch Plains-Fanwood High School, Scotch Plains, NJ
Hometown: Scotch Plains, NJ
Gender: Male
Race: Caucasian

Applied To
Boston College
Carnegie Mellon University
Cornell University
Dartmouth College
New York University
Tufts University
University of Pennsylvania
Yale University

Essay

Joseph used the following essay in each of his applications.

> *For most schools, he used the Common Application prompt: Select a creative work—a novel, a film, a musical piece, a painting, or other work of art—that has influenced the way you view the world and the way you view yourself. Discuss the impact the work has had on you.*

> *For his application to Cornell and a few other schools, the prompt was open-ended so he suggested the above question.*

> *On Penn's application, the prompt was: First experiences can be defining. Cite a first experience that you have had and explain its impact on you.*

Ah, *Figaro*! I am fortunate to at last have an opportunity to pour the gallons of zest inspired by that name into words that, hereto, have gone unexpressed. Perhaps, when complete, this essay will further serve to retort my parents' incredulous stares when "*La Vendetta!*" blares resolutely, in all its Mozartian glory, from those faithful woofers atop my dresser.

Mozart and Da Ponte's *Le Nozze Di Figaro,* The Marriage of Figaro, has done much for me It has ushered my musical palette forth with breathtaking speed. But within this single work there also exists a bevy of culture that touches all aspects of human interest! Where else but in the audience of an opera can one be diverted, learn music, language, and history all simultaneously? Can anything else residing on three modest compact discs take a person as many months to digest and fully enjoy? In my eighteen years I've experienced nothing like the thrill of the opera. The profits I have reaped from my experience with *Figaro* have been invaluable. For all of the listening, viewing, and reading that I have done- for all of those hours happily occupied- I am beginning to absorb the Italian language, socioeconomic class-relations of 18th century Europe, and Spanish dress and architecture. In this way, opera, and more specifically *Figaro*-my first- has spilt light upon previously shadowed intellectual interests.

Though I revere *Figaro*'s superlative educational utility, the piece synapses with me on a personal level as well. In its essence, opera seeks to communicate. In Peter Shaffer's play *Amadeus*, Antonio Salieri, describing the raw emotive puissance of Mozart's work, says, "I heard the music of true forgiveness filling the theatre, conferring on all who sat there a perfect absolution." Opera demands the synergy of all of mankind's methods of communication- song, acting, dance, oratory, and music. I was first introduced- truly introduced- to *Figaro* at the Metropolitan Opera in New York City. I invited my closest friends there for my eighteenth birthday. I had already read much of the libretto and heard Sir Georg Solti's *Figaro* on compact disc. But as I sat in the audience- subtitles steadily glowing from the LCD screen before me- I saw the majesty of opera blossom in real time. I saw comedy, tragedy, and villainy at once; invoking so many tools- so perfectly- to deliver the milieu of each and every scene. I had always held myself to be a person of communication; English and Literature had always been my favorite class. But I sat there, viewing the work of this man, who I'd always heard limned as 'great', in absolute control of his audience. And I whispered to myself- I recall this vividly-, "I get it." I understood why his bust was placed below the headline "The Great Composers" on that poster in 3rd grade music class. As I viewed John Relyea's Figaro bouncing to the pulse of *Non Piu Andrai* under James Levine's stewardship, I knew that this was an art form I could appreciate.

See page 322 to find out where this student got in.

JULIA HYPATIA ORTH

Julia was homeschooled for seven years. She won awards for woven work and for dog agility. She also received a National Merit Scholarship.

Stats
SAT: 1390 (750 Critical Reading, 640 Math)
SAT Subject Test(s): 730 Writing, 660 Math Level 2, 750 Biology
ACT: 32
High School GPA: 3.92
High School: Clonlara High School (home program), Ann Arbor, MI
Hometown: Cedar Hill, MO
Gender: Female
Race: Caucasian
Applied To
New College of Florida
Southampton College of Long Island University
University of California—Santa Cruz

Essay

Julia used the following essay in her application to New College of Florida. New College asked for four different one-page essays—this is her favorite.

Recommend a book to us and tell why you are recommending it.

Many books have touched my life and changed my perspectives, and choosing a single one to recommend seems not difficult so much as unfair to all the others. Jim Nollman's *Spiritual Ecology* has been the source of a great deal of enthusiasm, frustration, and irritation for me. Grace Llewellyn's *The Teenage Liberation Hand-*

book set me free. Even a few well-written textbooks, like Hopkins's *Ka Lei Ha'aheo: Beginning Hawaiian* and Haviland's *Cultural Anthropology* have inspired me to learn about worlds of knowledge I hadn't even been aware of before. That's not to mention the works of new and classical fiction (*Nineteen Eighty-Four*, *Portrait of Jennie*, *The Catcher in the Rye*, and *Dandelion Wine* being particular favorites) that I spent summer afternoons devouring in full. Yet . . . a book recommendation should be more than personal fancy, something that one feels compelled to share particularly with the recommendee(s). As I am quite unfamiliar with you, I wish to come up with something of fairly general interest as well as something that excites me. To my surprise, a particular book has presented itself to me for just such a purpose. I recommend *The Lorax*, by Dr. Seuss.

I can't in good conscience recommend it and be done with it though. This journey to "the far end of town where the Grickle-grass grows" with its environmental message might seem a touch moralistic or naive, out of context. Besides, Dr. Seuss wrote poetry, and it is poetry meant to be read aloud. I recommend that you do just that. I recommend that you check this book out of a library and take it outside. Stand on a hill-top or by the edge of a forest or in the middle of a park, perhaps under whatever local vegetation resembles Truffula Trees. Don't go alone. Bring your best friend or your younger brother or your cat or whatever neighborhood children are willing to listen. Dr. Seuss wrote *stories*, and stories are meant to be told to people. Chant the story with your best story voices to whomever will listen, and I can all but guarantee that bits of rhyme will lodge themselves in your head like the choruses of popular songs. Whatever you do, don't forget to look at the pictures.

The story itself is told by and about the Once-ler, the well-meaning antihero who chops down trees for his business. He means no harm, but undoubtedly causes much—a familiar situation indeed. (In the famous words of Walt Kelly's Pogo: "We have met the enemy, and not only may he be ours, he may be us.") The Lorax, defender of the trees, also does not follow any sticky-sweet good-guy stereotypes. He's ". . . shortish. And oldish. And brownish. And mossy", and speaks with a voice that is "sharpish and bossy." Finding himself entirely at odds with the Once-ler and his business, all the Lorax can do is shout out warnings and remonstrations at the top of his lungs. The perception gap between the two is tragicomically familiar, and leads exactly where one might expect. We would do well to learn not only from the Lorax's message, but also from the failure of his method of communication to result in anything but opposition.

It's food for thought, but don't get your thinker too excited. This is, after all, a children's story. It is my hope in recommending it that it will at worst provide you with a pleasant addition to your day, spent under the sun with a friend or two and a book that is, in the end, a great deal of fun . . . and that at best, it will provide you with inspiration—to plant a tree, to create and share your own artistic or literary worlds (a skill at which Dr. Seuss was adept), to spend more time outside, or more time reading to young friends, or perhaps even "only" to remember to not take even the most serious subjects *too* deadly seriously (again a bittersweet Kelly-quote comes to mind: "Don't take life too serious...it ain't nohow permanent."). Enjoy!

See page 322 to find out where this student got in.

JULIE YAU-YEE TAM

Julie was a three-time state spelling champion and a two-time state opera bronze medalist. She trained at the nationally renowned Houston Ballet Academy for nine years and finished the pre-professional program. Fluent in English, Spanish, and Mandarin and Cantonese Chinese, Julie attended Chinese language school until she graduated with honors in the twelfth grade. She also held offices in school clubs and community service organizations.

Stats
SAT: 1410 (660 Critical Reading, 750 Math)
SAT Subject Test(s): 740 Math Level 1, 680 Biology, 700 Chinese with Listening, 690 Spanish
High School GPA: 4.31
High School: Second Baptist Upper School, Houston, TX
Hometown: Houston, TX
Gender: Female
Race: Asian American

Applied To
Rice University (early decision)

Essay

The quality of Rice's academic life and the residential college system is heavily influenced by the unique life experiences and cultural traditions each student brings. What perspective do you feel that you will be able to share with others as a result of your own life experiences and background? Cite a personal experience to illustrate this. Most applicants are able to respond successfully in two to three pages.

Cebu City, Philippines

As I stare into my mirror, I see a face long and tired, worn out by distance, by time, and by too many things happening all too fast. The trip here was not easy. It took 27 hours in flight and airport waits – from Houston to Los Angeles, to Hong Kong, then finally to Cebu City, Philippines.

I was awestruck when my mother and I arrived here Tuesday morning and were taken directly from the airport to the funeral home. As I passed through the doors, I found myself in an atmosphere I had never before experienced. In the Philippines, funeral homes are like hotels. There are living quarters behind the grand hall, which is a large room with a sitting area where visitors can view the casket. Somber guards scrutinized me as I entered the grand hall, where my maternal grandfather, a former Taiwan senator and adviser of Head of State Chiang Kai Shek, lay in state. Although I am Chinese, to them, I looked different, walked differently, and even acted differently. I *was* different. As I entered the grand hall, I saw the banners, each four characters long and painted in traditional Chinese calligraphy, that extolled my grandfather's virtues. Flowers of every description, from governmental agencies, banks, schools, churches, and other organizations from all over the country and abroad, lined the walls. Newspaper articles, newsletters, and other notices announced the passing of my grandfather and listed the names of those who had given memorial contributions in his memory.

As I gazed into the casket, which was covered by a piece of glass because my grandfather's body was to lie there for over a week to be viewed by people from near and far, I saw how his face was hardened like clay. His loving spirit, his vivid smile, and his caring eyes had left his countenance, but not my memory. However, I still felt all these parts of him through the people and institutions he had touched so profoundly. At that moment I also realized how much he would be missed by them.

I slowly drew away from the casket and retired into the living quarters. A few guards carried our luggage into the back room, and several servants were at our attendance. Having someone constantly asking to serve me in any way possible was new for me.

During the next few days, I began to feel the discomfort of being continually in the spotlight, due to the attention I had received because of my grandfather's passing. Every time I wanted to refill my water bottle, I would have to don formal clothing, put on my uncomfortable high-heeled shoes, and fix my hair perfectly before leaving my room. At one point I took a chance and ran out in my pajamas and slippers. Unfortunately, my aunt saw me and upbraided me, saying that I "must look perfectly proper at all times in the event anyone important arrives." I found that being thirsty was easier.

Nightly memorial services at the funeral home had begun before our arrival and continued during our visit. On the first evening, my uncle, my aunt, my mother, and I thanked all who had come and received condolences. From both prominent and ordinary, I heard how my grandfather had treated all people with equal consideration. Humility and high office came in the same "package" for him.

We were up early the second morning to go to Cebu Eastern College, where my grandfather was Director for 32 years, for another ceremonial tribute to him. I told the students how my grandfather had inspired me. Because my grandfather was also a lover of music, I sang a song in his honor. Although most of the students had never met my grandfather personally (because he had retired at age 82 and died at age 91), they were definitely affected by his work in improving school facilities, erecting new buildings, increasing student population, and making Cebu Eastern College a premier force in secondary education in the Philippines. Their respect and admiration touched me deeply. At the end of the tribute, every student and faculty member individually offered words of sympathy.

My grandfather was cremated on the day of his state funeral. This morning our family and a few close friends used chopsticks to pick out his bones from the ashes. It hit me that, when I die I will just be, quite frankly, a pile of bones. Therefore, if my physical body is of little importance, then I need to cherish every day because what I contribute to society will be significant. Just as we took Grandpa's urn through the halls of Cebu Eastern College and the Lieh Fu Chen Building, named in his honor, I want to die knowing that someone will remember me for changing the world positively.

Now as I sit here in front of the mirror in "my" room, getting ready to leave Cebu City for home, I am thinking: Should I be feeling nostalgic for home? Do I miss being at school after a week in a far away land? I cannot say that I want to leave all this behind. Although most of the people here I have never seen or have only seen once or twice, they are almost like family to me. I can relate to them so well because of the language and cultural ties and our common regard for my grandfather. The Chinese, of course, emphasize the importance of family and respect for the elders, so this plays a role too.

I know my grandfather would be so happy to see me carry on his legacy of values. When he named me Yau Yee (幼 慈), he gave me more than a name. He gave me personality, meaning, and a heritage. I am reminded of my duty every day. My Chinese teacher has always said that I am one of the few who come to learn Chinese willingly – not forced by my parents – and that I have an authentic Chinese accent and realize the importance of learning the language of my ancestors. Reading some of the books my grandfather wrote has truly inspired me to pursue a political career to improve education and humanitarian values.

Now that my grandfather is gone, I will no longer have an immediate need for returning here. However, just as my mother has brought me here and to Taiwan to see the countries my grandfather influenced, I want to bring my children back through the halls my grandfather walked. If my grandchildren admire and remember me as I do my grandfather, then I know I will have continued his legacy, and my life will have been a success.

See page 322 to find out where this student got in.

KAREN A. LEE

In high school, Karen received a full diploma in the International Baccalaureate program and was a two-year "A" student on the Academic Decathlon team. She played the violin in the school's top orchestra, co-edited the literary magazine, was the secretary/treasurer of the French National Honor Society, and was a member of the National Honor Society and Mu Alpha Theta (Math Club). Outside of school, she studied piano and Mandarin Chinese.

Stats

SAT: 1600
SAT Subject Test(s): 800 Math Level 2, 690 Physics, 780 Chinese with Listening
ACT: 34
High School GPA: 5.46
High School: Garland High School, Garland, TX
Hometown: Garland, TX
Gender: Female
Race: Asian American

Applied To

Duke University
Johns Hopkins University
Rice University
Southern Methodist University
Stanford University

Essay

Karen used the following essay in her application to Stanford University.

How has the place in which you live influenced the person you are? Define "place" any way that you like . . . as a context, a country, a city, a community, a house, a point in time.

The Land Down Here

When it rains, the inhabitants where I live are the last to know. Welcome to Short People Land. At an early height of four feet eleven inches, I thought I had solidly established residence in the People of Average Height Land. Nonetheless, as I noticed myself moving toward the front of class pictures over the years and I remained four feet eleven inches on my twelfth birthday, I obtained Short Person status. While my personality has its roots in my childhood Average Height Land, becoming and remaining short has greatly influenced the person I am now.

Because I have not reached adulthood, human thought can naturally mistake me for someone younger. For instance, due to the limited size of our school's gymnasium, ninth-grade students are barred from peprallies. When I tried to attend my first one as a sophomore, students behind me shouted, "Freshman! Go back to class!" I never forget that this confusion will not end with graduation. Employers and coworkers may view me as immature and inexperienced based solely on my height. Keeping this possibility in mind, I consistently put forth extra effort to exceed expectations until perfectionism became automatic. My physics teacher handed back my second lab report of the year with a comment that my lab reports bordered on overkill. I hoped to transform my height into an asset, a trait to make me and my meticulous care stand out in others' memories. My work is by no means flawless, but living in Short People Land encourages my industrious attempts to prove that height and ability are not directly related.

On the other hand, being petite has always brought me the warmth of human companionship. As a short child, I had advantages in certain games, and my playmates welcomed the challenge of playing against me. In hide-and-seek, I would be the only one to fit under a table in the back of a closet under a staircase. I was one of the last people left in limbo. Many of these early diversions gave birth to long-standing friendships. When the stress mounts, we still rely on each other for commiseration. On another occasion, my Short Person citizenship helped me bridge the freshman-senior gap. When the seniors in the International Baccalaureate program at my school formed a club to tutor underclassmen, those who arrived for tutoring were too intimidated to ask for help. I joined a group of ninth-grade girls and casually discussed their biology lab with them. Until ten minutes into the discussion, they had thought I was just another freshman, but by that time, we had overcome their fear, and they gladly accepted me as their official biology tutor. I cannot describe my gratification when one of my protégées stopped me excitedly in the hall, "I made a B on my biology test! Thank you so much!"

While I accept my height with open arms, I recognize all the small annoyances packaged with it. For several years before I turned sixteen, I feared not being able to drive. I had difficulty seeing over the steering wheel and reaching the accelerator with my foot at the same time. In large tour groups at the art museum, I end up memorizing the back of patrons' shirts rather than enjoying the masterpieces. Window blinds are adjusted so that glaring sunlight just misses everyone's eyes but mine. Remembering my own frustrations, I developed a sympathy for others' aggravations and a sensitivity to others' needs. I can empathize with lefties trying to use a right-handed mouse or pale people who sunburn easily, both of whom, like me, suffer simply because of a physical characteristic. I remember to adjust the music stand in orchestra so that my stand partner can also read the music. At a pre-college summer program at Southern Methodist University, my apparent intuition for helping others earned me the nickname "Mother." People came to me for first aid, pocket change, or advice. Probably my limited caretaking talents did not quite deserve my honorable nickname, but I always did my best to help and always felt content that they appreciated my efforts. Despite their inconveniences, irritations of the vertically challenged mostly disappear before one of Short People Land's finest fruits, a sense of humor. Even I can laugh when someone quips, "You're so short you could pole vault with a toothpick." Knowing I would not take offense, my history teacher used me as an example for situations in which trying as hard as possible may still fail. He asked me to jump and touch the ceiling. I actually came within six inches, but I joined the class in laughing at the ridiculousness of his demand.

My residency in Short People Land has shaped my capacity for diligence, camaraderie, empathy, and laughter. Thanks to my height, I have nearly everything required to attack the ordeals of life and still maintain sanity. Neither have I lost respect for the people up there, so please do not hesitate to bend down. I'll meet you in the Land Down Here.

See page 323 to find out where this student got in.

KATHARINE ANNE THOMAS

Katharine was a four-year varsity tennis player. She was the number-two player on her team her junior and senior years and co-MVP her senior year. During her final year of high school she took two 200-level English courses at Franklin and Marshall College. In addition to community volunteer work during the scholastic year, she participated in a month-long volunteer program teaching English abroad in Poland during the summers of her sophomore and junior years. She won several Scholastic Writing Awards and won a first-place Gold Key award in the Short Short Story category her freshman year.

Stats
SAT: 1390 (740 Critical Reading, 650 Math)
SAT Subject Test(s): 710 Literature, 680 Math Level 1, 620 Math Level 2, 660 French
High School GPA: 4.15
High School: Lancaster Catholic High School, Lancaster, PA
Hometown: Lancaster, PA
Gender: Female
Race: Caucasian

Applied To
Bucknell University
Colgate University
Emory University
Georgetown University
Haverford College
Johns Hopkins University
Swarthmore College
Vassar College
Wake Forest University
Yale University

Essay

Katharine used the following essay in each of her applications.

Common Application: Topic of your choice.

My first real college writing assignment: five neat pages of argument and examples, insightful prose in black type and white space where my professor could write little words of praise. I replayed a little daydream I had developed of him reading the paper, pausing and nodding at the particularly insightful points, scribbling excitedly in the margins and finally closing it with a satisfied sigh. The reason I was looking forward to getting my work back was not that I truly believed it was a work of genius. My sleep-deprived, bleary-eyed misery refused to let me be a fan of my work. At that point I was cursing the uncountable nights of rubbing my temples in the unforgiving glow of the computer screen I had spent on it. Instead, my prediction was based on precedent (not to mention each aching bone's demand for restitution). Teacher's responses to my work had always been positive, and I grew increasingly confident about my ability. But in the process, my purpose in writing shifted from self expression as it should be in its purest form and instead to gaining recognition.

Upon reading the paper, my professor suggested that I take a second look at it. His comments clarified ideas that had always been beyond my grasp. So many of my papers with similarly obscured errors had gone without being criticized, but, strangely enough, no red-inked "Fantastic!" was nearly as gratifying as having my own vague sense of flaw verified. While other teachers' compliments had been flattering, what I appreciated more than anything, and what I would require to become any better in my craft, was a healthy dose of criticism. I realized that being selective enough in choosing my words would ensure that my ideas would never be misunderstood.

Envisioning the images that words have the power to create restored my passion for writing. What had made me love writing initially was the gloriously specific nature of words that enables them to provoke the exact response we intended them to and convey the most complex of emotions more so than any other outlet. Had I meant that Catholicism pervaded Irish tradition or was the religion embedded within culture? Did Joyce's Stephen Dedalus stray from the church or lose his faith? If there hadn't been a deadline I could have worked on that paper for weeks, editing day and night and probably still not being fully satisfied. I was at fault for having the haughtiness that led me to believe that I manipulated words, when in fact the opposite is true. Their role as the messenger of thought demands reverence. Words are for me what shapes and colors are for artists, what notes and beats are for musicians. But the medium by which we choose to express ourselves has little bearing; it need only fulfill its purpose. I gained from this experience a realization that I cannot be above laws that govern mankind's communication. The ability of words to touch one's core is timeless and beyond our grasp.

See page 323 to find out where this student got in.

KATHLEEN B. BLACKBURN

Kathleen was the salutatorian of her graduating class and served as her high school's yearbook editor during her junior and senior years. As vice president of the National Honor Society, she coordinated many volunteer activities for its members, including weekly tutoring of area children and multiple food drives. She was also an active member of the Spanish club and took part in five mission trips to Nicaragua with her youth group. When she wasn't busy with schoolwork or extracurricular activities, she worked as a waitress and babysitter.

Stats
SAT: 2030 (700 Critical Reading, 620 Math, 710 Writing)
SAT Subject Test(s): 740 Literature, 790 U.S. History
High School GPA: 4.3
High School: Lord Botetourt High School, Daleville, VA
Hometown: Daleville, VA
Gender: Female
Race: Caucasian
Applied To
Elon University
Washington & Lee University

Essay

Kathleen used the following essay in her application to the schools listed above.

Evaluate a significant experience or achievement that has special meaning for you.

It was an odd feeling, riding in the back of that dump truck, a coffin right beside me. As we bounced along the unpaved, potholed, Nicaraguan roads, it would unhinge just a bit, and I could see where Papá would soon be laid. After a long ride under the oppressive sun, the dump truck full of teenagers finally arrived at the tiny home that Mamá and Papá shared, and we unloaded our somber cargo. As I walked up their rocky, dirt yard, I was filled with memories.

I had met Mamá and Papá a year earlier, while on my first trip to Nicaragua with Because We Care Ministries. Both were in their eighties and living in filth. Stray dogs would come by their shack and roll in their meager food supply, actually passing mange to Mamá and Papá. The ministry found the poor couple and began to help them, providing food and medicine, teaching them cleanliness habits, such as not to eat food after a dog has urinated on it, and even building them a real home. I remember visiting while their home was under construction. Mamá gave everyone hugs and refused to sit down in the presence of her visitors, despite her dwindling health. Papá was healthy enough to stand and thanked each of us over and over again.

And now, just a year later, we were helping Mamá make the final preparations for Papá's death and burial. While the men lugged the coffin in and placed it in the corner of the one-room home, I rushed to the hammock to see Papá. His blank face stared back at me as he struggled to breathe. The air around him reeked of stale sweat, urine and vomit. I stroked his shriveled hand as his daughter attempted to give him a thimble full of water, but he was too ill to keep it down, and vomited it into a large pan filled with similar substances. At this point, I could not hold it back anymore, and slow tears fell down my face. It just did not seem fair. The only difference between Papá and me was where we happened to be born. Had I been Nicaraguan by birth, I would be in his situation; he would look upon me with pity. Then it was time to gather around Papá for prayer. We all held hands, and I rested my hand upon his bony shoulder. As we began to pray, it seemed as if a fresh breath of life blew into him. He began to pray with us, shouting "¡Gloria a Dios!" with the little strength he could muster. Fresh tears fell from everyone's eyes as the dying man whispered the Spanish words to "Amazing Grace" while we sang in English. Forgetting the strict rules about sanitation and disease, I kissed his sweaty forehead and whispered, "Vaya a casa, Papá. Go home, Papá."

The images of Papá on his deathbed praising the Lord will be forever imprinted in my mind. When I get frustrated with my blessed life in my comfortable Virginia home, I remember the amazing faith of this man. When I am disappointed, I remember the greater disappointments he faced. When I am weak, I remember how much weaker he was. And when I am joyful, I remember his immense joy, which makes me even gladder.

Papá did go home two days after I last saw him. Because of our shared faith, I firmly believe that he is in the presence of God. I cannot imagine how exciting heaven is for him. All he ever knew were the dirt roads of Nicaragua; now he walks along streets of gold. He was always ill; now he is in the presence of the Great Physician. He spent most of his life living in a trash bag; now he inhabits his own mansion. He never had quite enough beans and rice; now he has more than he could ever want. He taught me and so many others so much about life in the short time we knew him; I cannot wait to see him, wrap my arms around his thick, healthy body and say gracias.

See page 323 to find out where this student got in.

KELLY DUONG

Kelly spent her summers attending summer programs at many schools, including Harvard University and the University of Chicago. She also held a job as a waitress for one year, working mainly on weekends. In high school, she was involved in the theatre program, tutored at-risk elementary students weekly, and was co-President of the Asian-American club. In addition, she was involved in the National Honor Society and, by the end of her junior year, became an AP Scholar with Honor.

Stats
ACT: 32
High School GPA: 3.996
High School: Grandville High School, MI
Hometown: Grandville, MI
Gender: Female
Race: Asian American

Applied To
Brown University (applied early decision)

Essay

Kelly submitted the following essay to Brown University

Personal Statement

Standing barefoot in the cool, wet sand of Nha Trang Beach, I breathed in the fishy stench of the ocean. It was only a quarter past five, yet the beach had already come to life. Someone's father was gathering the morning's catch along the shore, while mothers were setting up shop nearby. These days, every minute boils down to money. This is one of the few things Vietnam and America have in common. It's hard to believe that this scene was once the beautiful, serene Vietnam of my parents' youth. Eyes closed, I tried to banish the image of high-rise cement ugliness from my mind. I took a deep breath and listened to the bittersweet melody of the ocean waves.

I was fourteen the first time I went back to Vietnam. It was the summer of eighth-grade. I would be heading off to high school soon, and my main concern for that summer was getting the perfect tan. I knew that I was in for more than I bargained for well before the plane made its landing in Ho Chi Minh City Airport. Uniqueness

The bird's eye view of the city was my first glimpse into the very soul of my native country. It was an unruly sight, resembling a Lego-town hastily put together, with random structures carelessly plopped on unoccupied land. My anxiety only magnified once I had landed. Never before had I seen so many people headed in so many different directions…and all on mopeds! I remember thinking that my first trip through the streets of Saigon could very well be my last.

The look on my parents' face didn't do much to calm my nerves. They had left their past behind thirteen years ago, and it was now apparent that their past had transformed beyond the point of recognition. Looking back, there must've been a certain point when it hit them that what they had been yearning for all these years no longer existed. The most obvious change was that Saigon was no longer Saigon. The cultural capital of Vietnam is officially named Ho Chi Minh City. But the changes ran deeper than that. After all, "a rose by any other name would still smell as sweet." This rose has been stripped of all its petals, with nothing left but the savage thorns held together by a bare stem; a carcass and a grim reminder of the beauty it once held. I'm sure they had acknowledged the inevitable ahead of time, but there's always a part of us that truly believes time will stand still in our absence and wait for our return.

Every now and then, my mind wanders back to my brief encounter with this long-lost friend; when I get a whiff of a steaming bowl of pho, the delicately prepared beef broth that is the signature dish of my homeland; or when I'm walking down South Division, and upon hearing the harsh jabbering of my native tongue, I'm instantly reminded of the smooth control it takes to perpetually switch from one tone to another (and how my skills are quite rusty still). Moments like these send me hurling back to a Vietnam I had heard about as a child—when Dalat was an intellectual playground and Saigon was rich in romance and art—but not the disappointing reincarnation I had witnessed firsthand. One day, I shall return. Maybe not to the romanticized country my parents had left to perish so long ago, but maybe, just maybe, to something even greater and more spectacular. My Vietnam.

See page 323 to find out where this student got in.

KEVIN JAMES TOSTADO

Kevin played varsity football and was recognized as a San Diego Union-Tribune Scholar Athlete. During his senior year, he was president of a community service club named Students For Social Action and director of a K–8 tutoring program at his local library. He was on the National Honor Roll, a National Hispanic Scholar, National Merit Commended, and an AP Scholar with Honor.

Stats
SAT: 1440 (680 Critical Reading, 760 Math)
High School GPA: 4.20 weighted
High School: Patrick Henry High School, San Diego, CA
Hometown: San Diego, CA
Gender: Male
Race: Latino
Applied To
Cal Poly
Franklin W. Olin College of Engineering
Massachusetts Institute of Technology
San Diego State University
University of California—Berkeley
University of California—Los Angeles
University of Notre Dame

Essay

According to Kevin, he responded to "the standard, give us your personal statement in 750 words or less, question."

I am a kicker on my high school football team. As a result, I do not receive much respect, if any, from my friends and teammates; however, I am a crucial part of my team. My main role on the football team is to kick a football through a neon-yellow goalpost while wearing a two hundred dollar helmet and pads. Nevertheless, kicking a football is very minor compared to some of the other roles that I have on the team.

During this last football season, I realized that I did not make the football team because I can kick the ball through the uprights; instead, I am on the team because I work hard at my varying positions and can adapt to the different situations that I come across.

All four years that I have attended Patrick Henry High School, I have played on the football team. I have been on winning teams (7-3, Eastern League champs) and losing teams (2-8, Eastern League chumps). I have played offense (wide receiver and tight end) and defense (middle linebacker and defensive tackle). I have smelled the sweet smell of success and suffered the harsh familiarity of defeat. With the exceptions of running back and defensive back, I have played every position on my team, the most notable of which being quarterback.

Last season, the head coach, Coach Jacobacci, confronted me. He told me that our starting quarterback was injured and that he needed a backup for our second-string quarterback.

"Why are you telling me this, Coach?" I inquired.

"Because you need to start learning quarterback."

I had never played quarterback before; I couldn't throw a spiral. I spent the next week working as hard as I could at practice so I could learn how to complete a pass, to handoff a ball, to read defensive coverages. During that week, our second-string quarterback sprained his ankle. The trainer said that our second-string quarterback would be unable to play in the upcoming game, our league opener against Scripps Ranch. I was slightly uneasy when I found out that I would be the starting quarterback that Friday night. I tried my best to lead the starting offense during the practices, but I would handoff the ball to the wrong person or get sacked. Most of my teammates were trying to figure out why the kicker was playing quarterback; I was too.

When George Long, our game announcer, began to read off the starting lineup at the beginning of the game, I was filled with nervous anticipation of the first snap. Not only was I starting at quarterback with a week-and-a-half experience, but also doing the kicking and punting. At halftime, we were ahead 14-0. In the first three plays of the game, I had handed off two balls for touchdown runs of 33 and 87 yards. We ended up losing the game 14-28, however, when the offense of Scripps Ranch came back to score four unanswered touchdowns the second half. However, my performance had proved to myself and all present at the game that I could be a quarterback.

I have learned a lot about myself by playing football. I have realized that I am willing to take positions of high risk (quarterback and kicker) and also positions that may be less glamorous (guard, offensive tackle). Wherever I am needed on my team, I always attempt to do my best.

Throughout my high school career, I have been involved in many different activities, including participating in Boy Scouts, being appointed Captain of the school academic team, and getting elected President of a school club that promotes service to the school and local community. These various experiences, especially the ones I gained on the football field, helped me to realize that it doesn't matter whether you have the starring role or a backup position to succeed in life. Whatever activity I participate in, if I continue to try my best to make a difference, I will come out on the winning team.

See page 324 to find out where this student got in.

KIMEN FIELD

Kimen played on her high school's volleyball and softball teams. She was a member of a philanthropic group and gave over 400 hours of community service. A lifetime Girl Scout, Kimen earned the Gold Award. She also worked each summer during high school and gained valuable experience working with technology.

Stats
SAT: 1530 (730 Critical Reading, 800 Math)
SAT Subject Test(s): 720 Math Level 2, 690 Chemistry
High School GPA: 4.20
High School: Irvine High School, Irvine, CA
Hometown: Irvine, CA
Gender: Female
Race: Caucasian

Applied To
California Polytechnic State University—San Luis Obispo
Rice University
Stanford University
University of California—Los Angeles
University of California—San Diego

Essay

Kimen used the following essay in her applications to Rice and Stanford.

How has the place in which you live influenced the person you are? Define "place" any way that you like . . . as a context, a country, a city, a community, a house, a point in time.

Each December a Christmas tree and Menorah share my family room and dreidels and Santa Clauses are juxtaposed on the coffee table. Each spring my family displays Easter decorations and prepares for the Seder. Such is the dichotomy of my family's religion: a division that has caused me much confusion and inward contemplation over recent years. When I was younger, I attended Sunday school at a local synagogue, but it was a duty and never a pleasure. I did not enjoy my time there and thus lost interest in Jewish philosophy. My friends and my mom's family exposed me to Christianity, yet its doctrines never captivated me. After long consideration of Judaism and Christianity I now realize that I am an atheist. I am also a secular humanist—a moral person trusting in human rights, education, and intelligence, not God, to propel us into the next millenium.

My family always promotes morality and integrity with a relative absence of spirituality, yet my mom occasionally remarks, "I have brought you up without religion, and I regret it." My parents wish for me to be religious, and I can feel my mom encouraging Christianity while my dad insists on Judaism. When my dad discovered I had been exploring atheism, he brought me books about Judaism to let me "give it a shot," but I do not think I ever could have. I lead a secular life and cannot find a reason to begin believing in an elusive God. Perhaps I am too scientific to comprehend the spiritual necessity of religion, but with billions believing, I understandably fear that I am missing out on a meaningful part of the human experience. While my family and childhood molded my theological beliefs, these same beliefs heavily impact and alter my family relationships. Hitler murdered my dad's family because they were Jews, and when I see my grandmother, the lone survivor, I feel like a traitor; I am not continuing the faith that my family died to protect. Christmas is my favorite holiday, and although we celebrate on a secular level, I feel hypocritical celebrating it when I do not believe in the religion. However, if I share my true feelings I fear I will be excluded from the family traditions I cherish. Throwing away a family's heritage might seem impossible, but with the candid words "I don't believe in God" so much of my family life might disappear.

I have come to understand the hardships of being an atheist and staying true to that title. Before a volleyball match last season, my teammates wanted to have a group prayer, and I said I felt uncomfortable. The looks that flashed back at me made me want to run off the court, but I stayed strong, and was relieved that they accepted my choice and moved on. This small incident foreshadows my future as I deal with the alienation that this declaration undoubtedly entails.

My overall childhood lacked religious upbringing, and I have shed my religious façade. The familial tension that resulted has led me to a balance between my religious beliefs and my family traditions. Having conquered this "crisis" at a relatively young age, I realize that I am more confident, strong, and honest. I can defend my beliefs (or non-beliefs) and I have truly discovered my convictions about the enormous spiritual cloud that hangs over us. I have had intensely uncomfortable discussions with my family about religion, but I am confident that choosing to be sincere about my lack of faith is the right choice. Being true to myself has proven to be a challenge, but a rewarding one. As a member of a philosophical minority, I have felt the effects of discrimination, yet I know I will persevere and become a stronger person from my assertion.

See page 324 to find out where this student got in.

KRISTEN T. MARTINEZ

Kristen was her high school valedictorian, as well as Band Captain, Executive Officer of the Marching Band, Principal Clarinetist of Wind Ensemble, Lead Alto Saxophone of Jazz Ensemble, President of National Honor Society, Vice President of Math Honor Society (Mu Alpha Theta), and Secretary of Science Honor Society. During this time, she also participated in an architectural internship and West Point's Summer Leadership Seminar. In addition, she was a member of Hershey's All-USA Honor Band, the All-County Honors Orchestra, the University of Miami's Honor Band, and served as Student Ambassador for the Parent Teacher Student Association.

Stats
SAT: 1950 (650 Critical Reading, 690 Math, 610 Writing)
ACT: 29
High School GPA: 5.665 (out of 4.0)
High School: Miami Southridge Senior High, Miami, FL
Hometown: Miami, FL
Gender: Female
Race: Hispanic

Brown University
Carnegie Mellon University
Columbia University
Cornell University
Georgia Institute of Technology
Harvard University
Johns Hopkins University
Massachusetts Institute of Technology
Northwestern University
Princeton University
Rice University
Rose-Hulman University
Stanford University
Tulane University
United States Military Academy
University of Pennsylvania
University of Michigan
University of Miami
University of Notre Dame
The University of Texas at Austin
University of South Florida
University of Washington in St. Louis
Yale University

Essay

Kristen submitted the following essay to the schools listed above.

Describe the world you come from, for example your family, clubs, school, community, city, or town. How has that world shaped your dreams and aspirations?

Every afternoon as I leave the school parking lot, I pop in my favorite CD by clarinetist, Benny Goodman. I listen to "Seven Come Eleven" and "Clarinetitis", which help relieve my stress. The music is upbeat. I tap my feet and I block out the world.

I was so excited when I received my first clarinet at the age of 11. I was familiar with music because I played piano, but I wanted to play the clarinet as well. Playing a woodwind instrument and interacting with other band students seemed thrilling. I wouldn't even take my clarinet out of the case until a professional instructed me how to do so. I opened the case and stared at the black, shiny clarinet and was mesmerized. It was just too fragile and beautiful to touch until my band director showed me how to put it together the second week of school.

I continued my clarinet studies in high school because I enjoyed playing in an ensemble. In marching band camp most of the seniors were also in jazz band, which played gigs wherever they could find an audience. I became friends with them and we would all hang out after practice and listen to jazz music. It really sparked my interest because I wasn't familiar with big band or swing music. That is where I first heard Benny Goodman.

Neither of my parents sing nor play an instrument so they don't understand the origin of my musical talent. When I was three I began asking for a piano, but my parents thought it would be better if I waited until I was able to read music. Also, my Mother didn't want me to learn to play through the Suzuki method; a method used to mimic sounds instead of reading music, and then have to relearn later through musical notation. My Mother wanted to wait and see if I was still as enthusiastic about playing piano and dedicated to music in a couple of months. When I was four, to appease me, my Grandmother gave me a keyboard and finally my parents provided piano lessons. I practiced those tedious, seemingly pointless exercises all week, but later I discovered their purpose.

I loved to practice. If I hit the wrong note, I started over again from the very beginning of the piece. I have come a long way. I now play clarinet solos composed by Mozart and Weber. I get out of the car and I run in my house after listening to Benny Goodman and pick up my clarinet to play. When I do my homework, Benny Goodman is often playing in the background. Even as I write this, Benny Goodman still plays in my head. Whether I'm playing or listening, studying or vacationing, music is an important part of my life.

See page 324 to find out where this student got in.

KRISTIN SHANTZ

Kristin was valedictorian of her high school class and a National Merit Finalist. She competed in piano and voice, winning first place at the California State Talent Competition in each division her junior year. She was granted the Arthritis Foundation Summer Science Research Fellowship the summer following her junior year, allowing her the opportunity to do ten weeks of research at Stanford University in the Department of Immunology.

Stats
SAT: 1520 (740 Critical Reading, 780 Math)
SAT Subject Test(s): 790 Math Level 2, 690 Chemistry
High School GPA: 4.00
High School: Valley Christian High School, San Jose, CA
Hometown: San Jose, CA
Gender: Female
Race: Caucasian

Applied To
California Institute of Technology
Claremont McKenna College
Harvard College
Pepperdine University
Princeton University
Stanford University
University of California—Berkeley
University of California—Los Angeles
University of California—San Diego

Essay

Kristen used the following essay in her application to Caltech.

What event or events have shaped your life?

It was the most agonizing moment of my life. I hesitantly climbed the three stairs that led up to the seemingly enormous piano and slowly approached the bench. As I sat down, my tiny hands shook and my face flushed with fear, but somehow I managed to get through my little song...and then the moment was over. Everyone clapped, and I sat down with my mom to watch the rest of the recital. As I listened to numerous other students play song after song, each progressively more difficult than the previous one, I began to feel more and more insignificant. My short, simple little song seemed worthless in comparison to the other amazing pieces performed with style. The experience was a bit too much for me, a mere five-year old, to handle, and I began to cry...and cry. But I kept practicing.

I have played the piano for twelve years. I have practiced for over three thousand hours. I have performed at least fifty times. But each performance is still pure agony. Each moment of performing is painful, as an intense fear of making a mistake or forgetting my song overwhelms my entire being. I fear utter and complete embarrassment more than anything in the world. And it has happened...I have made mistakes that seem to echo throughout the room, and I have forgotten notes so entirely that I am forced to start the song over. But I have kept practicing.

Some may wonder why I keep persevering through the pain, through the sheer agony of performing. I tolerate the trauma, because after my very first experience performing, I realized that success would only be achieved with hard work. Now, when I perform, the moment when it is over is the greatest feeling in the entire world. There is no moment like the one right after the final chord is struck, when the audience wildly applauds my beautiful ballads or spicy Spanish arrangements. As I take my deep bow, and the people clap, I realize that all my practice is worthwhile. No feeling is greater than the feeling after a successful performance. And at the very moment when the 1st place trophy was handed to me during my most recent competition, I knew that I had achieved my goal.

Piano performance has taught me so much that has truly molded and changed my mental perspective on life. When I was young, I used to think that I would be able to coast through life, and in the end, life's problems and challenges would work themselves out. After my first recital, however, I learned that just as the great, after-performance feeling must be preceded by pure torture, all great successes in life must be preceded by hard work and many struggles. I've realized that if I want to make a difference in this world, and make a contribution to society, I'm going to have to give it some elbow grease. But I don't mind...I'm ready for the challenge.

See page 325 to find out where this student got in.

LAUREN CATHARINE WEILER MOORE

Lauren was on the varsity water polo and swim teams for three years and editor-in-chief of her high school's literary magazine for one. She received several honors—AP Scholar with Distinction, National Merit Scholarship Program Commended Student, Honor Roll, and French Honor Society. She was a delegate to the Young Women's Leadership Conference and a youth delegate to the Insights Conference with world political, business, and educational leaders. Her longest extracurricular commitment was with a local volunteer organization for six years.

Stats
SAT: 1540 (740 Critical Reading, 800 Math)
ACT: 31
High School GPA: 4.05 weighted
High School: The Bishop's School, La Jolla, CA
Hometown: San Diego, CA
Gender: Female
Race: Caucasian

Applied To
Amherst College
Brown University
Duke University
Pomona College
Princeton University
Stanford University

Essay

Lauren is positive she used the following essay in her applications to Brown and Pomona. She is almost sure it also went to Amherst, Duke, and Stanford.

> *The prompt, from Brown's application, was: We ask that you use this opportunity to tell us something more about yourself that would help us toward a sense of who you are, how you think, and what issues and ideas interest you most.*

My make-up was done. My hair was set. My costume was perfect. All that was left to do was act… and act I did. In my eighth grade drama class, I took the title role in the play *Annie*. How did I land the vital part in the play? Simple: the role was perfect for me; Annie was a bouncy, cheerful, optimistic little girl with only good thoughts for the world.

That, and the fact that I had red hair and was one of a small handful who could actually sing.

My hair color and singing talents were hardly the reason that I could belt out "the sun'll come out… tomorrow!" like no one else, however. (Besides, there were at *least* two other redheads in the class.) I was the leading role because when I sang, I meant it. I bet my bottom dollar that tomorrow, there would be sun. And gosh darn it, I meant it. The sun *will* come out tomorrow. Things generally *do* change for the better. I am an optimistic person.

Optimism is a gift that was given to me by my family. My parents both come from larger families, so much of my time away from school is spent with aunts, uncles, or grandparents. The environment is always a happy one, with people laughing about Uncle Albert accidentally spitting his dentures into his water glass (honest, it really did happen!), or five-year-old Ana telling me about her "childhood" as a preschooler. And no matter how horrible a situation someone may be in, such as losing a pet Labrador of ten years or needing financial support to get pulled out of a rut, we find a solution or we create a positive outlook in the end to help, even if it just means buying good old Uncle Albert some stronger Polident. My family instilled this optimistic outlook in me while I was young. Even at the young age of four, having read *Alexander and the Terrible, Horrible, No Good, Very Bad Day*, I had learned my lesson: Happiness is a habit—cultivate it.

Each human being is good in some way; it is my job to find this goodness and, I think, to experience it in whatever way possible. To find good in someone not only benefits me and the recipient, but it also positively influences the people around us.

When people are around good people, good things tend to happen, as they do in my family.

I begin by trying to instill my optimism and love for life in other people. I really *do* point out beautiful skies after a thunderstorm, and I actually *do* stop to smell the rose bushes at school (much to my friends' horror). I laugh at every chance that I get and relish the time that I spend with my friends. I do cartwheels on grassy lawns. I often get smiles out of people; this means that the people around me are happy. Laughing at me, maybe; but happy nonetheless.

Don't get me wrong, though; I don't just sit around compromising my morals merely to squeeze a smile out of someone. Sometimes a situation does not warrant an optimistic attitude. If my friend Sam does all in his power to avoid doing his French homework, I will not sacrifice my homework time or my integrity to let him copy my answers. I also won't tell someone who has hurt herself by drinking too much at a party that everything will be okay; that is a sign of something worse that requires more than being cheerful. Larger, more global issues also resist a cheerful or optimistic approach. Do not think for a minute, for example, that I believe that issues such as genocide or the Holocaust happened for a positive reason.

Maybe I can't transform every situation into a good one. I accept this, however, and realize that I *can* change things right around me. Because I was raised in a positive environment, I tend to flourish in a positive environment. I do well when the people surrounding me are doing well. This is why I encourage people to enjoy themselves and the world around them. I will go to great lengths to make a companion happy, even if it means driving halfway across town to get milk-free ice cream for my lactose intolerant friend at the health food store. It means the world to me when I see someone smile who has been moping for the past hour; that smile is my reward. The phrase "look on the bright side" was made for me. Without my optimism, I do not know for sure what type of person I would be. (I certainly would not have scored the leading role of Annie.) Yet what I do know is that I would never be able to enjoy the roses and the cartwheels that I enjoy doing now. And without these things, life just would not be so precious.

See page 325 to find out where this student got in.

LILLIAN DIAZ-PRZYBYL

Lillian was an honors student and a four-year letterman in varsity swimming. She also played saxophone for her high school's wind symphony, jazz combo, and award-winning jazz ensemble.

Stats
SAT: 1520 (750 Critical Reading, 770 Math)
SAT Subject Test(s): 800 Literature, 720 World History, 800 Biology, 740 Chemistry, 740 Spanish
High School GPA: 4.46 weighted
High School: Lexington High School, Lexington, MA
Hometown: Lexington, MA
Gender: Female
Race: Latina
Applied To
Williams College (early decision)

Essay

Common Application: Topic of your choice.

I am a stargazer. Something about the sky, especially at night, intrigues me. The stars represent both science and poetry, two things I love. I remember one Christmas when I was little and I received a big, black telescope and a little blue dress with tiny silver stars on it. Both gifts made me want to explore, to make a difference in the world, discover a new solar system or maybe even track down far away signals from a little life form in a different blue dress looking back at me across the light years.

I grew older and out of the blue dress, but I couldn't outgrow the telescope or my love for the sky. The few times a year when we would bring it out to look at Saturn's rings, a distant nebula, or a double star, were always exciting times for me. I was fascinated by books about the sky and what was going on in it. There was so much wonder and mystery out there, only barely perceptible to the naked eye, which unfolded itself for the curious mind with a few lenses stuck on the ends of a tube. Stars change over time, and like humans, eventually grow old and die. Their mortality made them all the more beautiful to me, because in the gas jets of a supernova and glowing clouds of dust, new stars and solar systems are born. I read everything I could get my hands on, and even as I turned more to fiction than science, the way authors used the stars as metaphors for purity, distance, hope, or humanity itself captivated me.

However, in addition to the thrill exploring the heavens, astronomy involves a lot of sitting alone in the dark, waiting for stars to come up, skies to clear, instruments to function, or just for lightning to strike. Literature can be equally lonely, involving long searches through library stacks for references and literary criticism, and hours upon hours of reading and writing in isolation. There is adventure and joy to be found, it just takes time and patience.

Where in my life do I find companionship, then? Well, pretty much everywhere else: at school, at home, at swim team spirit parties, at jazz ensemble rehearsals. (Now that is one thing I love that is not at all lonely!) One of my favorite quotes is from Carl Sagan's novel, Contact; "For small creatures such as we the vastness is bearable only through love." I want to go to a college where I can find a community that will respect my interests and whose interests I will respect, where I can work with people who are interesting and challenging. I want to go to a college where I can find friendship and love to fill in the vastness (which really isn't so bad- everyone needs their space, after all). In short, I want to go to Williams College, for literature, astronomy, and love.

See page 325 to find out where this student got in.

LINDSAY CLAIBORN

Lindsay was involved in JV soccer and varsity gymnastics. She was section leader in marching band and band council president. A National Merit Finalist, she was a member of the National Honor Society for two years. During her senior year, she participated in an internship program at NBC Studios.

Stats
SAT: 1530 (750 Critical Reading, 780 Math)
SAT Subject Test(s): 750 Math Level 2, 700 Chemistry
High School GPA: 3.60 weighted
High School: Thomas Jefferson High School for Science and Technology, Alexandria, VA
Hometown: Vienna, VA
Gender: Female
Race: Caucasian

Applied To
Claremont McKenna College
College of William & Mary
Emory University
Pomona College
Stanford University
University of Southern California (College of Letters, Arts and Sciences)
University of Southern California (School of Cinema—Television)
Yale University

Essay

Lindsay used the following essay, with slight modifications, in each of her applications. The question was different for each school, but the essay fit all requirements. She initially wrote the essay for Stanford; their question asked the applicant to send a photograph and describe the meaning behind it.

"Can I hear a B flat please?" Our band director directs his question to the brass. "Now the woodwinds…" Then I hear it —the unmistakable squeal of four piccolos, skidding across the entire ensemble. I cringe and step out of line to look at my piccolo section. They look back with apologetic stares and one of them rummages for a tuner. These four girls are my responsibility. They must have their music memorized and their marching exact. They are a product of the time I have invested every year, from June to November, since 9th grade. We are part of a giant family that spends countless hours playing connect-the-dots on a football field. We are the marching band. We are each dots that move in unique patterns across a grassy game board. Each summer, June begins with individuals marching to unique patterns. In July, tempos start to coincide with one another, if only for a split second. In August, many tempos become one, blending all differences and creating a new cadence. From September to November we perfect our uniform tempo.

As my name thunders across the loud speaker amid the other leadership, I look no different than anyone else, one drop in a sea of uniforms. But my section knows that I am a darker dot, a bigger drop, like the checker piece that has reached the other side of the board and is coming back "kinged". I am the section leader. Leadership takes time to establish and more time to perfect. I have yet to perfect mine but our daily practices challenge what I know.

Thinking back to my freshman year, my section leader was a model of perfection. She seemed to know everything and everyone, and I felt privileged to be part of her section. Now I wonder if the freshmen feel the same way about me. They have yet to learn that my "perfection" comes from little more than experience, maturity, and dedication.

It is 10 minutes to show time. Anxiety runs high as the freshmen experience the rush of competitive performance. It's the last few seconds I will have to instill words of confidence in the minds of my flutes and piccolos. "Good luck, march your best." *Tap...Tap...* The solitary snare drum beats a solid tempo. Each drop adheres to another, collecting and combining. We are a mass; I am part of the sea again. We flood the dark alleys to the stadium. *Tap...Tap...* We are all united into one common goal; uniformity. *Tap...Tap...* We all appear exactly the same yet travel our specific paths. But that is impossible; to appear exactly the same is wearisome. Our own individualities create diversity, even when conformity is crucial. *Tap...Tap...* It's our turn; we may take the field in competition, in uniformity, in individuality. I locate my starting spot, dot #1. Downbeat, now my personal tempo is gone I must stay in step. Right, Left, Right. Where do I go next? Dot #2 . . . aha, four steps to the right. I am still traveling my personal path; my section follows me. They depend on every step I commit to. Left, Right, Left. I am alone in my directional movements but part of a whole picture. Dot #3, 4 steps diagonally left. Right, Left, Right. As the figures on the field ebb and flow with the musical tides, my individuality shifts with the demands of the performance. The show ends, and the drum tap resumes. *Tap... Tap...* Reality is beaten back into our heads, reminding us of what we have just accomplished. We are unified in an endeavor to entertain and impress.

As I stand on the field at the end of my final performance, my individuality comes back, my own rhythm returns. But a shred of the band's past unity remains. The bonds that we have formed do not split but stretch and evolve. Those of us who have led leave something behind for the next class and take with us the experiences of a lifetime.

See page 326 to find out where this student got in.

LINDSAY J. CUSHING

Lindsay interned for the Mayor's Office in her hometown and the Hampden County District Attorney's Office. She did community service with her high school's Key Club, participated in Debate League, and was a member of the National Honor Society. She was active in the music programs at her school and church.

Stats

SAT: 1420 (720 Critical Reading, 700 Math)
High School GPA: 4.60 (out of 5.00)
High School: Westfield High School, Westfield, MA
Hometown: Westfield, MA
Gender: Female
Race: Caucasian

Applied To

Claremont McKenna College
Duke University
Loyola University of Chicago
Muhlenberg College
Pepperdine University
Pomona College
Skidmore College
Stanford University
University of San Diego
Wittenberg University

Essay

Lindsay submitted the following essay to every school she applied to that accepted the Common Application. She revised it to fit the remaining schools' applications.

Common Application: Evaluate a significant experience, achievement, risk you have taken, or ethical dilemma you have faced and its impact on you.

The picture bobbing before me was of a seemingly happy 20-something year old man grinning for the camera, arm-in-arm with his buddies. But the numbers below told a different story: 1979-2000. As I walked through that balmy August night, I saw many of the same kinds of photographs on the shirt-backs of the people ahead of me. And the numbers below were in the same small increments; some as small as nine or ten years.

As a teenager, I had been exposed to the issue of suicide both in myself and in my friends, but felt powerless to stop this epidemic that was assaulting one million of my peers every year. That was until the day that I saw a television ad for a charitable walk called "Out of the Darkness."

"Out of the Darkness," a 26-mile walk through the night from Annandale, VA to Washington D.C., changed my perspective on suicide. Embarrassing as it was once to admit I, like most of my friends, had pondered how liberating it would be to stop having to deal with the stresses of teenage life. Even though I saw some of my friends suffering and glimpsed those same qualities in myself at times, I considered suicide to be a personal battle that only dwelt in reclusive misfits.

Those pictures changed my mind. If all of these beautiful, young, popular people could take their lives, then my stereotypes were completely wrong.

That was the purpose of "Out of the Darkness". To change people's attitudes about suicide. To make it a disease that people can talk about and seek help for without being ashamed. My money donors talked with me about suicide as if they'd never spoken the word before. They told me stories of personal suffering or the suffering of someone they loved without being ashamed that they were going to be judged.

A few days after the walk, making sure to tell my friends how much they mean to me, one of them asked, "Lindsay, why did you walk? What did you get out of it?" And I had to think. Did I want to educate people about suicide? Sure. Did I want to know I wasn't abnormal? Yes. But what was my ultimate goal? More than anything, I knew, I wanted to change the world. I wanted to know that once I set my mind to something, I could do it. In my small way, I learned that I could change the world both for me and for thousands out there just like me. I, Lindsay Cushing, had the ability to make a difference.

And as I remembered the pictures bobbing on the shirt-backs in front of me, I gave my friend a hug and said, "I don't want anyone to have to remember a loved one as a photograph."

See page 326 to find out where this student got in.

LYMAN THAI

In high school, Lyman was a National Merit Scholar and valedictorian of his class. He played clarinet in the marching and honors bands and captained his school's Academic Challenge team to the national level three straight years. He attended Cornell Summer College between his junior and senior years and participated in Junior Achievement and Academic Decathlon. He tutored during the school year and spent a summer as a teaching assistant for children with autism.

Stats

SAT: 1550 (770 Critical Reading, 780 Math)
High School GPA: 4.00 unweighted, 4.79 (out of 5.00) weighted
High School: Alief Hastings High School, Houston TX
Hometown: Houston, Texas
Gender: Male
Race: Asian American

Applied To

Cornell University
Duke University
Harvard College
Rice University
Stanford University
University of California—Berkeley
University of California—Los Angeles
University of Texas—Austin

Essay

Lyman used a variant of the following essay in each of his applications.

Common Application: Topic of your choice.

A Simple Reflection on My Father and My High School Years

My father has instilled in me the importance of being thrifty. Whenever I made an unwise purchase, he would lecture me, relating his experience as a refugee during the Vietnam War in an attempt to make me realize how not wasting anything – food, clothing, or money – had saved the lives of my family members during their perilous journey from Vietnam to Malaysia and from Malaysia to the United States. After arriving in the United States, my father worked long shifts at a steakhouse to provide for my mother and infant sister and to pay rent on my family's small, modest apartment. Four years later, my father began working for the United States Postal Service, which provided him a steady salary. He soon saved up enough money to buy his own house in southwest Houston. I was born a year after he moved my mother and sister into our new house. Because of my father's hard work and careful management of the family money, I was fortunate enough to have not faced economic hardship while growing up. Even so, my father's lectures stay within my heart. I never leave a grain of rice in my bowl, never throw away old shirts when they are out of style, and rarely purchase unnecessary items. So, I was completely surprised when, on my sixteenth birthday, my father decided to augment my limited possessions with my very own car.

Ever since my sister left home for college when I was nine years old, I have largely fended for myself. My mother and father work alternating shifts at the post office; my mother works during the afternoon, and my father works at night. During the day, my father, a devout Buddhist, makes a daily visit to his temple. Once he arrives home, he immediately goes to bed to rest up for a long night of sorting mail. When I entered high school, this situation made my extracurricular participation difficult. I relied on the bus to take me to and from school, which caused me to miss important meetings and events that happened in the afternoon. I often asked my friends for rides, but they had places of their own to go, and I felt awkward and burdensome. So, as soon as I could, I took a drivers' education course. On my sixteenth birthday, with my license safe in my wallet, I received the keys to my car. It was a four-thousand-dollar, seven-year-old Honda Accord that had been flooded during Tropical Storm Allison, gutted and repaired by my uncle, and sold to my father at a steep discount. Clearly, my father had noticed I was not taking advantage of the opportunities that his struggle to America had opened up for me. He hoped I would use the car to learn about volunteerism, to learn interpersonal, organizational, and leadership skills, to meet people outside of class, to make friends, and to experience all I would have never experienced if he had stayed in Vietnam. The car represented my father's values of social service and leadership, both of which soon became my own. With time, my car has become an extension of those values, for I use it to get to my tutoring jobs, my service projects, and my club meetings, in addition to just going to hang out with my friends.

Granted, I will not be taking my car with me when I go to college, but my father's life lessons and values will stay with me even without such a tangible symbol. I know I have much farther to go in life before I will truly have made my father's toil worthwhile, but I pray that receiving a college education will put me well on my way to doing so. Nothing I do will repay the debt I owe to my father, but when I emerge from college as a strong, independent, well-educated, moral adult, I am sure he will be fulfilled in knowing he raised me well.

See page 326 to find out where this student got in.

MARIA INEZ VELAZQUEZ

Maria was editor-in-chief of her high school's award-winning literary magazine, a participant in the Alpha Kappa Alpha Partnership in Math and Science Program, and president of her school's Amnesty International chapter.

Stats
SAT: 1400
ACT: 32
High School GPA: ~4.16
High School: Springfield High School of Science and Technology, Springfield, MA
Hometown: Springfield, MA
Gender: Female
Race: African American/Latina

Applied To
Connecticut College
Elms College
Smith College
Trinity College
Yale University
University of Massachusetts—Amherst
Xavier University of Louisiana

Essay

Maria used the following essay in each of her applications.

Please describe an experience of great personal importance to you.

In Search of Solitude

It is hard to come home again. I'm finding that out now. Over the summer I was stripped away, like an onion, a gradual pruning of all but the essentials. I became purified. I spent the summer as far away from home as I could get: two weeks in New Mexico as a Student Challenge Award Recipient, contemplating unknown constellations; four weeks as a scholarship student at Xavier University in New Orleans.

Leaving home was the scariest part. I have made myself malleable; I am the good student, the understanding friend, the dutiful daughter. I have always defined myself in terms of others: the ways they understood me was the way I was. It is so easy to do that. It is an easing of the mind, a process of surrender, a fading to oblivion, a surrender that kept me from thinking too hard about my self.

After building myself up from a heap of other people's thoughts and dreams, how shocking, then, to emerge into the stark fluorescent lights of an airport, to enter its crass brilliance, and discover I had no self, no one to define me. My plane ride to this new and foreign land of Albuquerque, New Mexico was my first solitary journey, my first layover, my first disembarking; I got off the plane in a cold panic, lost. I frantically tried to disappear once again, to hide from the harsh light. Huddled between the shelves of an airport bookstore I examined myself and found that I was empty. There was nothing there to see. Finally, the passage of time and the glare of the cashier ripped me from the grip of Nullity. Prompted by her look, I grabbed the cheapest, nearest book I could find. The book's weight in my hand was vaguely comforting.

In New Mexico, my book and I are left alone again. I spend the hot, noon bright days letting the glory of bone-white sidewalks burn away my pretensions towards identity. I play lightly with my voice, letting it flit and gravel-throat its way through stories and normal conversation. I experiment with the movement of my body, the inclination of my look. I discover I can be profound. I become outrageous, controversial, glinting glitter-bright fingernails every which way.

Two weeks later, my book and I leave New Mexico. I have memorized its cover: *The Hanged Man* by Francesca Lia Block. We travel onwards to New Orleans; its weight in my hands is again an anchor to reality.

In New Orleans, I am seduced by sepia, absorbed into a heaving mass of hued skin; I gladly lose myself in the balm of sweetly scented hair and cocoa butter. Here, again, I play with my identity. I leave my hair unrelaxed and wear it out. I learn to flash my eyes out, a coquette, and link arms with two girls I have befriended, we three ignoring the catcalls and hoots that track us down the street.

In New Mexico, I discovered the desert night. I let its silence fill me and transform me, until I was at once ethereal, eternal, serene. In New Orleans, I learn to be strong: I am the one the dorm girls come to at night when the black sky has descended and someone has ordered pick-up chicken; I am the one known for being unafraid. By now, I have let my nails grow out, long and blunt, colored them a crimson red – looking at them, I feel taloned and fierce, teeth blackened and filed to a point, like some old Mayan war story. I let my walk mime assertive strides.

It is hard to come home again, to once again surrender to the community of family, friends, and peers, whose chafing needs and desires chafe and brush against the skin with a subtle, bitter susurrus. It is hard to return to school, to the daily routine: I feel sometimes as though the person who claimed mountains is no longer there. But I try to remember this: the human soul is like a deck of tarot cards, and the mind is the dealer. Each card flipped is a facet of the potential self, each card a piece of a new person to be.

"Some of the faces will be mine. I will be the Hanged Man, the Queen of Cups. I will be Strength with her lions."

— *The Hanged Man*, by Francesca Lia Block

See page 327 to find out where this student got in.

MEGAN HERMAN

In high school, Megan participated in many extracurricular activities ranging from student government and varsity softball to marching band and a Christian Youth organization. She was also a member of National Honor Society and Orchard Park Pride, a local honor given to graduating seniors.

Stats
SAT: 1180 (590 Critical Reading, 590 Math)
SAT Subject Test(s): 590 Literature, 570 U.S. History, 520 World History
ACT: 26
High School GPA: 3.68
High School: Orchard Park High School, Orchard Park, NY
Hometown: Orchard Park, NY
Gender: Female
Race: Caucasian

Applied To
Hamilton College (early decision)

Essay

Megan used the following essay in her application to Hamilton College.

Topic of choice.

One of the Giants

My hand waved in the air. I was convinced I could finally answer a math question correctly. My eighth grade math teacher called on me, and when I answered, the class erupted in laughter. I had been asked what an isosceles triangle was. I confidently answered: a triangle with three sides! If I had told anyone then that in four years I would be taking the high school's hardest math class, no one would have believed me.

I had struggled with math since elementary school, but worked very hard to keep up with the smart math students surrounding me. In eleventh grade, much to my parents' surprise, I signed up to take pre-calculus BC, the hardest pre-calc class, leading to a senior year with AP calculus BC. That is when I met Mr. Dena and told him I would try my hardest despite my many math shortcomings. He was convinced I could succeed despite what family and friends were saying.

Mr. Dena had an unforgettable quote by Sir Isaac Newton on his chalk board: "If I have been able to see further, it is only because I stand on the shoulders of giants." He reflected on that quote throughout the year and was determined to teach us more than math, determined to have us make changes in the world knowing more than just calculus.

I once told Mr. Dena I didn't understand how I could do so poorly on a test when I had studied so hard. He looked right at me and explained it's not about the grades; it's about understanding the material. If studying didn't pay off on a test, it would someday. I knew then that beyond passing or failing tests, this was about hard work and effort. His class made me push myself harder than I ever had, and I learned so much from my classmates.

Mr. Dena occasionally gave partner tests, believing that we could help teach each other and solve hard problems together. Mr. Dena drew names out of a hat to assign partners. Students were praying out loud that he wouldn't pull my name with theirs. I understood! I wanted to have the best student in the class for my partner! A hush fell over the class as my name was drawn. Although my partner joked with the class about being stuck with me, we surprised everyone with our grade on this test. We worked very well together. Although Mr. Dena only hinted at the fact that he taught us about working with each other, I knew this was really why we had partner tests.

The final exam was Mr. Dena's final challenge to us. I failed his challenge but was in good company. I knew this would never be looked upon as a failure. I also knew that my overall average in the class showed my success. Mr. Dena taught me the important lessons, and, after all, Sir Isaac Newton didn't get it the first time or without the help of others. Most subjects had come easily to me, and to be challenged in math really changed the way I saw other challenges in life.

I am continuing AP calculus with Mr. Dena this year. Having made it half-way through the two-year challenge, I wasn't going to let a grade, a numerical rating, stop me from learning some of the best lessons of my life.

Will I pass the end-of-the-year AP exam? Mr. Dena would want me to be more concerned with the words of Sir Isaac Newton, to be more concerned that I push myself and "...see further..." He is one of the giants that Newton describes. He has helped me see not only more mathematical ideas than I thought possible, but who I can be. The question of whether I pass the AP exam or not is hardly as important as the question: How will Mr. Dena stretch me this year?

See page 327 to find out where this student got in.

MELISSA HENLEY

Melissa was on the varsity tennis team and was a member of the National Honor Society for two years. She worked a part-time job (about twenty to twenty-five hours a week) her junior and senior years and took part in a local tennis academy her senior year.

Stats
SAT: 1400 (690 Critical Reading, 710 Math)
SAT Subject Test(s): 640 U.S. History, 740 Math Level 1, 690 Math Level 2, 650 Chemistry
High School GPA: 4.00
High School: McMinnville High School, McMinnville, OR
Hometown: McMinnville, OR
Gender: Female
Race: Caucasian

Applied To
Dartmouth College
Lewis and Clark College
Linfield College
Stanford University

Essay

Melissa used the following essay in her applications to Dartmouth, Linfield, and Stanford. The essay prompt was approximately:

Use this space to tell us anything else about you that you feel we should know.

Although it may be difficult to tell, I hate talking about myself. I feel arrogant and self-centered and boastful when I go on and on about what I've done and what I want to do. And since I've had to answer the question "Tell us about yourself" on every other application, whether it's for a college or a scholarship, I've decided not to tell you about myself, but to tell you about my apple tree.

I grew up in the country, in a neighborhood where there were only three girls my age, but about ten boys two or more years older than I, one of whom was my obnoxious older brother. With this excess of torture, torment, and testosterone, I was often forced to find places where I could escape the plague of cootie-infested boys. Unfortunately, being both younger and a "girl", I could find no place the boys couldn't go. And so my mother, being the wonderful and patient woman she was, granted me sole access to our apple tree.

Before I continue, I feel I should describe my apple tree to provide you with a mental image as you read on. It's a young tree, no older than I am and so it's rather small, just a bit shorter than our old one-story house. It looks it's best in the summer, as most trees do, when it's laden with the greenest and sourest apples imaginable and it's covered with little white blossoms. With all the apples weighing them down, its branches would scratch the ground and form a curtain between the outside world and itself.

My apple tree first gave me respite from the harassment even before I was big enough to actually climb it. I spent days sitting at the base of the tree, writing the oh-so-juicy diary entries of a 7-year old and reading my Serendipity books, separated from the world by a few inches of shrubbery.

After I grew a bit and was able to climb the tree, I spent even more time in it, adding gymnastics and acrobatics (you gain a very unique perspective of the world when you hang by your knees in a tree) to the more peaceful activities of writing and reading. During the school year, when the weather was warm, I would do my homework sitting in my tree and enjoying a snack.

Once I reached middle school, I spent almost as much time in my tree as I did in my bedroom. My writing now included short stories and haikus, usually about nature and animals, and my reading had grown to books with several chapters and little or no pictures (a sacrifice I was forced to make in the effort to find more challenging books). Homework was done at the base of the tree since it was a bit difficult to drag the textbooks up into the branches.

Now, however, at the end of my high school career, I am no longer able to enjoy the comfort and serenity of my apple tree - unless, of course, I want to be prosecuted for trespassing. When my family and I moved from our home in the country, we left behind many things pertinent to the first thirteen years of my life, but my apple tree is what I miss the most.

My apple tree was more than just a refuge from the unbearable boys of the neighborhood. For years, it was my best friend. It was the best listener, with its trunk leaning companionably against my back and its branches hanging above, and it would never reveal any of my feelings or secrets. It was always there for me, strong and dependable, soothing and peaceful.

See page 327 to find out where this student got in.

MEREDITH NARROWE

Meredith was a one-meter springboard diver all four years of high school, placing third her freshman year, second her sophomore and junior years, and first her senior year in the state diving championship. She served as National Honor Society president, played in the school band, and twirled flags with the color guard.

Stats
SAT: 1370 (710 Critical Reading, 660 Math)
SAT Subject Test(s): 730 U.S. History, 650 Math Level 1
ACT: 29
High School GPA: 4.14
High School: King Kekaulike High School, Pukalani, Maui, HI
Hometown: Pukalani, Maui, HI
Gender: Female
Race: Caucasian

Applied To
Brown University
Columbia University
Occidental College
Pomona College
Scripps College
Stanford University

Essay

Meredith used the following essay in her application to Stanford and modified it for her application to Pomona.

> *How has the place in which you live influenced the person you are? Define "place" any way that you like . . . as a context, a country, a city, a community, a house, a point in time.*

Da Kine Diversity

He sauntered over from the neighboring display at the National History Day competition at the University of Maryland with an air of superiority.

"So," he drawled, "you three won this category last year? Refresh my memory; what was your project's title?" We turned our attention away from our current History Day display and focused on our competitor.

"It was called *Da Kine Talk: Migration to Hawaii Creates Pidgin English . . . And Controversy*," I replied.

"That's right," he conveniently remembered. "What does *da kine* mean, anyway?"

"It's a word you use when you don't know the actual word," I explained. "If you can't remember what color your shoes are, you would say their color is *da kine*."

"It's vague, kind of like 'stuff' or 'whatever,'" interjected my teammate. "For example, when asked what your day's activities will be, your answer would be, 'I'm gonna go *da kine*."

"It's kinda like 'whatchamacalit'," added my other teammate. "If you are frantically searching for your homework assignment and someone asks, 'What are you looking for?' you could reply, 'I can't find my *da kine*!'"

"Oh, I get it," he sneered. "You won last year without knowing what your title means." Haughtily, he turned away. We looked at each other and raised our eyebrows. Although we had given three different answers, each was correct and symbolic of a language that sprouted from Hawaii's unique cultural diversity. Designed as a means for the *lunas* (overseers) of the canefields to communicate in general terms with laborers of different ethnicities, cultures, and languages, Hawaii's Pidgin English often fails to yield the clear definition our fellow competitor expected.

Hawaii is known as the ethnic and cultural melting pot of the Pacific. It is a place where my parents are Mainland "immigrants," and, I suppose, a place where as a *haole*

(Caucasian), I am a minority in my public high school. After growing up in Hawaii, I can discern a thick line between our "island style" and Mainland "normalcy." Like a *keiki* (child) of split custody, I experience both worlds regularly. Sure, I have no clue how to operate a rice cooker, but I do know the difference between Island sticky rice and Uncle Ben's. A good luck cat figurine is absent from my home, but my family follows the custom of removing our rubber slippers before stepping onto our linoleum floor. When I speak with my local friends, I end statements with, "Yeah?" — the customary request for affirmation that your opinion is valid. While attending a three week summer writing program at Carleton College in Minnesota, however, I was surprised to learn that this habit was noticeable and thought of as a Hawaiian "accent" by Mainland students.

Few of my Maui friends would have elected to spend a month of their summer in Minnesota doing *more* schoolwork. In fact, even fewer of my schoolmates, when confronted with the lure of palm-tree lined beaches, would have opted to spend seven months of sunny Sunday mornings enclosed in a house analyzing the effects of Pidgin English on a century of Hawaiian history as my two teammates and I did. By taking advantage of our unique, isolated culture and the abundant amount of information available, we discovered that history is not old and stale, but is a living, personal part of every society. The possibility of supplementing this discovery in a place where everybody has a similar intellectual curiosity and where a never-ending pool of information exists is mind-boggling and exciting. Imagine a child — whose only video viewing experience has been a black and white silent movie — suddenly allowed an unlimited selection of cartoons at the local video store. Stanford is my ultimate video store, an institution in which my beliefs and ideas will be challenged and augmented by more developed views from different backgrounds and perspectives, both inside and outside the classroom. I will find a new *ohana* (family) of people who, like myself, crave new experiences and diverse intellectual pursuits. Again, there will be a variety of answers to any question, all describing *da kine* (truth).

See page 327 to find out where this student got in.

MICHAEL HARRIS

At his high school, Michael was captain of the varsity tennis team, editor-in-chief of the school newspaper, treasurer of the Mock Trials Club, and vice president of the Math Club. Outside of school he taught piano to six novice-level students and prepared them for recitals.

Stats
SAT: 1380 (620 Critical Reading, 760 Math) **ACT:** 32 **High School GPA:** 4.70 weighted **High School:** Plymouth-Whitemarsh High School, Plymouth Meeting, PA **Hometown:** Lafayette Hill, PA **Gender:** Male **Race:** Caucasian

Applied To
Boston University Brandeis University Duke University Emory University George Washington University Lehigh University New York University Tufts University University of Pennsylvania Washington University in St. Louis

Essay 1

Michael used similar versions of the following essay in his applications to Brandeis, Duke, Emory, and Tufts.

Describe the environment in which you grew up and how it has shaped your personal goals.

So here I am: another Saturday night, one where I should be out with my friends, enjoying myself, but I am home. I am not here because I am grounded, or because I want to be: instead, I am here to make sure I write the best essay I can and, consequently, be admitted to Tufts University. I realize I only have myself to blame: I have allowed my desire to achieve overtake my longing to be a "normal" high school student.

Upon reaching high school, many students enter the "rebellious teenage years—" the years that disobeying parents is "cool" and having the mentality that less than the best is acceptable. However, I have maintained my drive to achieve despite the temptations to be bitten by the "teenage bug."

Although my friends wonder how, I know exactly why I am just as motivated now as I was ten years ago. Everyone in my family has been extremely successful: they attended top universities and have succeeded in the professional world. Needless to say, from a young age, there was always pressure for me to do just as well. Nothing less than an "A" would suffice, and not a single tangible reward came from my academic achievements.

That personal drive continues to "haunt" me now. Although my family no longer applies nearly as much pressure, I still have that drive to succeed. I accept nothing less than my best, and when I do not achieve up to my capability, I know I have only myself to blame. While the benefits of having a strong work ethic are obvious, I am often jealous of other students who have the luxury of an "average" teenage life.

I often wonder if I should not have allowed my family environment to have that great an impact, and, in turn, let myself learn how to tolerate failure. I no longer have just a desire to succeed: I often feel that I have no choice but to succeed. My stress level often goes off the charts as my goals to achieve and be at my best sometimes make me mentally exhausted.

So, as I sit here on Saturday night, writing this essay, I wonder who really has been bitten by the teenage bug: me, or the rest of my graduating class. Should I have let my environment influence me the way it has? Will my drive to succeed actually make me more prepared for the professional world? And, should I have set my personal goals as high as I have?

I do not yet know the answers to my questions, but I truly believe I can find them in my years as an undergraduate student at Tufts. My environment has manifested itself in me, and has become internalized in my own mind. In writing this essay, I have come to realize that it is a mixed blessing: I am fortunate to have such a strong work ethic and desire to achieve, but have not yet experienced the aspects of failure that may await me in the real world.

Essay 2

Michael used the following essay in each of his applications.

First experiences can be defining. Cite a first experience that you have had and explain its impact on you.

"Do you think I'm going to do well, Mike?" I was sitting on the edge of my auditorium seat, anxiously waiting for the recital to begin. I then noticed the familiar face of Rachael, a six year-old girl who nervously asked me this question.

Suddenly, my mind wandered to a time earlier in the year when I never thought I would be at the recital with my six prepared piano students. I recalled one of my most disappointing conversations when a parent informed me that her child wanted to stop taking lessons. My goal for the year had been to make piano fun for all of my students, and I felt like I had failed. Although my teacher told me not to take the situation personally, I still felt responsible for a student not enjoying the piano.

That encounter also made me question why I had accepted the day my piano teacher asked me to teach her beginner piano students. Although I had never taught anything previously, I liked the idea of sharing my love for the piano and experiencing something I enjoy from a teacher's standpoint.

I quickly realized that piano was much different as a teacher. My first few lessons were more difficult to teach than I could have ever imagined. I did not anticipate having to review the alphabet with my students before teaching them the notes! My frustration also grew when I noticed some students learning the notes more quickly than others. I wondered why this was the case, and consequently questioned my teaching techniques.

Surprisingly, I still found myself smiling at the end of most lessons. My moments of disappointment were frequently eclipsed by the many times when my students played well and I could reward them with a sticker. Slowly, I noticed each of them improve.

Yet, as the recital approached, I grew increasingly nervous. I wanted my students to have a positive experience in their first performances. I was thrilled when each of my students was able to tell me that they felt prepared for the "big day."

After a short period of silence and recalling the highs and lows of my year teaching, I glanced back at Rachael. "Of course I think you'll do well. You've worked hard to prepare, and I've enjoyed every minute of teaching you. You'll be great!" At the time, all I could really think about was not allowing my anxiety to surface!

The recital could not have gone better. Each of my students played flawlessly. A year of hard work felt so rewarding, for both my students and me. I realized that I meant every word I said to Rachael; in fact, I enjoyed the challenges of teaching all of my students.

I could not have anticipated how much I would learn from my first teaching experience. Now, I appreciate the efforts of all my teachers, especially my piano instructor. I also have matured as a teacher and am proud of my ability to interact positively with my students, even when I am frustrated.

When the next piano recital comes around this spring, there will be no reason to be nervous. In fact, I learned the real accomplishment is not how my students play at a recital, but how we work together throughout the year to make teaching and learning piano a rewarding experience.

See page 328 to find out where this student got in.

MICHELE CASH

At her high school, Michele was president of the Interact Club and the Latin Club. She played tennis and ran cross-country, was an attorney on the mock trial team for three years, and organized school-wide blood and canned-food drives. She attended the California State Science Fair twice and won first place her junior year. She worked as a research assistant at NASA Ames Research Center the following summer.

Stats

SAT: 1450 (690 Critical Reading, 760 Math)
SAT Subject Test(s): 670 U.S. History, 710 Math Level 1, 750 Math Level 2, 720 Physics
ACT: 29
High School GPA: 4.00
High School: Abraham Lincoln High School, San Jose, CA
Hometown: San Jose, CA
Gender: Female
Race: Caucasian

Applied To

Harvard College
Harvey Mudd College
Princeton University
Rice University
Stanford University
University of California—Berkeley
University of California—Davis
University of California—San Diego
University of Rochester

Essay

Michelle used the following essay in each of her applications, with the exception of her Stanford application. The essay prompt was approximately:

Tell us something about yourself.

I came home from summer camp to find another foster child in our home. Noel had returned to his parents and Christian had replaced him. He was a quiet, shy, four-year-old who never made a sound. His past rendered him scared of adults, and when he spoke, it was barely an audible whisper. When I first met him, Christian did not faze me as anything other than another foster kid, with whom we would be sharing our home and love until a more permanent home could be assigned by the court. My parents were emergency foster parents and I had seen foster children come and go, some stayed only two days, others lived with us for several months. In the end, they all left.

At first Christian's presence did not impact me. With my busy schedule it was easy to let the cowering child who wanted to be left alone go unnoticed. But Christian's sad face and puppy dog eyes sang to me. Before long I found myself reading <u>If You Give a Mouse a Cookie</u> to him every night before tucking him into the little miniature bed in my brother's room. The dark held monsters which scared Christian. Every night I made sure that the soft yellow nightlight beside his bed was casting its friendly glow on the walls, protecting him from the monsters concealed in the dark. I did not want Christian to wake up scared and frightened; he was so fragile and sweet I could not stand to see him upset.

Weeks passed and Christian found comfort in my active and compassionate family, slowly he shed his shell of fear and insecurity and transformed into an assertive four-year-old demanding attention. Christian willingly tried new activities. There were many common childhood experiences Christian never had. I taught him how to hold a crayon and color imaginative pictures, how to throw a softball and kick a soccer ball. We sat together on the family room floor and built Lego towers. We explored the mysterious corners of the backyard, creating secret magical lands for us to play in. I enjoyed Christian's inquisitive mind and loved watching his reactions to the surrounding world.

Christian fit perfectly into the makeup of our family. He even continued the pattern set by our ages: 16, 13, 10, 7, 4; obviously he was meant to be part of our family. In every way Christian became my little brother. I protected him from harm and held him in my arms if he was ever hurt or upset.

In August of that summer my family went on a trip to Washington where we hiked up a steep trail toward the glaciers on Mount Rainer. Even Christian and my youngest sister, Gayle, made it most of the way up without whining to be carried; but before we reached the desired glacier, more than half our party decided they would rather rest than continue up the steep ascending path. Christian anxiously sought to play in the glistening snow, but he was too tired to climb any higher. I wanted him to encounter the cold softness of snow, so my brother, Stephen, and I plodded up the steep slope on a mission to bring back snow for Christian. Hiking up the mountain was not as difficult as coming down. The icy snow burnt my hands and soaked my heavy sweatshirt. I didn't mind the stinging numbness in my fingers; the pain dissipated upon seeing Christian laugh as he built three-inch snowmen and participated in our miniscule snowball fight. The genuine happiness Christian displayed that day playing with snow made my trek to the glacier one of my most meaningful achievements.

Christian stayed with my family through Halloween and Christmas and into February of the next year. Once school started I no longer had countless hours to imagine marvelous kingdoms and explore hidden worlds with Christian, but I still managed to read to him and tuck him in bed on a regular basis. One cold Friday in February I came home from school to find a Polaroid picture of Christian on my desk with the caption, "To Michele" written in his shaky writing. The authorities had taken Christian away and I had not even had the opportunity to say good-bye. The loss of Christian devastated me. He fit so logically, so perfectly into our family; he made it balanced and whole. Christian's deep inquisitive mind and genuine shyness reminded me of myself at his age. I wanted Christian to have all the opportunities life held open for him, but circumstances snatched him away from me.

When people find out that my parents are foster parents they often ask how we can take care of foster kids, don't we get attached to them? I only have one answer for their question: I have loved them all, and have cared for them all, but some have left an aching hole in my heart.

See page 328 to find out where this student got in.

MIEKO Y. BEYER

Mieko served on the editorial staff of her high school's literary magazine and as an officer in the Quizbowl Club. She won awards in Latin and played tennis on her school team. She also spent a year abroad in Japan.

Stats
SAT: 1390 (740 Critical Reading, 650 Math)
High School GPA: 93.0 (out of 100)
High School: Orchard Park High School, Orchard Park, NY
Hometown: Orchard Park, NY
Gender: Female
Race: Asian American/Caucasian

Applied To
Boston University
Columbia University—Columbia College
Loyola University New Orleans
New York University
Smith College
State University of New York at Buffalo
State University of New York College at Purchase
University of Chicago

Essay

Mieko used the following essay in her applications to BU, Chicago, Columbia, Loyola, NYU, and Smith.

Chicago's application asked applicants to compose their own essay question. Mieko proposed the following: Due to internal and/or external weirdness, sometimes you may feel like you just don't belong. A commonly heard reaction to an individual's weirdness may be, "Are you from a different planet or something?" Now, there are those who react with offense or jest, but there are others for whom this comment triggers deep introspection. (Am I from a different planet?). Suppose you are the second sort of person, describe how you found out about your alien status and what your home planet is like.

I don't think normality is overrated. I think it must actually be a very nice sensation. Because normality isn't who you are, it is how you feel. Normality to me is a sense of belonging.

Certain things commonly indicate your ease at belonging; our physical appearance is oftentimes the best indicator.

I am perfectly healthy, my mom brags about how she used no anesthesia when giving birth to me. Yup, my existence was pure from the moment I left the womb. I am average weight, height, looks, coloration....everything! I can run, not too fast, but not too slow. I can lift heavy things, but not really heavy things. You know, just healthy. I am average smart too, I even had tests done to prove it (you have them for your perusal).

But alas, I am strange.

How did this happen? Am I a genetic oddity? All of my physical and mental categorizations show that I should feel comfortable in my life...but I do not.

Oh, not in a bad way! I love everyone, and I don't want to die. I am just, odd. The worst thing is to look normal, have people act to you as they would any normal person, and then have to offend their efforts with your abnormalities.

I have always been aware of these things, and I have now gotten to the bottom of it; I am an alien.

Once, in childish play, my sister performed tests on me, to determine what species I was. It was a rigorous procedure where I tried talking to animals, telekinesis, taste tests, tree-climbing, and was timed at being silent. All results indicated, according to my sister, that I was indeed an alien. That's a pretty strange childhood memory. Even more strangely though, the FBI seized those records from my then nine year old sister. Then they tagged me on the bottom of my foot, telling my parents that it was "for my own protection."

I am greatly influenced by my family's way of regarding my eccentricities. They smile indulgently at me as they pull a jar of kosher pickle spears from a grocery bag, "Guess what we got for you Mieko!" And when they told stories of our perils to relatives, it was always "Mieko who, strange child, was riding down the stairs in a laundry basket for fun." When I got stitches, on my knee cap, on my nose-bridge, on my brow bone, it wasn't treated with worry, but with chuckles and knowing nods. I always found this interesting, because shouldn't those abnormalities be washed out of a child? My friend used to eat her own hair, so her mother would tie her hair in tight French braids all the time. I have never seen her chew her hair since. Why didn't my parents refuse to buy me pickles? Why didn't they take away the laundry baskets? Why didn't they dress me up in protective equipment to prevent lacerations? I think I know why. My alien core shined through and they realized resistance was futile. Everyone knows the saying, "You can't make a sow's ear into a silk purse." I am a sow's ear.

I'll try to envision my home –planet, my people, by taking the opposite version of all my sources of discomfort here. Basically, they come down to two major things, sharp edges and sporadic verbal outbursts.

I think on my planet we are all amorphous putty. We hover approximately 1 to 2 feet in the air, energetically floating around mazes of compartments and chattering weirdness. Some compartments are just like Earth, offices, apartments, stores, etc. But the rest are unique to my planet. There are Laughing rooms and there are Sighing rooms. They are self-explanatory. The two categories make up the range of emotion found on the planet outside of Contemplation. Contemplation is carried out in the caudal end of our bodies, and can be detached, almost like an intellectual fart, and dispersed like one. However, it has no odor, and is very pleasant to happen upon.

I really do love your planet; I think it might actually suit me better than my native one. By encasing my being in the more structured human form, it limits the degree of damage I can do. My sudden bursts of thought on my planet might have caused a tidal wave of cogitative emittances that might have wrought physical destruction. Here, I must take the time to laboriously write them down or articulate them in speech (though sometimes I do tend to babble very randomly) by which time the power of the thought is weakened by my other physical efforts. Here on Earth, one's thoughts must be first manifested physically outside the mind to have any effect on the environment at all It was Emily Dickinson who realized this signature mode of Earthling thinking when she wrote "A word is dead when it is said, some say. I say it just begins to live that day"

Despite all my complaints about feeling a bit alienated sometimes by my er, alien origins, I realize that having a streak of weird on an otherwise ordinary human form isn't a bad thing, but just another part of me. I guess it's not as bad as I thought at first, because you know what? Everyone is an alien somewhere. The next time someone says to me "Are you from a different planet or something?" I think I will say to them "Yes, and on my planet, I'd say to you 'Are you from a different planet or something?'"

See page 328 to find out where this student got in.

NITIN SHAH

Nitin was editor-in-chief of his high school newspaper and president of its Amnesty International chapter.

Stats
SAT: 1590 (800 Critical Reading, 790 Math)
SAT Subject Test(s): 760 U.S. History, 800 Math Level 2
High School GPA: 4.60 weighted
High School: La Costa Canyon High School, Carlsbad, CA
Hometown: Carlsbad, CA
Gender: Male
Race: Asian American

Applied To
Harvard College
Stanford University
University of California—Berkeley
University of California—Los Angeles
Yale University

Essay

Nitin used the following essay in his applications to Harvard and Yale.

Evaluate a significant experience, achievement, or risk that you have taken and its impact on you.

Christmas in India

I never understood how my culture and background were different from everyone else's until a visit to my parents' mother country of India opened my eyes. Before that, I was just another kid in Southern California's suburban wilderness, in which parking spaces, large backyards, BMWs, and a strange sense of surrealism abound.

As I, age nine, stared out of the jumbo jet's window at the puffy white cloud tops and into the pale blue late December sky, I pondered back over the intense activities of the previous few days, including Christmas. That holiday was always perplexing for me as a child. Judging by what I could gather from my primary source of reliable information, cartoons, this Christmas thing involved a confused fat man forcing a bunch of moose to be his partners in crime as he broke into people's homes only to leave things, instead of take them. The most puzzling feature of all to me, as a San

Diegan, was that white substance everyone was walking in and building real live snowmen out of.

It was all oddly interesting, but what did all this have to do with me? I asked my mother, my backup data source. Christmas, she told me, can mean certain things to certain people, but to most people, it's a religious day. Is that what it is for us? I asked. No, she said flatly. Upon further pressing, all she would say was that we believed different things than some people. She would not explain those different things, though. My parents never did much explaining; they preferred rather that my sister and I figure things out for ourselves in our own way.

Things in India were a far cry different from back home. This was apparent from the moment we departed from the airport into a hot Bombay night so muggy there was no need to stop for a drink; I need only open my mouth to take in all the moisture I would need.

It was like this, with my mouth and eyes and ears wide open, that I took in the tastes and sights and sounds of India, conscious for the first time of my background and identity. I watched from a filthy, rust-covered train as a tiny cross-section of Indian life passed me by, a virtual slide show of the people here and their way of life, much removed from my own.

Dozens of dark-skinned naked children, many about my age, engaged in a play-ful shoving match in a waist-high brown-colored river. They cared not about getting dirty or sick or about the passing train they undoubtedly saw many times a day; their only care was about the moment. On an overlooking hill, old and wrinkled women watched them coolly in the sweltering heat as they milked cows and swiftly unleashed words that I could not have understood even had I been able to hear them over the train's drone and the children's screaming. Nearby, the women's husbands repaired the proud yet cramped dried-mud homes that stood chipped and battered from a recent earthquake. The men functioned as a single unit, concentrating completely on one building before moving on to the next. The entire village had perhaps twenty of these constructs, and the cows and bulls grazing in the surrounding pasture seemed to outnumber the people 2-to-1.

I realized that this place, not the life back home, was where I really came from, yet I was still awed with the people's contentment. They had so little in the way of material possessions, yet were so happy. They didn't need a car, or fence, or swanky home to be satisfied. Every day was their Christmas, and the gift was life.

See page 329 to find out where this student got in.

PETER DEAN

In high school, Peter played baseball and football and was captain of both teams his senior year. He was involved in Student Government all four years and was a member of his school's Executive Committee.

Stats
SAT: 1340 (650 Critical Reading, 690 Math)
SAT Subject Test(s): 600 U.S. History, 680 Math
High School GPA: 3.90
High School: James Madison High School, Vienna, VA
Hometown: Vienna, VA
Gender: Male
Race: Caucasian

Applied To
Davidson College
Gettysburg College
Rhodes College
University of Virginia
Valparaiso University
Vanderbilt University
Wake Forest University
Washington and Lee University
Wheaton College (IL)

Essay

Peter used the following essay in each of his applications.

Common Application: Evaluate a significant experience, achievement, or risk that you have taken and its impact on you.

No underarm hair, no facial hair, baby fat, and a mouthful of baby teeth is how I spent my first two years at James Madison High School. In the middle of my sophomore year, when most of my peers had begun shaving, I was getting the last of my baby teeth removed, because at age 16, I had "the mouth of a 12 year old," my dentist told me.

My older brother was big, strong, mature, and only a year ahead of me. Therefore, I was continuously asked, "what happened to you?" I always tried to answer the question optimistically - as I tried to do with the question, "do you shave your legs?" After long anticipation, Mr. Puberty finally arrived at the end of my sophomore year. Since that time I have grown at least eight inches, lost my baby fat, gained some underarm hair, and become the starting quarterback on the Varsity football team. Starting my senior year I can now look back and appreciate the lessons I learned before puberty, and I am glad that puberty did take so long.

Delayed puberty helped build my character. It taught me a lot about humility. In the halls during my freshman and sophomore years I was always looking up to, or being pushed around by, everyone. Now that I am bigger than most of my peers, I do not feel that I am better than they are. Lacking appearance, size and strength I was also forced to develop other character traits such as friendliness, a sense of humor, and kindness to attract friends - especially those of the opposite sex.

Delayed puberty eliminates many worries that usually are associated with entering high school. In the morning I did not need to shave, because the peach fuzz was still sparse. I did not worry about my wisdom teeth having to come out, because I had just lost all my baby teeth. I did not need to worry about braces, because I was on pace to get them in graduate school. I did not have to worry about any girl problems, because I learned from experience that girls are not interested in guys that remind them of their younger brothers.

Delayed puberty also postponed and shortened my adolescent conflicts with my parents. Of course, I have tormented my parents with petty arguments about use of the car and curfew. However, my adolescence has been efficient. My brother tortured them for four full years, but I achieved the same results in a few short months.

As I look back on my pre-puberty days there are many reasons why I am glad Mr. Puberty visited me late. I realize that there is no way to control when he comes, but if he ever chooses to visit you later than your peers you should be thankful. Even though you might spend a few years on the "short" end of jokes, in the end it will only make you better.

See page 329 to find out where this student got in.

PHILIP JAMES MADELEN RUCKER

Between the ages of 10 and 16, Philip lived away from home in Lake Arrowhead, California, for competitive figure skating training. Following his sophomore year of high school, he moved home to Savannah, Georgia, to be with his family. In school, Philip was actively involved in the production of his class yearbook, National Honor Society, Rotary Interact Club, and many other organizations. In the Savannah community, he was a Junior Block Captain with his local neighborhood association and a staff writer for his local newspaper. He also held a part-time job as a legal assistant at a small law firm.

Stats
SAT: Philip did not include his score in any of his applications
SAT Subject Test(s): 650 U.S. History, 740 Math Level 1
ACT: 30
High School GPA: 94.0 (out of 100)
High School: St. Andrew's School, Savannah, GA
Hometown: Savannah, GA
Gender: Male
Race: African American/Caucasian

Applied To
Boston College
Brown University
Emory University
Georgetown (early action)
Harvard College (early action)
Tufts University
Tulane University
University of Chicago (early action)
University of Rochester
Yale University

Essay

Philip used the following essay in his applications to BC, Brown, Chicago, Georgetown, Harvard, Rochester, and Yale. The essay prompt was different for each, but the prompts from his three top-choice schools are below.

Harvard College: Supplemental essay on a topic of your choice.

University of Chicago: In a pivotal scene of a recent American film, a videographer—a dark and mysterious teen-aged character—records a plastic bag blowing in the wind. He ruminates on the elusive nature of truth and beauty, and suggests that beauty is everywhere—often in the most unlikely places and in the quirky details of things. What is something that you love because it reflects a kind of idiosyncratic beauty—the uneven features of a mutt you adopted at the pound, a drinking glass with an interesting flaw, the feather boa you found in the Wal-Mart parking lot? These things can reveal (or conceal) our identity; so describe something that tells us who you are (or aren't).

Yale: There are limitations to what grades, scores, and recommendations can tell us about any applicant. We ask you to write a personal essay that will help us to know you better. In the past, candidates have written about their families, intellectual and extracurricular interests, ethnicity or culture, school and community events to which they have had strong reactions, people who have influenced them, significant experiences, personal aspirations, or topics that spring entirely from their imaginations. There is no "correct" response. Write about what matters to you, and you are bound to convey a strong sense of who you are. (As with the first essay, observe the 500-word limit.)

My Moment of Reckoning

The blistering sun shines through the tall fir trees onto a mound of frosty snow that sparkles like diamonds. As the heat of the summer day melts the snow, the snow forms a stream that curls down the hillside onto the quiet road below. I walk up the hillside with my skates over my shoulder, the sun shining on my black pants. It is hot. I enter the rink to the familiar sounds of sharp blades etching the ice to the beat of Beethoven. Indoors, the air is chilly; the ice is glistening; the heat from outside meets the icy coolness of the rink at the tall, wide windows.

Hour after hour, day after day, the same Zamboni brings white snow from inside the rink to the outside, dumping it into the same spot, creating the same flowing stream down the hillside. Seen from outdoors, the mound of snow is an aberration in the summer heat, but seen through the windows from indoors the same snow, framed by the trees, suggests a crisp, sunny, winter day. Even though the snow has been there every morning since I started coming to this rink, it struck me on this particular morning both how lovely and how strange it appeared.

The snow is clean and fresh, the residue of the early morning practice of young, promising, and often famous, figure skaters. Not yet sullied like most snow by the time that it is taken away, it is still pristine. It clings to its frostiness in the hot sunshine – a futile effort. This snow has lived a short life. It began as the smooth, shimmering ice that first catches one's eye and then catches the edges of the skaters' blades. As the skaters worked harder, the ice became snow, and within an hour or two of its beginnings it was removed. The snow rests now in this mound like millions of tiny diamonds, vulnerable to the rays of the sun and awaiting its fate.

As I stop to notice the incongruous beauty of the snow, the evergreens, and the glaring summer sun, I reflect on an affinity that I feel towards this snow. I, like the snow, am a bit misplaced. It has been wonderful to be a part of the life at this beautiful rink, this elite training center that grooms champions, but it is not really my element. I long to be with my family and have a more "real" life, not the sheltered, specialized one that this rink offers, where one's purpose is so limited. I stare at the snow for a moment and consider that soon it will melt into water and flow down the hillside to regions uncertain. Yet, perhaps, it will land where water and snow naturally belong and where the season of its life fits the season of its setting. As I watch, I realize that, perhaps, it is time for me also to leave, to leave this rink and this rarefied life of competitive skating, to go down the hillside and return to my roots.

See page 330 to find out where this student got in.

RISHABH CHANDRA

Along with being valedictorian of his high school's graduating class, Rishabh was also the captain of the tennis team, a member of the Arista honor society, and helped in the guidance department for two years. After school, he was a volunteer worker in Central Park and also campaigned for Mayor Bloomberg's reelection.

Stats
SAT: 2080 (640 Critical Reading, 800 Math, 640 Writing)
SAT Subject Test(s): 800 Math II, 800 Physics
High School GPA: 4.0
High School: John Bowne High School, Flushing, NY
Hometown: New York, NY
Gender: Male
Race: South Asian

Applied To
City University of New York—Macaulay Honors College
The Cooper Union for the Advancement of Science and Art
Columbia University
Cornell University
Stevens Institute of Technology

Essay

Rishabh used the following essay in her application to the schools listed above.

Common Application: Topic of Your Choice.

My Educational Journey

I remember feeling really small. The occasion was a visit to the military airbase in Gwalior, India. As the teacher led us through rows of airplanes on the concrete hangar, my sense of awe grew beyond the space among jostling children that I physically occupied as an eight year-old. The whirring engines and the offer of transporting me to a different world had me hooked to planes and engine technology from that day on. While I remember my first response to technology, I am now beginning to realize my growing intellectual curiosity and scientific appetite. To me, Mathematics and Physics are not a succession of courses taken at school and standardized tests, but a way of organizing my thoughts around an otherwise overwhelming world of science-led breakthroughs.

My years of formalized education have opened doors for what I view as a quest. Sometimes, I have felt the need to please my parents with exam scores and subsequently gain their praise, but the scientific quest has always been mine alone. The internalization of scientific concepts in high-school has provided me a "base" with which to begin. However, I still have to understand the economic and social issues that might be involved in the advancement of science.

The global debate on the "impending energy crisis" has got me thinking about the future utilization of fossil fuels and the development of energy alternatives. The long-term challenges facing the aviation industry make me wonder about the future of globalization. How will the "global village" be a reality without efficient transportation? Can we respond to disasters such as the hurricane Katrina, the tsunami, the earthquake in Kashmir without adequate means of transportation?

Living in a multi-cultural community, I also appreciate that human relationships cannot be sustained through virtual networks alone. Longing to see one's family or the transportation of consumer merchandise i.e. global commerce, remain important to sustaining both irreplaceable human bonds and improve standards of living.

The framework for my quest, however, will always remain scientific. I believe that efficiency in design is the right approach to deal with issues of productivity and resource utilization in the world. I seek in the American scientific community the free exchange of ideas and tolerance for exploring new frontiers that have made it diverse and famous. Therefore, formal training in mechanical engineering in your institute would help me accomplish my goals.

See page 330 to find out where this student got in.

ROBYN ROSE SCHNEIDER

During high school, Robyn was twice named Orange County Impromptu Speech champion. She held leadership positions in the French and Drama Clubs, as well as in the Aspiring Authors Society and a humor magazine, The W.C.—both of which she founded. Robyn was also varsity team mascot and house manager for school plays. Outside of school, she donated more than 1,000 books to children's homes, served as a volunteer library storyteller, and wrote an advice column for the local newspaper.

Before sending out her transfer applications, Robyn signed a book deal with Random House to publish a young adult novel, created a website based on her search for a literary agent, and worked on an anthology of humorous short stories.

Stats
SAT: 1410 (710 Critical Reading, 700 Math)
High School GPA: 3.60
High School: Northwood High School, Irvine, CA
College GPA: 3.75
College attended: Hofstra University Honors College
Hometown: Irvine, CA
Gender: Female
Race: Caucasian

Applied to
Barnard College
Boston University
Brandeis University
Brown University
Harvard College
New York University
Smith College
University of Pennsylvania
University of Southern California
Yale University

Essay

Robyn used the following essay in each of her applications.

There are limitations to what grades, scores, and recommendations can tell us about a candidate. Write a personal essay on a topic of your choice that will help the Admissions Committee to know you better.

The Forbidden Art of The Personal Essay:
A Personal Statement on the Subject of Campus Life,
200-Level Love, and the Pursuit of the Perfect Course Description

243: Art of the Personal Essay seemed like the perfect course. The instructor was Phillip Lopate, that famous essayist. I flipped through the course catalog, positive there had to be something wrong with 243—something I wasn't catching. After all, Hofstra only offered five creative writing courses, and none of the others encompassed non-fiction. Why was Lopate's course description so incredible?

I met with my Honors College advisor to sign up for my honors seminars, and he asked me which other courses I was considering. Flipping through the catalog, I pointed out Philosophy and International Economics, then finally showed him Lopate's course. That's when I found out what the problem was. Apparently those numbers before the course title actually mean something, because "200" means graduate course. Art of the Personal Essay was officially off-limits to me. My advisor, trying to come up with some consolation, offered that he'd heard of undergraduates being allowed to take graduate courses in special circumstances. I took his words to heart.

A week later, the creative writing department had their annual luncheon. I figured out who Professor Lopate was (he looked the same as he did on all of his book jackets), and went over to introduce myself.

"Hi, Professor. My name is Robyn Schneider and I'd like to sign up for your personal essay writing course, but I'm an undergraduate."

He stared at me, and then asked the dreaded question, "What year are you?"

"I'm a freshman, but I'll be a sophomore next semester because of advanced standing."

"Absolutely not."

"Would it make any difference," I persisted doggedly, "if I had a novel forthcoming from Random House and was represented by one of New York's top literary agents?"

"Well of course. Then the circumstances would be quite different."

"They're different," I told him, trying to convey with my eyebrows that I hadn't just asked him a hypothetical question.

"Oh, erm, hmmmm." He scratched his ear. "Okay then, why don't you submit a writing sample, a ten page personal essay should suffice, to my Hofstra Pride Mail, and I'll see." He winked.

"Thanks," I said.

Fifteen minutes later I was back in my dorm checking my email. An email from my agent read, "I've sent your manuscript to be edited by Sally Arteseros; she's one of the best. She mentioned to me that she edited Art of the Personal Essay by Phillip Lopate, and that you should sit in on one of his classes or at least get in touch with him."

Fate! It was fate! I sent Lopate my writing sample, mentioned our common editor, and got an email back the next week saying that my writing passed the test and welcome to his course.

I went to the English department to sign up for the course. What followed was a treasure hunt through the different offices, all over campus, to see two different deans, until I was finally told by the Honors College that undergraduate students could never take graduate classes, exactly the opposite of what I'd heard when I learned what 200-level meant. Dejected, I slunk back to my dorm. It was a lost cause. I'd never get to study under Professor Lopate, learn how to write non-fiction properly from an expert, or enjoy the immense satisfaction of being at least five years younger than the other students while still remaining at the top of the class.

My roommate's friend knocked on the door.

"She's not here!" I hollered, but he turned the knob anyway.

We talked for a while. It turned out he was taking an independent study in creative writing, which meant he designed the course himself and got credit for a workshop. I asked him how he got that approved and he told me the steps to follow: find a professor to sponsor you, write up a course description, present it to the head of the department. I thanked him and began typing—Personal Essay and Modern Memoir, a course that was made up of Phillip Lopate's 243 as well as reading works by five modern memoirists, compiling a non-fiction manuscript of my own, and attending a non-fiction venue in New York City each month.

I presented my course to the head of the department and he approved—how could he not? I was offering to do the inexplicable: take on a graduate course as a freshman and then do extra outside work just to get undergraduate credit. It was the most challenging independent study the department had ever seen.

When I told my Honors College advisor what I'd done to get into the graduate course, he just laughed. "That's the thing about you, Robyn. I never doubted you'd find a way to get what you wanted."

See page 330 to find out where this student got in.

SEAN MCCLELLAN

In high school, served as captain of his high school swim team, a member of mock parliamentary and mock trail, an ASB Parliamentarian, and took six different AP courses. In addition, he also worked for two years as a camp counselor at the Oregon Museum of Science and Industry.

Stats
SAT: 1390 (690 Critical Reading, 700 Math)
High School GPA: 3.65
High School: Walla Walla High School, Walla Walla, WA
Hometown: Walla Walla, WA
Gender: Male
Race: Caucasian

Applied To
Bates College
Grinnell College
Lewis & Clark College
Macalester College
University of Washington (honors program)
Wesleyan University

Essay

Sean submitted the following essay to the schools listed above.

> *Describe a character in fiction that has had an influence on you,*
> *and explain that influence.*

A while ago, probably sometime last year, I was browsing through a great local bookstore here in Walla Walla, Earthlight Books. At the time, I happened to be looking for something to read for my own enjoyment so I busily scanned through the "used fiction" section looking at anything that caught my eye. As it happened on that fateful day, I ended up purchasing that provocative piece of prophetic British literature, Brave New World, by Aldous Huxley. This novel, especially because of the character Helmholtz Watson, enabled me to see society, and particularly high school society, in a wholly new manner.

While reading the book, I empathized with Watson, as Huxley surely intended, because of Watson's ability to see Huxley's futuristic society for what it was. Near the beginning of the novel, Watson acts the perfect image of an Alpha Plus male; yet, as the plot continues, Helmholtz realizes that he is not finding fulfillment living the high life and pleasing everyone but himself. Now granted, I have never been the popular, athletic, ladies' man that Watson is. Nevertheless, Mr. Watson inspired me because he reaffirmed my belief that I need not worry about being "cool" in the manner that peer pressure and pop culture proclaims everyone should. Rather, enjoying close friends, appreciating family and being passionate about things I love to do, such as swimming, being out of doors, and participating in mock legislature and mock trial, have become progressively more important over the course of my high school career. Just as Watson became a truly unique individual upon realizing that Huxley's society was stifling his creativity, I have come even more to find the daily routine of high school life monotonous and shallow.

That said, I would like more than almost anything to enroll in an establishment of higher education where people care about learning simply for learning's sake, where people keep their minds truly open, where people find honest, intellectual debate thoroughly stimulating and where I can be an individual and be normal, at the same time. I want to follow Helmholtz Watson's footsteps at the end of Brave New World and enter an "island" full of the best thinkers of the time and times past. And perhaps more importantly, I want to have an adventure on this island, a fantastic one totally different from anything I have ever experienced; I believe Wesleyan University can be the site of that adventure.

See page 331 to find out where this student got in.

SERIN IPEK SECKIN

Serin was the science columnist for her school paper, violinist in a musical chamber group, a member of the math team, and taught English in China. She also conducted research work at Columbia-Presbyterian Hospital and is an accomplished pianist, having received a Gold Award at the Rockland County Music Competition.

Stats
SAT: 2260 (720 Critical Reading, 800 Math, 740 Writing)
SAT Subject Test(s): 800 Biology, 770 Chemistry, 740 Math I, 750 Math II
High School GPA: N/A
High School: Saint Ann's School, Brooklyn, NY
Hometown: Brooklyn, NY
Gender: Female
Race: Caucasian

Applied To
Brown University
Columbia University
Cornell University
Dartmouth College
Harvard University
Johns Hopkins University
Princeton University
Stanford University
Tufts University
University of Chicago
Washington University in St. Louis
Wesleyan University
Williams College
Yale University

Essay

Serin used the following essay in her application to Brown University.

In reading your application we want to get to know you as well as we can. We ask that you use this opportunity to tell us something more about yourself that would help us toward a sense of how you think, and what issues and ideas interest you most. Your statement should not exceed 500 words, and it may be done in your own handwriting or typewritten.

I looked into the microscope and gracefully fumbled around with the tweezers and scissors, attempting to assist my lab mentor tie two arteries together. Although this was only an experimental micro-graft onto a sedated rat's thigh, the tension and excitement in the lab reminded me of the day I watched an actual laparoscopic surgery, nervously standing behind a surgeon as he carefully operated through a high-resolution monitor on a human being.

I reflected upon the extreme purposefulness and determination I felt during those micro-surgeries. My back might have ached, my eyes might have been sore and weak, but I never even noticed this pain until I came home. For, even though this was just a rat, I felt convinced that success in our experiment might one day translate into the difference between life and death. In fact, I thought of that every morning that summer, when I would begin my workday at the lab by checking the hospital database to see if the many patients I had interviewed for a survey were still alive.

Yet, it was clear to me that my determination was driven not only by my compulsion to help, but also by my compulsion to learn, to know. Why were we harvesting arteries from the thigh? How did the antioxidant drug we were using prevent cell growth? And it struck me what a great coincidence it is that science has turned out to have such an enormous benefit to humanity, since I think we would still pursue it for the sake of knowledge alone. "Curiosity has its own reason for existence."

A year ago, I wanted to do an independent research project comparing various traits of the ubiquitous New York City subway rats to those of lab-bred rats. The science teachers rejected it. "Too risky" one said. "The school can't legally house those diseased rats, Serin." I didn't let it go that easily- I talked to every biology teacher in the department, but it was a no-go. I confess that I had no motive for this project other than pure curiosity. But in that, I am certainly not alone. For example, the scientists who discovered Thermus Aquaticus, the bacteria that live in coral springs, surely had no idea that their work would one day lead to the discovery of a heat-resistant enzyme now used in Polymerase Chain Reaction machines to solve violent crimes and exonerate innocent "criminals."

But then, of course, there are the many times when I wished my curiosity hadn't gotten the better of me, as when I have begged someone to tell me a secret that ended up agonizing me. More significantly, the once divine mysteries of the universe, inexplicable symbols of God's power, have been diminished somewhat by our knowledge that we know we are merely agents of DNA replication on an insignificant planet wheeling around an insignificant star in a universe destined to collapse upon itself.

I sometimes wonder if we would still pursue science so doggedly if we could prove beyond any doubt (scientifically, of course) that so much knowledge is bad for us. But I do not take that question too seriously. Perhaps science is not incompatible with faith after all.

See page 331 to find out where this student got in.

STEPHANIE CROSS

Stephanie played JV softball for one year, played varsity softball for two years, spent two years on the varsity bowling team, and participated in numerous summer leagues for both sports, including ASA and YABA. She was a member of the National Honor Society and the National Spanish Honor Society, and was treasurer of the National Art Honor Society. She was also awarded the Bausch & Lomb Science Award and earned the Silver Award and the Gold Award in Girl Scouting. She played the viola for nine years and was selected to the District Orchestra and the Regional State Orchestra three years in a row.

Stats
SAT: 1510 (710 Critical Reading, 800 Math)
SAT Subject Test(s): 700 Math Level 1, 720 Biology
High School GPA: 104 (out of 100)
High School: Lewisburg Area High School, Lewisburg, PA
Hometown: Lewisburg, PA
Gender: Female
Race: Caucasian
Applied To
Swarthmore College (early decision)

Essay

Write an essay about people who have influenced you, situations that have shaped you, difficulties or conflicts with which you have struggled, goals and hopes you may have for the future, or something else you consider significant.

At times I hated Mrs. Shambaucher, at times I admired her, but to this day I thank God that she was my fourth grade teacher. I didn't know at the time how much she would influence me as a student or as an individual, but Mrs. Shambaucher provided me with more aggravations and realizations than anyone else I have ever met. Many view her too authoritarian and too tough, but she has a great sense of humor and a great understanding of what is needed in our youth for them to succeed in the future. She instills great ethics and habits in her students, but she can also cause the most frustration.

As I soon learned, Mrs. Shambaucher wasted no time. I remember entering her classroom for the first time and being given a small notebook. It was the first day of school and our make-shift classroom had no black board but she was teaching within the hour. Our first science lesson was on cell structure and organization, terms I wouldn't see again until sixth grade. I was confused, lost, and overwhelmed. What kind of person would expect a fourth grader to know what a nucleus was or what cilia did? I was scared for my life on that first day but I know I am better because of it. Other science lessons of the year would include rocks, Moh's scale of hardness, the development of a chicken, and the solar system. The other fourth graders never had to study so much or complete so many worksheets, but they also never even heard of some of the terms I knew until they reached high school. Mrs. Shambaucher was the first person to ever teach me history. I was always interested in the Erie Canal and I had limited access to information on topics I had only scarcely heard of before. The brief overview of Pennsylvanian and American history that I had that year was better than what I received in eighth and ninth grade. I often found myself looking through my tattered notebook to find facts that I had learned over five years earlier.

Another area that I grew to love was literature. Up until this point we had never read a book over one hundred pages long in school, unless it was for a personal book report. I still remember O'Henry's short stories, The Secret Garden, Black Beauty, Amos Fortune, The Witch of Blackbird Pond, The Adventures of Tom Sawyer, and The Westing Game (one of the best books I have read to this day). Most of these classics are never taught in my school and I don't know how I would be today if it hadn't been for the passion for reading that Mrs. Shambaucher instilled in me. She also taught me how to write a biography and how not to write an essay. These helpful hints are never considered in most curricula yet the students are expected to know it. The work load was atrocious when it came to reading and writing. Most students complained, but we continued to read in class as well as at home. My reading skills were sharpened dramatically during that year. One assignment we had was to write instructions for making a peanut butter and jelly sandwich. A classmate would then follow the instructions and we would have to eat the result. Lets just say that I never forgot to include every last step in the future after I was presented with a mass of peanut butter and jelly on one piece of bread.

She had a great sense of humor and learning was supposed to be fun. There were always contests to find an answer to a math problem or research facts on famous people. We were the only class to perform school plays, complete with costumes, sets, and pages of memorized lines. Worksheets were assigned to sharpen our reasoning and spark creativity. I learned so much in that year and because of her I have developed a greater appreciation for all aspects of life and learning. The skills that she fostered have been so useful throughout my schooling and in my interactions with other people. I know that I would have been unable to handle so many situations and assignments if it had not been for her emphasis on study habits, attention to detail, and that everything be your personal best. My drive and the quality of my work all stem from her teachings and influence. If it had not been for her, I would never have valued the classics so highly or learned about African American history, algebra, or the stage until at least eight grade.

Despite the effects of her teachings, there were times where I was ready to scream. The homework was intense and there were no excuses for not completing or trying what was taught. Numerous projects and reports were assigned in addition to regular classroom work. The automatic A was no longer a reality and everything that was handed in was expected to be of your best caliber. Instructions had to be followed and just about everything was expected to be typed. She would almost always point out your flaws, even though she could have been reprimanded if a student were to complain. She knew what we were capable of and she would never settle for less. Although a great philosophy when applied to the future of the child, it made life a little more difficult. At times I would think her so unfair and so strict, especially when other classes had two recesses or extra time to talk and play Connect Four. I hated when my name would go on the board for talking in class, or when I wasn't allowed to go to recess because I had missed a quiz. Through it all she would shrug off any complaints and continue teaching at a rate she knew we could handle if we would apply ourselves.

Politicians today often complain about the state of our public educational system and I would have to agree with them most of the time. However, no amount of money or state regulated guidelines will fix the problems that exist in our schools. I personally feel that we need more Mrs. Shambauchers in the elementary schools. Children should see what they can accomplish and be pushed to their limits time and again until they too desire to learn and yearn for knowledge. I have been shaped in ways I can't fully comprehend by one teacher who taught what she felt was important and at a rate that even parents were questioning. No principal could have forced her to change a lesson or teach ridiculous state courses without a fight. She knew how to work with children and bring out the best in them in a hope for the future. I admire her so much for changing the world one child at a time. Its a noble goal that no politician can achieve through laws and the fact that she continues to influence over twenty-five children a year is reassuring when faced with so many ill-prepared students. She is one of a kind and her spirit is unparalleled to any teacher I have had thus far. Mrs. Shambaucher influenced me in so many ways outside of education that I know I would not be who I am today if it hadn't been for her constant prodding and high expectations.

See page 331 to find out where this student got in.

STEPHANIE WUN-LEE CHOW

Stephanie was president of her high school's Spanish Honor Society for two years and vice president of its Science Club her senior year. She was also named Most Valuable Player of the Mathematics League two years in a row and captained the tennis team her senior year.

Stats
SAT: 1480 (690 Critical Reading, 790 Math)
SAT Subject Test(s): 800 Math Level 2, 740 Biology, 730 Chemistry
High School GPA: 3.88
High School: Wethersfield High School, Wethersfield, CT
Hometown: Wethersfield, CT
Gender: Female
Race: Asian American

Applied To
Boston University
Brown University (PLME Program)
Columbia University
Cornell University
Harvard College (early action)
Massachusetts Institute of Technology
Princeton University (early action)
Rensselaer Polytechnic Institute
University of Connecticut
Yale University

Essay 1

Stephanie used the following essay in her application to MIT. The essay prompt asked the applicant to make up a question and answer it. Stephanie posed the question:

Which more describes your personality, a Cheerio or a Snickers bar?

Drawing parallels between both Cheerios and Snickers bars and myself is no problem; I find both foods agreeable to my personality quirks. Pressure to select one, however, favors the chocolatey Snickers bar over the wholesome Cheerio. The former's multitude of ingredients, physical structure, and rise to fame bear a stronger resemblance to the circus of thoughts entertained in my mind.

Cheerios sports the healthier nutrition label; having this cereal's "healthy, whole-grain" personality marks an untiringly responsible, straightforward individual content to live an ordinary life, free from wild excitement. The simpleton Cheerio, lacking the domineering clutter of flakes and raisins, connotes a humble and uncomplicated life. These qualities portray a very stable and worldly individual.

Snickers cannot compete with the nutritional "virtuosity" of its opponent but combatively wields wonder weapons of its own. The ingenious combination of Snickers's delectable ingredients: chocolate, caramel, and peanuts, evokes strong sensations of pleasure in the blissful consumer.

The chocolate coating washes the restless soul like morning tides over a sun-baked sandcastle, problems and concerns reconciled with each passing mouthful. Likewise, my mind bears the task of extinguishing problems, my own and of others.

My imagination finds representation in the caramel, rich and flexible. Leisurely pulling each bite of Snickers from the origin and watching the gooey strands stretch their fullest, glistening in the light with sticky, sweet happiness, ensures maximum exposure of the golden luxury.

The highlight of my Snickers adventure lies largely in the presence of the crunchy peanuts, sharp contrast to their creamy confectionery counterparts. These crispy hidden treasures rejuvenate my optimism and jocularity by replenishing my mind with imaginative ideas and perspectives. I also entertain the thought that the peanuts allude to my slightly "nutty" personality.

One may elect to analyze the physical structure of the two foods to draw additional comparisons; Cheerios sport the infallibly circular doughnut shape while the Snickers take on a more rectangular prismatic skeleton. Circles commonly serve as symbols of perfection and complete unity; presumably, the Cheerio's circular shape as a representation of the personality of an individual implies a continuing contention for a life of perfection. Nevertheless, I do not care to fall victim to a life of endless struggle in achieving and maintaining a state of utopia; I prefer the company of the natural, reliable, Snickers figure, so mundane and simple yet an ingeniously constructed idea; countless architectural structures utilize the strength and practicality of the rectangular prism.

The much famed Honey Nut Cheerio flaunts an attractive honeybee mascot; Snickers relies simply on rewards of its taste for promotion through the ambitious ladder of success. While the Cheerios are the more publicized and celebrated, Snickers has managed to make a name for itself through simple hard work and strife for excellent taste.

Although Cheerios embodies the qualities of the ideal and perfect individual, to possess such a resume of virtues leaves no room for improvement and consequently offers no fire for motivation. Thus I select the Snickers candy bar as the better representative of my personality.

Essay 2

Stephanie used the following essay in her application to Princeton.

> *What one class, teacher, book, or experience can you point to as having really changed the way you think?*

I discovered one of my favorite books, *The Westing Game,* by Ellen Raskin, in fourth grade. I read it because I was looking for something to read and my teacher had recommended it to the class, and because he had told us that those students whom he knew had read the book needed to reread the story a few years later before completely understanding the complex plot. I admit now that I bought the book more for the second reason than the first although I still maintain that I was a mystery-love-struck fourth grader with a voracious appetite for reading.

The plot revolves around the "murder" of the eccentric millionaire Samuel W. Westing and the challenge the "deceased" man poses to his sixteen potential heirs to uncover the identity of his killer. In the end, it is the neglected thirteen-year old Turtle Wexler who deciphers the Westing Game riddle and wins the inheritance. Her triumph was especially important to me because it instilled in my pliant young mind a strong belief of succeeding in areas where one is not expected to succeed. Westing's meticulously planned "murder" and "game" confounded all the heirs but young Turtle, whose clever thinking and resourcefulness enabled her to piece together the complicated mystery.

Turtle's spunky character also left a deep impression in my mind. In reading of her smart-alecky mouth, her flaring temper, and her independence, I felt myself applauding her "un-girl-like" behavior so shunned in other children's novels. I did not believe that I would begin kicking people in the shins when someone provoked my temper, but I did treasure the idea that I did not have to bear the sweet, obedient facade of the "classic ladylike girl" as I had witnessed in *The Babysitters' Club* series or in stories like *Little Women.* As a girl with a burning spirit of independence and resolve, *I* believed that I could outwit Supreme Court judges, doctors, and private eye detectives if I was brave and clever enough for the task!

Essay 3

Stephanie used the following essay in her application to Princeton.

If you could hold one position, elected or appointed, in government (at any level), which one would you want it to be and why?

In my opinion the most important and nationally influential position of government is one that affects the economic structure and stability of the country. The United States of America relies on the strength of its booming economy to bolster the nation's wealth and prosperity, hence establishing the health and survival of the nation's economy as an item of utmost importance. With this perspective in mind, to be appointed Federal Reserve Chairman of the United States would bring me the greatest honor and personal satisfaction.

As chairman of the Federal Reserve, I head the organization that controls the flow of money through the economy; by raising or lowering the nation's interest rates I can cut down on inflation or encourage businesses and individuals to invest. I wield the executive axe that influences levels of employment and stabilities of prices, interest rates, financial, and foreign exchange markets. The Federal Reserve System serves as the "central bank and monetary authority of the United States" in that it has the power to regulate and set the interest rate standards for the nation's banks.

I see the position of Federal Reserve Chairman as an office existing for the survival of the nation, dictating economic growth and prosperity, or possible financial disasters dating back to the period of the Great Depression. The Federal Reserve System supports the United States of America like a shell protecting an egg; without the Federal Reserve to reinforce and "calcify" the shell of the economy, the economy would crack and shatter. With America relying so heavily on the economy for employment and living, a ruptured economy would invariably result in a formless and withering nation, weak and easy prey to be exploited by other countries. As appointed chairperson I would make it my duty to protect the nation from such misuse and guide the United States into a new millennium of prestige.

Essay 4

Stephanie used the following essay in her application to Princeton.

What one or two suggestions would you have if asked about how to improve race relations in this country and around the world?

In improving any relationships, the best way for individuals to accept one another is to understand the background, culture, and beliefs of the other person; I believe that this "ethnic comprehension" is best conveyed through education. In a broad sense, such education encompasses both actual classroom learning of the culture and incorporation of that foreign race into the student body. Schools around the world should practice the concept of desegregation, breaking down ethnic barriers and establishing "homogenous student mixture-type" school systems. Foreign exchange student programs should be encouraged as well as the integration of inner city schools into more "well-rounded" school systems. My high school currently enrolls approximately ten to fifteen foreign exchange students and I would like to see the numbers increase as we move into the next century. Wethersfield High to my knowledge does not practice integration, but this concept too would play an influential role in spreading awareness of different ethnic cultures.

One cannot expect an immediate change in race relations by simply instigating a few measures. Aside from exposure to the different ideas and beliefs of foreign cultures, one must accept the difference psychologically; wars and friction always begin "in the minds of the people." By incorporating ethnic diversity into the daily life of a young student, society is molding the child into a bastion for racial tolerance. Teachers claim that "students are the future," and I must agree. When the youth of the world is exposed to a multitude of racial differences as a part of everyday life, discrepancies become the norm and any and all prejudices and stereotypes will hopefully melt away. We are all different only by mindset; once we learn to accept others on basis of their humanity and character, we will unlock the secret to the planet's racial tolerance.

See page 332 to find out where this student got in.

STUART PETER DEKKER

In high school, Stuart was an avid golfer, a student pilot, and Board President of his high school band. He also owned his own landscaping and handyman company that operated during the summer.

Stats
ACT: 33
High School GPA: 4.33 weighted
High School: Downers Grove North High School, Downers Grove, IL
Hometown: Downers Grove, IL
Gender: Male
Race: Caucasian

Applied To
College of William and Mary
Georgetown University
New York University
Tulane University
University of Illinois

Essay

Stuart sent the following essay to each school to which he applied. The prompt below is from Georgetown's application.

> *The admissions committee would like to know more about you in your own words. Please submit a brief essay, either autobiographical or creative, which you feel best describes you.*

It was a cold, gray day in January not all that many years ago, when my father and I woke early and made the one hour drive to Palwaukee Airport, just a few miles north of O'Hare. It was the day of my first flight lesson, and I was painfully excited. I met Tom, my flight instructor outside of the Service Aviation hangar, and was immediately struck by the beauty of the shiny aluminum aircraft. We walked towards the smallest plane, which was parked on a small plot of grass, a Cessna 150.

The Cessna was a tiny single engine aircraft, and it was so light that Tom was easily able to pull the plane off the grass and onto the taxi-way by hand. He showed me how to do a pre-flight inspection, and then climbed into the co-pilot's seat. It was at that moment that the full realization that I would actually be flying the aircraft and not just a passenger in it struck me. I began to feel nervous for the first time since my father scheduled this lesson for my birthday, and my hands began to sweat despite the sub-freezing temperature.

I climbed into the pilot's seat and again was struck by how miniature the plane was. My left shoulder was against the door, and my right was snugly against Tom's. Behind our two seats was a luggage compartment no larger than that of a compact car's, and even my five foot two inch frame felt cramped with a lack of leg room. We put on our radio headset, and Tom informed me that he would take care of contacting ground and flight control so I could concentrate solely on flying. I pushed the primer into the stop several times, as instructed, and turned the key. The roar of the engine was deafening despite our insulated headsets, and the vibration that it caused on the flight yoke was painful on my wet, freezing hands.

I listened to Tom's instructions, and we slowly taxied to the runway, steering with the two rudder pedals on the floor. We reached the end of the runway, and I heard over the radio that we were cleared for take off. I slowly turned the plane onto the long slender runway, and pushed the throttle to its stop. The engine roar grew almost unbearably loud and the plane accelerated quickly down the runway. I gripped the yoke as if my life depended on my not letting go, and when the speedometer read sixty knots, I slowly pulled it back towards my abdomen. I felt the front tire lift off the ground, and slowly rise so that I could no longer see the ground. I thought for a moment that we were up, but then suddenly I felt the rear tires bounce on the runway, and lift off the pavement.

The feeling was like nothing that I had ever experienced, and I wondered how a small plane could feel so different from the large jetliners that I had often flown on before. I had always felt safe and secure during takeoffs in those monstrous flying cylinders, but this small Cessna, no larger than a refrigerator, did not pass along that feeling of safety and comfort. I began to sweat profusely, and my stomach felt as if I was riding a roller coaster despite the relative smoothness of the flight.

We climbed to three thousand feet, and glided over the beautiful city of Chicago. I was beginning to get used to the feeling the plane created, and I was comfortable with the controls. Suddenly, Tom announced that we would be making a touch and go landing at Meigs Field, an airport located on a small peninsula just north of the city. The plane began to bounce through heavy turbulence, and when we were less than 100 feet above the frozen waters of Lake Michigan I realized that I was going to be sick. I glanced at Tom, and was about to announce my impending illness, when I lost it, vomiting all over my ill-fated flight instructor. He immediately took control of the plane, and flew us back to Palwaukee Airport.

When we landed I was excruciatingly humiliated, and I began to wonder if a hobby of flight was really best for me. I contemplated my choices, and weighed my love of flight with my ironically violent motion sickness, and decided my motion sickness would have to be overcome. I have since flown over eight hours in the Cessna, and several hours in engineless gliders. I intend on receiving my private pilot's license within the next several years, and hope that flight will always be one of my strongest passions.

See page 332 to find out where this student got in.

TRACY SERGE

Tracy directed and performed in several plays in high school. Her other activities concerned original oratory, sales, and forensics.

Stats
SAT: 1480 (780 Critical Reading, 700 Math)
SAT Subject Test(s): 800 Literature, 690 Math Level 1
ACT: 35
High School GPA: 4.00
High School: Fairmont Senior High School, Fairmont, WV
Hometown: Fairmont, WV
Gender: Female
Race: Caucasian

Applied To
Yale University (early decision)

Essay

Tell us something about yourself that we couldn't learn from the rest of your application.

Waltzing Over the Border With a Paintbrush in My Hand

One of my favorite books is The Little Prince by Antoine de Saint-Exupéry. The narrator of the novel states that adults never ask the important questions about a person, such as "What does his voice sound like?" or "What games does he like best?" Often, in applying for scholarships and, now, for college, I have felt that perhaps no one was asking the "important questions." I believe I have been shaped more by those profound experiences which have become my anecdotes, than I am of my grades and ACT scores, which reveal only one aspect of my life that is important to me. So, when asked to state something about myself that the admissions committee would not be able to gather from my application, I found I was unable to limit myself to just one interest or story. After all, twenty-four straight hours on a bus with twenty-one classmates has influenced my life far more than even a perfect score on the SATs ever could.

To elaborate on the above, my eighth grade class had only twenty-one students. We all knew each other as no one else could (eight hours a day, five days a week, for nine years, will do that) and decided to celebrate (or mourn) the impending gradu-ation from our close-knit, sheltered group to the larger world of high school with a bus trip to Canada. As it happened, the bus broke down about twenty-five feet from the Canadian border. This was the greatest exercise in patience I have ever had to endure. It took four hours for our driver to realize the problem and inform us that we had run out of gas. I love absurdity...and truckstops.

The patience I learned in this situation has served me well in another area of my life: ballroom dancing. In the seventh grade, I decided that I preferred the beauty and grace of the stylized ballroom dances to the repetitive back-and-forth sway of the usual teen moves. My partner was a fellow student, and we weren't sure it was going to work out when we arrived at the first class and discovered that we were the only couple there not contributing to our retirement plans. However, the problem was soon solved when preference grew into passion. I have now been a avid ballroom dancer for nearly six years and have learned much more than just the proper sequence of steps in a samba. Aside from the obvious self-discipline of many hours a week spent in training, learning dance requires patience. Everyone learns at a different speed and in different ways. A dancer must understand that while she has trouble with the waltz, her partner may be equally perplexed by the fox-trot. The two must then cooperate to become comfortable and confident. From dancing, I have learned the incomparable value of teamwork. After all, it does take two to tango.

Another experience that has had a lasting impact on my view of myself has been painting murals. From the time I was three and couldn't color inside the lines, through the many days in geometry I spent trying to draw at least a respectable imitation of a circle, I was certain I had no artistic talent. It's amazing how an overabundance of white walls will bring out the artist in anyone. I don't know exactly what made me decide to paint the girl's dressing room in our theater department, but my friend and I decided that it had to be done, and we were the ones to do it.

We started the day after the idea occurred to us, deciding that a sunset over mountains must be respectably simple. It wasn't. Within the first ten minutes, we realized we were in way over our heads. We did manage to make the sun somewhat circular, but could not get it any color resembling nature's pale yellow. Of course, we'd started and we knew we couldn't stop—not until walls, floor, and ceiling were completely transformed. In my head, I often likened the painting of a mural to the stages of grief: denial (This certainly wasn't my idea!); anger/rage (Why did you pick mauve? Any fool knows the sky is never mauve!); envy (Why can't I be as talented as Michelangelo?); resentment (You started this because you knew it would make me look bad!); bargaining (If I mow your lawn, will you finish my mural?); depression (What's the use? It's never going to look good.); and acceptance (Wait a minute...this actually does looks good!).

We struggled for weeks, teaching ourselves art basics such as shading, blending, and highlighting. We began to absorb ourselves into the painting. The excited chatter of the first days died down, replaced by the soothing sound of brush strokes from the hands of two teenaged girls in meditative concentration. Slowly, the mural began to take form and our confidence began to grow. The room brightened, and the harsh fluorescent lighting seemed to fade into the background behind our luminous sun. The last part, the ceiling, was perhaps the most difficult. We spent hours a day, heads at 90-degree angles to our necks, trying not to be so presumptuous as to compare ourselves to Michelangelo.

Finally, it was complete: sun, valley, mountains, and the sprawling colors of the sunset. As the first freshman walked into the room this year and said, "Oooh...that's really good. Who painted it?" I realized that there is an additional stage beyond acceptance: wisdom. The painter is rewarded not only with pride, but with a sense of the power of passion and perseverance.

These activities and events have contributed substantially to the person that I am. With every decision I make, every responsibility I am given, and every strange circumstance in which I find myself, I gain a little more wisdom. Academic learning is central in my life, but it is only one aspect of the person I am. I haven't told you what games I like best, and you may still not know what my voice sounds like, but I think I have begun to, at least partially, answer the important questions.

See page 332 to find out where this student got in.

VICTORIA MARIEL BARONE

Victoria was the editor of her school newspaper. She also played water polo for three years and helped her parents take care of three foster babies at home.

Stats
SAT: 1410 (700 Critical Reading, 710 Math)
SAT Subject Test(s): 770 Math Level 2
High School GPA: 4.35 weighted
High School: Lauralton Hall Academy, Milford, CT
Hometown: Stamford, CT
Gender: Female
Race: Caucasian

Applied To
University of Michigan
University of Notre Dame
University of Southern California

Essay 1

Victoria used the following essay in her application to Notre Dame. According to her, the essay prompt asked the applicant to tell the admissions committee something interesting about him or herself that could not be revealed anywhere else in the application.

Don't Worry About the Girl

I looked around as I walked into the unfamiliar pool area and spotted "the guys" from my team sitting in the bleachers. I felt a hand on my shoulder and heard someone say, "Excuse me, you have to pay to get in." Trying to stay calm, I looked at the woman and politely explained that I was playing in the tournament, which meant I did not have to pay for a ticket. Confused and embarrassed, she mumbled, "Oh, good for you." I knew I would be the only female player that day so I understood her mistake; however, I was still annoyed that I had to explain my presence.

When I play water polo, both my teammates and my opponents are members of the opposite sex. On most occasions, I am the only woman, refreshingly unlike the all-female environment at my school. Although I am regularly a starter for the B-team, I have been selected to join our A-team this year for most of the games. I do not play much during the toughest matches, but I enjoy cheering for my teammates from the bench.

Three years ago, I was an unlikely water polo player until my older brother suggested I join his team, in the Eastern High School Water Polo League. I was sore and tired when I first started practicing. I was lost in the water and afraid to ask the older boys on my team for help, but I was enjoying myself. On the third night of practice, I was hit in the face by a pass from one of the boys. My nose began to bleed profusely. I cried from pain and embarrassment. I thought that would be the end of my water polo career, but my coach convinced me to get back in the water. Once I recovered from that incident, I knew I had finally found a sport I loved.

Over the years, I have learned to deal with being different. During games, opponents overlook me as not being a threat. There are few feelings more satisfying than scoring a goal or stealing the ball after hearing them say, "Don't worry about the girl, go guard someone else." I capitalize on the ignorance of boys who feel I am not good enough to play with them. I do not let it bother me when some opponents do not respect me enough to shake my hand after a game. These experiences have taught me how to handle narrow-minded people.

Being on the team has become a very important part of my life. I have proven myself capable to my coach and my teammates. Without being a tomboy, I found my place among the men and maintained my femininity. My self-confidence has grown with the knowledge that I can play such a rough sport. Water polo has taught me to be aggressive, both in and out of the water. I am not be intimidated by people who look bigger or stronger. I have learned not to be too sensitive and to accept a certain amount of teasing. Water polo has been a great source enjoyment for me while helping me develop into a well-rounded person.

Essay 2

*Victoria used the following essay in her application to Notre Dame. According-
ing to her, the essay prompt involved reading a brochure on the Catholic
Church's views on abortion and euthanasia.*

A Winning Alternative

When a young woman made the courageous decision not to abort her unplanned
baby girl, my life was enriched. My family, a licensed foster family, was chosen to
care for Madelene, who lived with us from the day after she was born until she was
adopted ten weeks later. I formed a special bond with our baby, as I was deeply
involved in caring for her. I loved to feed her and rock her to sleep on my chest.
Wherever I was out with Madelene, I faced many questions from both strangers and
acquaintances. I explained that my family takes in foster babies to do our part in
offering women an alternative to abortion. We have had three foster babies so far,
and each one still has a special place in my heart.

Madelene has already positively affected the lives of many people. I cannot
imagine my life without her in it. When she lived with us, she became a part of our
family. Each of my five siblings, my parents, and my cousin, who also was living
with us, loved Madelene and will never forget her. When I saw her new parents at
her Christening a few months after she was adopted, I realized what a wonderful
gift she was. Madelene brought untold happiness to the young couple, unable to
have children of their own. Viewing the Christening, I was moved by my mother's
dedication and commitment to supporting life. I realized that my mother must have
a boundless amount of love to give.

My mother has been an inspiration to me. She has taken into our home both old
and young to show her children how important it is to respect life at these fragile
times.

When I was eleven years old, my grandmother was ill and confined to a wheelchair.
My mother insisted that she live with us when she was no longer able to care for herself.
I remember how special it was when I came home from school and my grandmother
would be there. I was still small enough to cuddle on her lap in the wheelchair. It was
difficult near the end of my grandmother's life to watch her mental and physical health
deteriorate and feel the strain on the relationship between my mother and her mother,
but I knew that my mother felt good about her decision. She taught me to be there for
those who need me no matter how difficult the situation.

The message in the statement of the Bishops, Faithful for Life, coincides with my
personal belief that life of any kind deserves respect. My experiences with Madelene

and my grandmother taught me much about this. Caring for these individuals has given me a means of tapping into my heart to share the love that I have. I realize that some people do not share my feeling on these issues, but everyone should be aware when making a moral decision that there are options.

See page 332 to find out where this student got in.

WENDY WEINERMAN

Wendy was active in her high school's theater productions, thespian society, and choir. She also played tennis and was a member of the National Honor Society. Outside of school, she took choir and voice lessons, tutored middle school and high school students, worked at Baskin-Robbins during the year, and worked at an arts camp during the summer. She volunteered every other weekend, delivering food to senior citizens. Awards and honors included: National Merit Scholar, second place in her division at a district-wide vocal competition, and third place at a local community college's high school math competition.

Stats
SAT: 1540 (800 Critical Reading, 740 Math)
High School GPA: 4.00
High School: West Linn High School, West Linn, OR
Hometown: West Linn, OR
Gender: Female
Race: Caucasian

Applied To
Whitman College (early decision)

Essay

Common Application: Topic of your choice.

Click. Click. The last two feet fall into position with 42 others, thus ending the procession of shoes and leaving only their echo to fill the ancient stone monastery. Slowly, even this remnant of sound departs the room and only an expectant silence is left. For a brief moment, there is no motion, no breath, no sound. Then, almost imperceptibly, twenty-two pairs of eyes rotate upwards, each following the arc of one hand in its purposeful rise. Suddenly an organ chord bursts through the silence. The single hand sweeps downwards, three rows of mouths open, and the concert begins.

Perhaps each of us hopes for a moment or two like this in our life. That special day, or hour, or minute where we can not only claim that we were a witness to magic but that we actually took part in creating it ourselves. Myself? I more than hope; I live for these moments, and in all fairness can probably claim more than my fair share. Why? Because I'm a performer. As many who have come before me, my love is in creation, my art in expression, my joy in the toil to achieve these goals. Don't get me wrong. I'm not attempting to pretend I'd rather practice lines for 12 hours a day than perform the final play on stage. Honestly, no one in his or her right mind would. However, through the experiences in my life, I *have* come to appreciate that there's a great deal more to learn and gain from process than from performance.

Magic actually comes in many forms, not just from the second or two of anticipation while waiting for a song to begin. Magic also is in looking back, in realizing how far I've come and what an immeasurable impact so many experiences have had in shaping who I am today.

When I first entered the Oregon Children's Choir and Youth Chorale in the beginning of 4th grade I knew nothing of harmony, balance, blend, or intonation. However when I graduate in just a few short months I will honestly be able to claim that these words have gained a much deeper significance than simple musical terms.

Singing in choir taught me how to blend, both with the voices of singers from 1st through 12th grade and with people of all different ages and backgrounds. It's proof that there are times in life when one must accept being purely background music for the good of the whole and times when it is best to run with the melody and count on others for support. It has shown me the two sides to every solo—the fear in carrying a song almost alone, and the pride of leading a choir through the highs and lows of the notes. To this group alone do I owe my deep belief that the emotion behind music and life is always more important than any amount of complexity or pretense within it.

Through my years of growth within the OCCYC, I have learned not just how to create harmony in music but how to overcome vast differences to create harmony in *life*. Truly, what could be more magical?

See page 332 to find out where this student got in.

WENJUN JING

Wenjun was a varsity athlete in volleyball, squash, and crew and was voted captain of the volleyball team her senior year. She also recorded a CD and went on a singing tour of France with her high school's concert choir.

Stats
SAT: 1500 (740 Critical Reading, 760 Math)
SAT Subject Test(s): 700 Math Level 2, 720 Chinese with Listening, 660 French
High School GPA: N/A—Wenjun's school graded with a "group" system; she had an A average
High School: St. Andrew's School, Middletown, DE
Hometown: Cherry Hill, NJ
Gender: Female
Race: Asian American

Applied To
Barnard College
Carnegie Mellon University
Columbia University
Connecticut College
Harvard College
Massachusetts Institute of Technology
Rice University
Rutgers University
Tulane University
Washington University in St. Louis
Wellesley College
Yale University

Essay

Wenjun used the following essay in her applications to Wellesley, Harvard, Rice, and Washington.

Common Application: Topic of your choice.

Personal Statement: Coming out of the Cave

When I left for boarding school, Sasha and I promised to write to each other and keep in touch through email. She and I had become best friends ever since she rescued me from an empty seat on the school bus in the beginning of 7th grade. About a week into my new high school, after I finally learned how to use the email system, we started emailing each other every day. She would update me on things going on at home, and we would trade stories about our schedules. She was horrified at my Saturday classes and the fact that we were required to play sports. We found it ironic that our schools could be so different, and yet we were so much alike. We exchanged the normal amount of silly emails—complaints about homework, lack of sleep, guy trouble, etc. I assumed that her life back at home was about the same as it was last year.

Then, one evening, as I was checking my email, there was a message from Sasha. It began, "Wenjun, there's something I have to tell you. I'm gay." I was shocked. I was scared. I thought, this is a joke. Sasha? Gay? My best friend of three years was gay and I hadn't had a clue. In that email, the longest I've ever read, she told me everything. She had known she was gay for almost two years, and she had told very few people, only those she could trust would support her. She hadn't told her parents, and wasn't planning to. She said she couldn't bring herself to tell me in person because she couldn't be sure of my reaction so she was doing it over email. I thought to myself, where have I been for the past two years? On another planet? I had been totally oblivious. I was in shock. How could I not have known? There were so many clues. She never wore skirts or dresses. Never wore makeup. Never crushed on the same guys that we crushed on.

All this time, I had been in the dark to Sasha's identity. Either through assumption or deception, I had never thought that she was gay. As Plato, in his Allegory of the Cave, spoke of those in the cave who mistook shadows for reality, I mistook Sasha's true self. I only saw her shadow, the outward appearance of the Sasha that *I* knew, and not the Sasha that *she* was. With this email, I was drawn into the "light", and I felt blinded. But I realized that I wasn't friends with Sasha simply because she was a heterosexual person. No, I was friends with her because she was funny, witty, kind, generous, and sweet. As I got used to the "blinding light", my eyes adjusted, and I wrote back to her, telling her I didn't care if she was gay. The next time I saw her I wouldn't treat her any differently, I said.

I also was drawn into the light about her mental problems. She had been having such a hard time keeping her secret to herself, on top of having family problems, that she had been contemplating suicide. I had no idea. The entire time that I knew her, I never once thought she was anything but happy and stable.

Presently, our friendship is strained by this new revelation, and I worry about being PC around her. Many times, I wish I were back in the cave, mistaking shadows for reality. It is so easy to just overlook the difficult issues or pretend things don't exist if it's advantageous for yourself. However, I know that had I been kept in the dark, Sasha and I would have always had a chasm between us. Now, we both work hard to remain best friends, knowing that a friendship built on truth is stronger than one built on shadows.

See page 333 to find out where this student got in.

XUEYANG (SEAN) LI

Having played the violin for 12 years, Sean has sat concertmaster for numerous orchestras including the Georgia All-State Orchestra, Georgia's Governor's Honor Program Orchestra, and the Atlanta Metropolitan Youth Symphony. In addition to this, he also works as a violinist in the Sunrise Quartet, a group formed with some friends that plays weddings, parties, and charity events. In high school he was on the debate team, during which time he and his partner won many awards and tournament championships. His active leadership in the Tutors-in-Action Network (TAN) has allowed him to put his passion for teaching into action, as has his work tutoring at the Kumon Reading and Math Center.

Stats
SAT: 2350 (770 Critical Reading, 780 Math, 800 Writing)
SAT Subject Test(s): 800 Chemistry, 790 Math I, 800 Math II, 800 World History, 790 Chinese
High School GPA: 4.0
High School: Northview High School, Duluth, GA
Hometown: Atlanta, GA
Gender: Male
Race: Asian American

Cornell University
Dartmouth College
Duke University
Emory University
Georgia Institute of Technology
Northwestern University
Princeton University
Stanford University
University of Georgia
University of Pennsylvania
Washington University in St. Louis
Yale University

Essay

Sean submitted the following essay to Princeton, Yale, and a modified version to the University of Pennsylvania.

Topic of your choice

Every day, the news is filled with stories of brilliant politicians and gorgeous Hollywood actors. Society chooses to give its million-dollar bills to football players and pop stars, and even my parents want me to jump on the bandwagon of fame and wealth by becoming a lawyer, a neurosurgeon, or a business magnate. Yet somehow, I know I would not feel quite right spending my life as a glamorous celebrity or an affluent doctor, but I hope to be a somebody someday. After all, who doesn't want to make their mom and dad proud?

Throughout my life, I have always asked myself the question that all adults ask kids, "What do you want to be when you grow up?" Back when I was five, I was thrilled with the thought of being a farmer, growing my own food in my own backyard. That quickly changed, however, especially after I realized how cool it would be to own a gas station and whiff that gasoline odor all day. But even something as awesome as that could not interest me forever, and I quickly went through other stages when I decided to become an astronomer, a lawyer, and a marine biologist.

But until now, I never even considered aspiring to be like those who I have had most contact with throughout my life – teachers. Looking back, I can still smell the six-molar ammonia when Dr. Warren stayed after school for two extra hours just so we could finish up our AP Chemistry labs. I can still taste the donuts that Mr. Tomlin bought those Saturday mornings when he drove us to middle school Academic Bowl tournaments. And I can still recall those warm afternoons when my kindergarten teacher, Mrs. Osteen, randomly stopped by my house just to say "hi." Such are the teachers who have shaped my character these past twelve years in school, and such are the teachers who build the foundations of our communities, guiding the paths of those who become our divas and CEOs. Such are the teachers who are my heroes.

Little boys and girls always say they want to be like their heroes some day, and as a boy still growing up, I hope to be like my heroes one day - not a wealthy NBA player or a distinguished Congressmen, but just an ordinary teacher. I have actually thought about it for quite some time. As a tutor of my school and a past teaching assistant at Kumon Math and Reading Center, I have had my share of teaching, and I know how rewarding it is. Still vivid in my mind is the voice of pure joy when one of my students called to thank me for helping her get a four on the AP Chemistry exam. In the background, I could hear her mom screaming to offer me homemade chocolate chip cookies. Furthermore, I dream of being a teacher because I know how delightful it feels to see those light bulbs pop on. I still remember aiding an algebra student in grasping logarithm concepts one day. Everyone had left school already, and it was just my tutee and I in the classroom. Both of us were dead tired, but I knew I would go home unsatisfied without my tutee understanding the change of base rule. After I explained the concept for the ninth time, he suddenly jumped up and shouted "got'em!" and I knew I would drive back home content that evening.

And finally, those grateful "thank-you's" and expensive coffee baskets on the last day of the semester – I have had my experiences of those, and I know how gratifying it feels, like you are on top of the world because you have made a difference in someone's life, that you are not only a teacher but a somebody after all.

See page 333 to find out where this student got in.

ANONYMOUS 1

The applicant was a letterman in soccer and earned the rank of Eagle Scout while in high school. He also volunteered regularly at a local food bank and was a bowling enthusiast. He worked a variety of minimum-wage jobs, including: cooking at a small bar and grill, working as a cashier at Arby's, and working in retail sales at an Abercrombie and Fitch clothing store.

Stats

SAT: 1530 (730 Critical Reading, 800 Math)
SAT Subject Test(s): 800 Math Level 1, 800 Math Level 2, 720 Biology, 770 Chemistry
High School GPA: 4.00
High School: Porter-Gaud School, Charleston, SC
Hometown: Charleston, SC
Gender: Male
Race: Caucasian

Applied To

Clemson University
Davidson College
Duke University
Princeton University

Essay

The applicant used the following essay in his application to Duke. He chose the most open-ended essay option.

We had hiked for over five miles and were getting close to our campsite when it began to rain. The younger Boy Scouts had packed too much gear and were getting very tired. We needed to get to our campsite before dusk, so we could not afford to slow down. After I draped my poncho over my backpack so that my tent and sleeping bag would stay dry, I helped the new scouts cover their backpacks and offered to help carry some of their excess gear. After I had taken some of the weight off two scouts' backs, we continued the trek, looking forward to a break at the end of our hike and hoping that the rain would stop. Once we had reached our campsite and set up camp, we were able to find enough wood to have a small campfire before we retired for the night. My membership in the Boy Scouts has been full of similar challenging and rewarding experiences.

I started out as a Cub Scout at age seven, following in the footsteps of my father who had been an Eagle Scout and wanted me to join the scouting organization as soon as I could. The Boy Scouts of America is an institution that promotes trustworthiness, loyalty, reverence, service, and spirit. I was attracted to this organization immediately, and I am still active in the scouting program to this day.

The goal that I set for myself when I joined the Boy Scouts was the same as the hope that my parents had for me: to earn the rank of Eagle Scout. Throughout my climb through the ranks of scouting, I had to "live" the Scout Law in my activities and service. I had to prove my trustworthiness and determination as well as my eagerness to help others. I went on many camping trips with my troop where I learned various skills to complete merit badges. As I began to prove myself, I became a leader in the troop. As a patrol leader, I had to help plan camping trips and determine what supplies would be needed. I had to set an example for the younger scouts in my troop as well.

As I grew older, I began to widen my participation with the Boy Scouts. I took part in Eagle Scout service projects as well as other service opportunities such as food drives and working in a soup kitchen. I have continued my community service with the scouts and outside of scouting through my entire high school life. Finally, after going on many hikes and earning over 21 merit badges, I was ready to become an Eagle Scout. All that was left was my Eagle Scout service project. After much thought, I decided to build eight benches near an outside basketball court at my school. I had to plan the dates of the project, get the materials, make a design for the benches, and get other Boy Scouts to help me in the undertaking of this project.

My Eagle Scout project was the most important part of my life in scouting. It allowed me to prove my skills as a planner, an organizer, and a leader. After the project had been planned and organized, I continued by buying the materials that we would need and planning the dates that the project would take place. The younger scouts volunteered to help me with my project, and when the time came to begin, I delegated the individual jobs to my fellow Boy Scouts. We built the benches during the summer before my ninth grade year and secured them in poured concrete the following fall. The project was completed without a hitch, and I am proud of that accomplishment, especially when I see students using the benches.

Throughout my years as a Boy Scout, I came to understand and love the ideals that the scouting organization stresses. The environment that this organization provides gives me a wonderful feeling. I can be around honest, kind people who respect each other and who are energetic and involved. For these reasons, I have continued in the Boy Scouts and I have actually expanded my participation. While in the eleventh grade, I was elected President of the Venturer Scouts, a branch of scouting for older

Boy Scouts. I have continued to work on extra merit badges to earn palm awards to add to my Eagle Award. Recently, I was elected as my troop's Junior Assistant Scout Master. Having this position allows me to help the adult leaders of my troop to plan events, meetings, and campouts.

For as long as I can remember, my parents have taught me how to distinguish right from wrong. They taught me how to have good morals and a high ethical standard. I learned from them the great feeling that comes from helping others in need. My parents always urged me to complete any challenge I had accepted. Since I had this wonderful foundation of love, morals, service, and determination, the Boy Scouts of America was perfect for me.

One of the rewards of staying in the Boy Scouts is seeing younger scouts advance in the program. As an Eagle Scout, I enjoy helping the younger scouts complete requirements for higher ranks and merit badges. I know how demanding the trail to the Eagle Scout Award is, so I am always happy to help potential Eagle Scouts strive to achieve their personal goals. My future goal is to continue to be involved in my community as a volunteer and a leader.

See page 333 to find out where this student got in.

ANONYMOUS 2

The applicant was an all-county cross-country runner and captain of his high school's cross-country and track teams. He was involved in school plays, both as an actor and as a stage manager, and won school-issued awards in fine arts. He was captain of his school's Quiz Bowl team and the president of the National Honor Society. The student government's liaison to the Secaucus Board of Education, the applicant attended Jersey Boys State—a hands-on program imparting the rights and responsibilities of citizenship, and earned the Eagle Scout award.

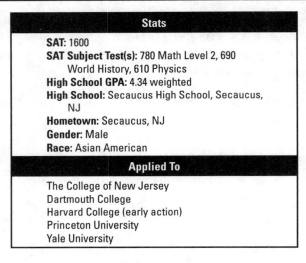

Stats
SAT: 1600
SAT Subject Test(s): 780 Math Level 2, 690 World History, 610 Physics
High School GPA: 4.34 weighted
High School: Secaucus High School, Secaucus, NJ
Hometown: Secaucus, NJ
Gender: Male
Race: Asian American
Applied To
The College of New Jersey
Dartmouth College
Harvard College (early action)
Princeton University
Yale University

Essay 1

The applicant used the following essay in his applications to Dartmouth and Princeton. The prompt, from the Princeton application, requested a "conversational" response.

One of the highest compliments that can be paid someone is that he or she has "good character." What's your idea of what "good character" is? Give examples if you like.

This past summer, I considered getting a tattoo. A simple, Oriental kanji character which, loosely translated, means "true to oneself." Ultimately, I didn't get the tattoo because I decided that I didn't need an ink-drawn symbol on my arm to show the world that I am true to myself. Honesty and integrity is the highest measure of character in a person. For example, it can be said in one breath that a bristled veteran of reconnaissance missions who risked his life for his country has "good character," and that an ardent supporter of humanitarian efforts and global pacifism has "good character." Both the militant activist and the anti-war pacifist display "good character" because they are loyal to themselves and their own beliefs. Each follows his own moral compass and then guides himself to help others in the manner that he feels is noble and just. Once you are honest with yourself, you have the ethical standards to be compassionate with others, determined to reach your goals, and virtuous in the pursuit of your ambitions.

Essay 2

The applicant used the following essay in his applications to Dartmouth and Princeton. The prompt, from the Princeton application, requested a "conversational" response.

> *If you were given the time and resources to develop one particular skill, talent, or area of expertise, what would you choose and why?*

An awe-inspired fan once told a famous master of the flamenco style, "I would give my life to play as well as you do." The guitarist responded, "I already did." To me, music is the language of the mind, and the melodious arpeggio of a burnished walnut instrument speaks what cannot be written in words. I would love to be able to speak through the strings of a guitar, be able to combine my thoughts into a symphony of metal, wood, and broken air. I can play the guitar, at an elementary level, but I have not reached that plateau where I can truly play with feeling. It is the emotion behind the instrument that transforms it into an artistic creation, an extension of a tuned ear, a tapping foot, and a trained hand. If I could give my life, as that musician did, to practice and study the guitar, I would.

Essay 3

The applicant used the following essay in his applications to Dartmouth and Princeton. The prompt, from the Princeton application, requested a "conversational" response.

> *What one person, class, book, or experience would you point to as having had a significant effect on the way you think about something? Explain.*

"Dream as though you'll live forever but live each day as though you'll die tomorrow." That statement is more than a quote I put in my online profile. The words of the late Jimmy Dean are the motto by which I live. My Father's passing is an experience that is very hard for me to discuss, but I can say that this was the single most important event in my life. It was a coming-of-age, as I changed from the sixth grade boy who felt like he was on top of the world to the seventh grade teenager who suddenly saw everything in better perspective. I changed from the exuberant playground football player who dove for extra yardage on each play to the reserved student who put in an extra effort into schoolwork. From his memory, I realize that too often dreams are lost and regrets are made in life, only when it is too late. As a result, I have become inspired to put my best effort into everything that I do, because sometimes there's only one chance.

Essay 4

The applicant used the following essay in his applications to Dartmouth and Princeton. The prompt, from the Princeton application, requested a "conversational" response.

> *Those of us in admissions are often asked what are the two or three things in a student's application to which we give the greatest weight. If you were in our shoes, what are the two or three things in an application to which you would give the greatest weight? Explain why.*

A college is primarily an institution of learning, and the highest importance in college admissions should be placed on the curriculum a student has selected for himself and the grades received in those courses. The curriculum includes the breadth of courses selected, as well as the extracurricular and co-curricular activities in which the student has participated. A college is also a place for the growth and development of one's character, and the character that one has already developed should be influential in the admissions process, determination can be shown in the course selection, drive from involvement in extracurricular activities, enthusiasm in the recommendations, and energy in the essay. The final question should be a sum of these qualities. The admissions staff may ask, for example, "Is this applicant an amicable and intellectually curious person that I would not mind having as a roommate?" or "does this applicant enjoy learning for the sake of learning, and would this applicant be an asset to the classroom?" If these questions, along with the rest of the application, are able to elicit a positive response, than the admissions staff should place that application in the "admit" file and look forward to seeing that applicant during orientation week.

See page 333 to find out where this student got in.

ANONYMOUS 3

The applicant earned the Girl Scout Gold Award and graduated with honors from high school.

Stats
SAT: 1440 (800 Critical Reading, 640 Math)
ACT: 30
High School GPA: 3.70
High School: Henry M. Gunn High School, Palo Alto, CA
Hometown: Palo Alto, CA
Gender: Female
Race: Caucasian

Applied To
Lewis and Clark College
Kenyon College
Knox College
Oberlin College
Occidental College
Pomona College
University of Puget Sound
Whitman College

Essay

The applicant used the following essay in each of her applications.

Common Application: Topic of Your Choice.

I needed to come out of the closet—literally. When I was eight years old, I hid in my grandmother's closet because I was too shy to face the guests who were visiting. I feared the cheek pinching and I feared having to talk to them. I emerged from the closet (at least it was a walk-in), but only after everyone had arrived and I could be more unobtrusive.

Yes, I was shy. I was very shy, for as far back as I can remember. I only spoke when I was spoken to. I hardly ever started conversations with nice kids or stood up to that frightening stock character, the school bully. I had a hard time meeting people with whom I would want to be friends. I joined activities, which everyone says is a great way to meet like-minded people, but a kid as shy as I was could fade into the background, unnoticed. Up until about eighth grade, I was either unknown, or "the shy girl." No one saw me as *me*: A sweet kid who despite being shy didn't have stage fright and loved singing and acting. A kid who loved animals and was a little obsessed with "saving the Earth", who was intrigued by Ancient Egypt and drew cartoons of dinosaurs that reviewed movies. I wanted people to see beyond "the quiet girl," and they didn't see me at all. I was angry, and I was tired. Being shy actually takes effort and is exhausting, both physically and mentally. I was sick of it.

When I entered high school, I finally thought, "I'll show them! I'll work on becoming more outgoing. Maybe I can make more friends and fit in better." That was all I wanted. Every day I gave myself a pep talk: "Say 'hi'; be friendly." Around school, I tried my new attitude. I smiled at people, cheerfully said "hi," and attempted to start conversations. Being friendly wasn't always easy, and it could sometimes be frightening, but I kept trying because I knew my life could be the better for it.

My behavior did change, but not all of a sudden. It happened so slowly that I can't believe I was overcoming my shyness. But, looking at myself now compared to ten or even one year ago, I realize how incredibly far I've come.

At the end of my sophomore year, I was at my first meeting with my new Girl Scout troop. We went to hear a speaker who would teach us "how to follow our dreams." We sat down in the audience full of Girl Scouts from our town. I felt a little uneasy with my new troop because before this evening, I had never met most of them. The speaker began, trying to energize the crowd.

"Any sixth graders?" She asked.

A rousing cheer from the sixth graders.

"Any seventh graders?"

A roar of kids.

"Any eighth graders?"

They yelled and clapped spiritedly.

"Any ninth graders, freshmen?"

My troop clapped halfheartedly; too "cool" to scream like the younger kids. We were the only high school troop in Palo Alto, and I was the only sophomore. At that moment, I realized the speaker wasn't going to say "sophomores." Just as the speaker was about to move on, I stood up from my chair and yelled, "TENTH GRADE! SOPHOMORES!" Would anyone else join in, showing some solidarity even if they weren't sophomores? I knew from the moment I stood up that no one would. People looked at me as if I was crazy, but as I sat down, a smile grew on my face.

I remember this event because it was a major breakthrough in conquering shyness. I've had many other "non-shy" moments since then and will definitely have more in the future. After a few months with my new troop, one of the girls told me, "You fit in really well because you're so outgoing." Me, outgoing? That word surprised me, but the words I liked even more were "fit in."

I'll admit that being constantly outgoing isn't who I am, and I can't and won't change that. Sometimes I just want to be by myself, and there are some instances when I still don't feel like being friendly. I'll never be loud or boisterous or a show-off, which is fine with me. Who I was never changed. The difference is that now I can show something more genuine to the world, because shyness no longer controls me. My personality and spirit won't fit inside the confines of shyness. Nor will they fit inside a closet. No matter what happens in my life, I'm never going back in there.

See page 334 to find out where this student got in.

ANONYMOUS 4

The applicant created autonomous robots and was actively involved in a computer science program in which he won the U.S.A. Computing Olympiad's Junior First Prize. He also worked to develop and implement a pilot project to teach Visual Basic to at-risk kids. In addition, he volunteered at engineering camps for children, owned his own computer business, played varsity rugby, and taught downhill skiing.

Stats
SAT: 1470 (680 Critical Reading, 790 Math)
SAT Subject Test(s): 800 Math Level 2, 690 Physics
High School GPA: 94.8 (out of 100)
High School: Woburn Collegiate Institute, Scarborough, Ontario, Canada
Hometown: Scarborough, Ontario, Canada
Gender: Male
Race: Asian Canadian

Applied To
Brown University
Columbia University
Cornell University
Dartmouth College
Harvard College
Massachusetts Institute of Technology
Princeton University
Stanford University
University of Pennsylvania
Yale University

Essay

The applicant used the following essay in each of his applications.

Write an essay which conveys to the reader a sense of who you are. Possible topics may include, but are not limited to, experiences which have shaped your life, the circumstances of your upbringing, your most meaningful intellectual achievement, the way you see the world—the people in it, events great and small, everyday life—or any personal theme which appeals to your imagination. Please remember that we are concerned not only with the substance of your prose but with your writing style as well.

Childhood Dreams

When I was a little boy, I really wanted to be a professional baseball player. Who didn't? In the glory days of the Toronto Blue Jays, life revolved around baseball for us 7 year olds. Everyone knew Roberto Alomar had 53 steals and Joe Carter had 33 home runs. I dreamed of being at bat on the 7th game of the World Series, in the bottom of the 9th inning with the bases loaded and 2 outs. I dreamed of the millions of dollars I would make playing a game I loved. Then, the baseball players went on strike, and the baseball craze died. So, I decided that I would become the next best thing – a rocket scientist. Of course, I had no clue as to what this entailed, but my interest in screw drivers, vacuum cleaners and lawn mowers was enough to have me convinced that I was destined for that career.

Ever since I started to walk, I loved everything that moved or made sounds. For that matter, I loved everything that helped build or fix anything that moved or made sounds. This was an early indicator of things to come, but my dream became closer to reality with the European godsend: Lego. Year after year I would write letters to Santa for the newest and greatest Lego kits. And year after year I would sit down and spend hours on end assembling and disassembling my prototype spaceships. My love for Lego eventually developed into a love for robotics. It started in the beginning of the seventh grade. I picked up a book at the local bookstore that had an interesting looking cover. Little did I know that this would spark the beginning of a six year quest. The book described how to build a simple robot out of cheap Radio Shack parts. Eager to move on from the realm of Lego, I dragged my dad out to five different Radio Shack stores to buy all of the required components. I struggled with building the robot for a few weeks on my own, as no one in my family had the experience to help me. Finally, after I had my first functional prototype, I realized that I had found a genuine interest in building things that moved and acted independently. Having the robot avoid crashing and emulate humanlike behavior were two basic things I worked on. After two years and many different iterations and ideas, I deemed my project complete and submitted it for review in our City's science and technology fair. The judges were impressed with the simple collision avoidance and behavioral functions I had built into the robot – it won the Institution of Mechanical Engineers' Engineering Excellence award. This was the first major accomplishment towards my rocket science/engineering goal.

Throughout high school I continued to experiment with different aspects of robotics. I joined my school's FIRST Robotics team, and have been a key contributing member in the development of our team's robot. My continued interest in small robots has led to my current senior year Computer Science project on autonomous robots. For my school project I hope to enter the Trinity College Fire-Fighting Home Robot Competition in Hartford with a good chance of success having built in all of the optional robot features. This ongoing project is proving to be a complicated test of both my knowledge of hardware and my programming skills. Operating quite nicely in parallel with my school project is my developing mentorship with the University of Toronto Institute for Aerospace Studies studying robotics for space exploration. At the Institute, I will be exposed to more current approaches that are used to tackle large scale robotics problems. I will work with other graduate students developing things like cellular automata and neural networks that will eventually be implemented on the Institute's robots. It will be a very exciting and valuable experience to be able to work with some of the most technologically advanced equipment with the country's brightest researchers.

It may not exactly be rocket science just yet, but robotics has played a large role in my intellectual development. It has showed me just how virtuous patience really is through solving problems systematically and logically. It has provided me with a vehicle to apply and enrich my abilities in creativity, maths, and sciences; robotics has become one of my passions. I may not have built a Mars Rover (yet), but the realization of this dream is something I will definitely pursue further in college.

See page 334 to find out where this student got in.

ANONYMOUS 5

In high school, this applicant was the Editor-In-Chief of her school newspaper, captain of the Speech and Debate Team, a member of the National Honor Society, treasurer of the Marching Band, a class representative to the Student Council, and volunteered on a regular basis in the local community.

Stats
SAT: 2200 (690 Critical Reading, 750 Math, Writing 760)
High School GPA: 3.6
High School: Acton-Boxborough Regional High School, Acton, MA
Hometown: Acton, MA
Gender: Female
Race: Asian American

Applied To
Boston College
Boston University
Brandeis University
Dickinson College
George Washington University
Georgetown University
Hamilton College
Johns Hopkins University
Tufts University
University of Massachusetts—Amherst
Wellesley College

Essay

This applicant submitted the following essay to the schools listed above.

Evaluate a significant experience, achievement, risk you have taken or ethical dilemma you have faced and its impact on you.

Tighter Abs in Eight Days with Windsor Pilates!

I represent a minority that has been persecuted by society for ages. I am one of the few individuals who actually like watching infomercials. Although most people believe infomercials are merely a waste of airtime for junk nobody ever buys, I am entranced by knives that can cut through bricks with one fair swipe and fascinated by cleaners that can clean red wine from carpet with merely one squirt! Since I began eating solid food, I have refused to consume anything without the accompaniment of a sales pitch in the background.

My unique affinity for commercials became more than admiration one Saturday morning. A carefully staged ambush during my father's croissant and orange juice allowed me to gain control of the television remote. Before long, an advertisement for a Shark vacuum that could swallow a cluster of nails in one gulp caught my eye. I was at the edge of my seat, spellbound by the vacuum's ability; meanwhile, my father sat comfortably on the sofa and, as expected, harshly discredited the vacuum's accomplishments. To my surprise, my unusually stubborn father dialed the toll free number and ordered the product. Instead of viewing my father as a hypocrite for succumbing to the infomercial, I desperately wished to hold the power that could influence strong-willed people like my father. It was my desire to learn this art of persuasion that drove me into the world of Speech and Debate. I knew the team would introduce me to new ideas, but I never expected it to take me to America's cheese capital: Milwaukee, Wisconsin.

It was another early Saturday morning. Standing in front of thirty fierce competitors in my three-inch Steve Madden pumps this past May, it required all of my brainpower to hide the anxiety that their presence produced. Although armed with my yellow legal pad full of intelligent comments, I fumbled over simple words and could not share my thoughts about social security with my fellow mock Senators. I mentally punished myself for my performance, and I was determined for another show to redeem my reputation and pride. When the opportunity for my second attempt came, I buttoned up my crisp, charcoal blazer and smoothed out the wrinkles in my knee-length skirt. This time the room was different. My peers simply melted away when I gave my opinions about the genocide occurring in Sudan. Finally, the butterflies ceased to flutter in my stomach. I felt the control and power of my words. The poise and confidence of the outspoken advertisers that I had seen so many times appeared. I realized that I could only persuade the three judges and the students ranking me when I believed what I had to say. All I had to do was believe in myself. When I was certain of what I had to sell, the points I addressed smoothly connected themselves into a coherent argument without a struggle. With my jet-black hair pulled back into a ponytail, I couldn't help but smile.

After countless Saturday speeches, I have moved closer to my childhood dream of being compelling and articulate. I had anticipated that Speech and Debate would teach me the skills I needed to become an effective public speaker. Instead, I have discovered that the very talents that I yearn for are already within myself. With my skills, I have convinced unwilling neighbors to buy poinsettias, cheesecakes, and even video rental coupons. However, I have yet to master the skill to persuade my resilient father to visit the Boston Museum of Fine Arts or to switch out of dial-up Internet. Until then, I will continue to watch and learn exactly how Daisy Fuentes urges viewers that Windsor Pilates tapes are part of the equation to achieving tighter abs.

See page 334 to find out where this student got in.

Part 4

WHERE THEY GOT IN

AARON ANTRIM

Bard College* Class of 2006

Applied to:

Amherst College	denied
Bard College	accepted
Hampshire College	accepted
Harvard College	waitlisted, denied
Humboldt State University	accepted
Reed College	accepted
Stanford University	denied
Yale University	denied

* Following his freshman year at Bard, Aaron transferred to Humboldt State. The information in this book, however, pertains only to his applications for freshman admission.

ADAM BERLINSKY-SCHINE

Cornell University, Class of 2005

Applied to:

Cornell University	accepted

ALISON KAUFMANN

Amherst College, Class of 2003

Applied to:

Amherst College	accepted
Brown University	accepted
Stanford University	accepted
Swarthmore College	accepted
Wellesley College	accepted
Wesleyan University	accepted
Yale University	accepted

ALLISON KAY RANGEL

Reed College, Class of 2010

Applied to:

Reed College	accepted
University of California—Berkeley	accepted
University of California—Los Angeles	accepted
University of California—Santa Barbara	accepted

AMY BERG

Claremont McKenna College, Class of 2008

Applied to:

Claremont McKenna College.. accepted

Colby College.. accepted

Haverford College.. accepted

Lewis and Clark College .... accepted

Pomona College... waitlisted, removed name

University of Oregon—

   Clark Honors College... accepted

Whitman College.. accepted

ANDREA SALAS

Dartmouth College, Class of 2004

Applied to:

Amherst College.. waitlisted, removed name

Bates College .... accepted

Bowdoin College... accepted

Dartmouth College... accepted

Tufts University.. waitlisted, removed name

University of California—Berkeley.. accepted

University of California—Los Angeles.. accepted

University of California—San Diego .... accepted

University of California—Santa Barbara... accepted

University of California—Santa Cruz .... accepted

Williams College .... accepted

ANDREW COLLINS

Duke University, Class of 2005

Applied to:

Duke University... accepted

Georgetown University.. accepted

Harvard College .... denied

Princeton University.. denied

Stanford University.. denied

University of California—Berkeley... denied

University of Virginia .... accepted

Vanderbilt University.. accepted

ANDREW H. GIORDANO

Brandeis University, Class of 2008

Applied to:

American University.. accepted
Brandeis University.. accepted
Carleton College.. withdrew
Colorado College.. accepted
The Johns Hopkins University.. accepted
Muhlenberg College.. accepted
Oberlin College... accepted
State University of New York—Binghamton......................... accepted
University of Delaware .... accepted
University of Rochester .... accepted

ANDREW MAXWELL MANGINO

Yale University, Class of 2009

Applied to:

Brown University .... accepted
Columbia University—Columbia College.............................. accepted
George Washington University .... accepted
Georgetown University.. accepted
Harvard University..waitlisted, denied
New York University .... accepted
Northwestern University .... accepted
Princeton University..waitlisted, denied
Syracuse University .... accepted
Tufts University.. accepted
University of Chicago... accepted
University of Pennsylvania... accepted
Washington University in St. Louis .... accepted
Yale University.. accepted

AUDREY NATH

Rice University, Class of 2005

Applied to:

Harvard College .... denied
Massachusetts Institute of Technology................................. accepted
Rice University .... accepted

BRANDON MOLINA

Harvard College, Class of 2004

Applied to:

Columbia University.. accepted
Elon University.. accepted
Harvard College .... accepted early action
Stanford University..denied
Tulane University .... accepted
University of Pennsylvania...denied
United States Military Academy .... accepted

BRIAN TRACY

University of Notre Dame, Class of 2005

Applied to:

University of Notre Dame............................... accepted early decision

CANDACE SEU

California Institute of Technology, Class of 2005

Applied to:

California Institute of Technology.. accepted
Harvey Mudd College... accepted
Illinois Institute of Technology..lost application
Pomona College .... accepted
University of Southern California .... accepted

CAROLINE ANG

Brown University, Class of 2004

Applied to:

Brown University .... accepted
University of California—Berkeley... accepted
University of California—Los Angeles....................................... accepted
University of California—San Diego .... accepted

CAROLINE HABBERT

Brown University, Class of 2004

Applied to:

Brown University .... accepted
Stanford University... accepted
University of Michigan.. accepted
Washington University in St. Louis .... accepted
Yale University.. accepted

CAROLINE MELLOR

Reed College, Class of 2009

Applied to:

Bard College .... accepted early decision

Reed College .... accepted early decision

CAROLINE LUCY MORGAN

Davidson College, Class of 2007

Applied to:

Davidson College .... accepted early decision

CHELSEA STITT

Duquesne University, Class of 2010

Applied to:

Duquesne University .... accepted

University of Pittsburgh .... accepted

Villanova University .... waitlisted, removed name

CLAUDIA GOLD

Massachusetts Institute of Technology, Class of 2006

Applied to:

Brown University .... denied

Cornell University .... accepted

Massachusetts Institute of Technology .... accepted

New York University .... accepted

Rice University .... waitlisted, removed name

University of Chicago .... accepted

Yale University .... denied

CLAYTON KENNEDY

Bard College, Class of 2005

Applied to:

Bard College .... accepted

Colorado College .... accepted

Goucher College .... accepted

Hampshire College .... accepted

Lewis and Clark College .... accepted

New College of Florida .... accepted

Pitzer College .... accepted

Truman State University .... accepted

University of Puget Sound .... accepted

DANIEL FREEMAN

Yale University, Class of 2004

Applied to:

Yale University.. accepted early decision

DANIEL MEJIA

Harvard University, Class of 2007

Applied to:

Amherst College... accepted

Georgetown University.. accepted

Harvard College .... accepted

Princeton University.. denied

Rutgers University—New Brunswick .... accepted

Tufts University... accepted

DAVID AUERBACH

Carleton College, Class of 2004

Applied to:

Carleton College.. accepted

Dartmouth College... accepted

Macalaster College.. accepted

Willamette University... accepted

DAVID GIBBS

Tufts University, Class of 2010

Applied to:

Tufts University.. accepted early decision

Tulane University .... accepted early decision

DIANA SCHOFIELD

Northwestern University, Class of 2004

Applied to:

Boston College .... accepted

Cornell University... accepted

Emory University .... accepted

Georgetown University .... denied

Harvard College .... denied

Northwestern University .... accepted

University of North Carolina—Chapel Hill... accepted

University of Pennsylvania... denied

Washington University in St. Louis .... accepted

Elizabeth Jeffers Orr

Kenyon College, Class of 2010

Applied to:

Bates College .... accepted

Colby College .... waitlisted, removed name

Kalamazoo College .... accepted

Lewis & Clark College .... accepted

Macalester College .... waitlisted, removed name

Oberlin College .... accepted

University of Denver .... accepted

University of Puget Sound .... accepted

Ellison Ward

Princeton University, Class of 2004

Applied to:

Brown University .... accepted

College of William & Mary .... accepted

Connecticut College .... accepted

Duke University .... accepted

Harvard College .... waitlisted, denied

Johns Hopkins University .... accepted

Princeton University .... accepted

Yale University .... waitlisted, removed name

Emily Allen

University of California—San Diego, Class of 2005

Applied to:

Georgetown University .... accepted

Harvard College .... denied

University of California—Berkeley .... accepted

University of California—Los Angeles .... accepted

University of California—San Diego .... accepted

University of Pennsylvania .... denied

University of Southern California .... accepted

Yale University .... denied

Emma Fricke

Smith College, Class of 2004

Applied to:

Mount Holyoke College .... accepted

Smith College .... accepted

Sweet Briar College .... accepted

Vanderbilt University .... accepted

Wellesley College .... waitlisted, removed name

ERIC OSBORNE

Amherst College, Class of 2004

Applied to:

Amherst College.. accepted early decision

FAITH NANCY LIN

Yale University, Class of 2008

Applied to:

University of California—Berkeley.. accepted

University of California—Los Angeles... accepted

University of California—San Diego .... accepted

Yale University... accepted

FATIMAH KAUSAR ASGHAR

Brown University, Class of 2011

Applied to:

Brown University .... accepted early decision

GAURAV P. PATEL

University of Pennsylvania, Class of 2004

Applied to:

Dartmouth College.. accepted

Harvard College .... denied

Princeton University.. waitlisted, removed name

University of Pennsylvania... accepted

Yale University... denied

GIANNA MARZILLI

Williams College, Class of 2004

Applied to:

Amherst College... waitlisted, removed name

Brown University .... waitlisted, accepted

Carleton College.. accepted

Colby College... accepted

Macalester College... accepted

Skidmore College... accepted

Smith College... accepted

Tufts University.. accepted

Washington University in St. Louis .... accepted

Wellesley College .... accepted

Williams College .... waitlisted, accepted

HALEY A. CONNOR

Washington University in St. Louis, Class of 2005

Applied to:

Washington U. in St. Louis .... accepted early decision

HANNAH REBECCA STERN

University of California—Los Angeles, Class of 2011

Applied to:

California State University-SanFrancisco .... accepted

University of California-Davis .... accepted

University of California-Irvine .... accepted

University of California-Los Angeles .... accepted

University of California-Santa Barbara .... accepted

HEATHER FIREMAN

Massachusetts Institute of Technology, Class of 2004

Applied to:

California Institute of Technology .... accepted

Massachusetts Institute of Technology .... accepted

Stanford University .... waitlisted, removed name

University of California—Berkeley .... accepted

JAMES GREGORY

Duke University, Class of 2004

Applied to:

Duke University .... accepted

Harvard .... waitlisted early action, denied

Princeton University .... denied

University of North Carolina .... accepted

Yale University .... denied

JAMIE BUSHELL

Hamilton College, Class of 2009

Applied to:

Hamilton College .... accepted early decision

JAMIE MANOS

Cornell University, Class of 2004

Applied to:

Cornell University .... accepted early decision

Jane Sha

University of California—Los Angeles, Class of 2010
Applied to:

New York University .... denied
Stanford University .... denied
University of California—Berkeley .... accepted
University of California—Davis .... accepted
University of California—Irvine .... accepted
University of California—Los Angeles .... accepted
University of California—Riverside .... accepted
University of California—San Diego .... accepted
University of Pennsylvania .... denied
University of Southern California .... denied

Jessica Lau

Harvard College, Class of 2004
Applied to:

Brown University .... accepted
Dartmouth College .... accepted
Harvard University .... accepted
Pennsylvania State University .... accepted
Princeton University .... denied
Rutgers University .... accepted
Tufts University .... accepted
University of Pennsylvania .... accepted
University of Michigan .... accepted
University of Virginia .... accepted

Jessie Seymour

Dartmouth College, Class of 2004
Applied to:

Cornell University .... accepted
Dartmouth College .... accepted
Middlebury College .... accepted
University of Maine .... accepted

Jing Yi Hon

Brown University, Class of 2011
Applied to:

Brown University .... accepted
Columbia University .... denied
Northwestern University .... denied

JoAnn Rebecca Gage

Bryn Mawr College, Class of 2005
Applied to:

Bryn Mawr College..accepted early decision

Joseph A. Rago

Dartmouth College, Class of 2005
Applied to:

Brown University ....accepted early action
Dartmouth College..accepted
Princeton University..waitlisted, removed name
Yale University..waitlisted, denied

Joseph I. Malchow

Dartmouth College, Class of 2008
Applied to:

Boston College...accepted
Carnegie Mellon University ....accepted
Cornell University..accepted
Dartmouth College..accepted
New York University ....accepted
Tufts University...accepted
University of Pennsylvania...denied
Yale University...denied

Julia Hypatia Orth

New College of Florida, Class of 2003
Applied to:

New College of Florida ....accepted
Southampton College of Long Island U...accepted
University of California—Santa Cruz ....accepted

Julie Yau-Yee Tam

Rice University, Class of 2003
Applied to:

Rice University ....accepted early decision

KAREN A. LEE

Stanford University, Class of 2004

Applied to:

Duke University .... accepted

Johns Hopkins University .... accepted

Rice University .... accepted

Southern Methodist University .... accepted

Stanford University .... accepted

KATHARINE ANNE THOMAS

Haverford College, Class of 2005

Applied to:

Bucknell University .... accepted

Colgate University .... accepted

Emory University .... waitlisted, removed name

Georgetown University .... denied

Haverford College .... accepted

Johns Hopkins University .... accepted

Swarthmore College .... denied

Vassar College .... waitlisted, removed name

Wake Forest University .... accepted

Yale University .... denied

KATHLEEN B. BLACKBURN

Washington & Lee University, Class of 2011

Applied to:

Elon University .... accepted

Washington & Lee University .... accepted

KELLY DUONG

Brown University, Class of 2011

Applied to:

Brown University .... accepted early decision

KEVIN JAMES TOSTADO

Franklin W Olin College of Engineering, Class of 2006

Applied to:

Cal Poly.. accepted

Franklin W. Olin College of Engineering...................... accepted

Massachusetts Institute of Technology......................... accepted

San Diego State University.. accepted

University of California—Berkeley............................... accepted

University of California—Los Angeles......................... accepted

University of Notre Dame.. accepted

KIMEN FIELD

Stanford University, Class of 2004

Applied to:

California Polytechnic State University—

    San Luis Obispo.. accepted

Rice University... accepted

Stanford University.. accepted

University of California—Los Angeles......................... accepted

University of California—San Diego............................ accepted

KRISTEN T. MARTINEZ

Massachusetts Institute of Technology, Class of 2010

Applied to:

Brown University... accepted

Carnegie Mellon University.. accepted

Columbia University.......................... waitlisted, removed name

Cornell University.. accepted

Georgia Institute of Technology.................................. accepted

Harvard University.. denied

Johns Hopkins University... denied

Massachusetts Institute of Technology......................... accepted

Northwestern University... accepted

Princeton University... denied

Rice University... denied

Rose-Hulman University.. accepted

Stanford University............................ waitlisted, removed name

Tulane University.. accepted

United States Military Academy.................................. accepted

University of Miami.. accepted

University of Michigan... accepted

University of Notre Dame... accepted

University of Pennsylvania.................. waitlisted, removed name

University of South Florida .... accepted

University of Texas at Austin .... accepted

University of Washington in St. Louis... accepted

Yale University.. denied

KRISTIN SHANTZ

California Institute of Technology, Class of 2004

Applied to:

California Institute of Technology .... accepted

Claremont McKenna College... accepted

Harvard College .... accepted

Pepperdine University... accepted

Princeton University... denied

Stanford University... denied

University of California—Berkeley .... accepted

University of California—Los Angeles... accepted

University of California—San Diego .... accepted

LAUREN CATHARINE WEILER MOORE

Pomona College, Class of 2005

Applied to:

Amherst College.. denied

Brown University .... accepted early action

Duke University... waitlisted, removed name

Pomona College .... accepted

Princeton University... denied

Stanford University... denied

LILLIAN DIAZ-PRZYBYL

Williams College, Class of 2004

Applied to:

Williams College .... accepted early decision

LINDSAY CLAIBORN

Claremont McKenna College, Class of 2005

Applied to:

Claremont McKenna College.. accepted

College of William & Mary .... accepted

Emory University .... accepted

Pomona College... waitlisted, removed name

Stanford University...denied early decision

University of Southern California—

(College of Letters, Arts and Sciences) .... accepted

University of Southern California—

(School of Cinema-Television).. accepted

Yale University .... denied

LINDSAY J. CUSHING

Claremont McKenna College, Class of 2008

Applied to:

Claremont McKenna College.. accepted

Duke University .... denied

Loyola University of Chicago .... accepted

Muhlenberg College.. accepted

Pepperdine University..waitlisted, denied

Pomona College .... denied

Skidmore College.. accepted

Stanford University... denied

University of San Diego .... accepted

Wittenberg University .... accepted

LYMAN THAI

Harvard College, Class of 2008

Applied to:

Cornell University.. accepted

Duke University .... accepted

Harvard College .... accepted

Rice University .... accepted

Stanford University... denied

University of California—Berkeley.. accepted

University of California—Los Angeles.. accepted

University of Texas—Austin .... accepted

Maria Inez Velazquez

Smith College, Class of 2004

Applied to:

Connecticut College .... accepted
Elms College .... accepted
Smith College .... accepted
Trinity College .... accepted
University of Massachusetts—Amherst .... accepted
Xavier University of Louisiana .... accepted
Yale University .... accepted

Megan Herman

Hamilton College, Class of 2009

Applied to:

Hamilton College .... accepted early decision

Melissa Henley

Dartmouth College, Class of 2005

Applied to:

Dartmouth College .... accepted
Lewis and Clark College .... accepted
Linfield College .... accepted
Stanford University .... denied

Meredith Narrowe

Stanford University, Class of 2004

Applied to:

Brown University .... accepted early action
Columbia University .... waitlisted, removed name
Occidental College .... accepted
Pomona College .... accepted
Scripps College .... accepted
Stanford University .... accepted

MICHAEL HARRIS

Duke University, Class of 2008

Applied to:

Boston University.. accepted

Brandeis University.. accepted

Duke University... accepted

Emory University... accepted

George Washington University.. accepted

Lehigh University... accepted

New York University.. accepted

Tufts University... accepted

University of Pennsylvania... denied

Washington University in St. Louis... accepted

MICHELE CASH

Stanford University, Class of 2004

Applied to:

Harvard College .... waitlisted, denied

Harvey Mudd College... accepted

Princeton University.. denied

Rice University .... accepted

Stanford University... accepted

University of California—Berkeley.. accepted

University of California—Davis... accepted

University of California—San Diego .... accepted

University of Rochester .... accepted

MIEKO Y. BEYER

New York University, Class of 2008

Applied to:

Boston University.. accepted

Columbia University—Columbia College...................................... denied

Loyola University New Orleans... accepted

New York University.. accepted

Smith College... accepted

State University of New York at Buffalo.................................. accepted

State University of New York College

at Purchase.. accepted

University of Chicago.. waitlisted, denied

Nitin Shah

Harvard College, Class of 2004
Applied to:

Harvard College .... accepted
Stanford University .... waitlisted, removed name
University of California—Berkeley .... accepted
University of California—Los Angeles .... accepted
Yale University .... accepted

Peter Dean

Washington and Lee University, Class of 2004
Applied to:

Davidson College .... accepted
Gettysburg College .... accepted
Rhodes College .... accepted
University of Virginia .... accepted
Valparaiso University .... accepted
Vanderbilt University .... accepted
Wake Forest University .... accepted
Washington and Lee University .... accepted
Wheaton College (IL) .... accepted

Philip James Madelen Rucker

Yale University, Class of 2006
Applied to:

Boston College .... accepted
Brown University .... accepted
Emory University .... accepted
Georgetown University .... deferred early action, denied
Harvard College .... deferred early action, denied
Tufts University .... accepted
Tulane University .... accepted
University of Chicago .... deferred early action, accepted
University of Rochester .... accepted
Yale University .... accepted

REBECCA BROWNGOEHL

Middlebury College, Class of 2007

Applied to:

Bowdoin College.. accepted

Brown University .... denied

Colby College... accepted

Columbia University... denied

Harvard University.. denied

Middlebury College .... accepted

Pennsylvania State University—

    Schreyer Honors College .... accepted

Trinity College... accepted

Tufts University.. accepted

Wesleyan University .... accepted

RISHABH CHANDRA

The Cooper Union for the Advancement of Science and Art, Class of 2010

Applied to:

City University of New York—Macaulay Honors College...................... accepted

The Cooper Union for the Advancement of Science and Art................ accepted

Columbia University.. waitlisted, removed name

Cornell University.. accepted

Stevens Institute of Technology... accepted

ROBYN ROSE SCHNEIDER

Barnard College, Class of 2008

Applied to*:

Barnard College .... accepted

Boston University... accepted

Brandeis University.. accepted

Brown University .... accepted

Harvard College .... denied

New York University .... accepted

Smith College... accepted

University of Pennsylvania... denied

University of Southern California .... accepted

Yale University.. denied

*   The outcomes listed for Robyn refer only to her applications for transfer admission.

Sean McClellan

Wesleyan University, Class of 2007

Applied to:

Bates College .... denied*

Grinnell College .... accepted

Lewis & Clark College .... accepted

Macalester College .... accepted

University of Washington .... accepted

Wesleyan University .... accepted early decision

*Bates College withdrew Sean's application after he was accepted early decision by Wesleyan University.

Serin Ipek Serin

Brown University, Class of 2011

Applied to:

Brown University .... accepted

Columbia University .... waitlisted, removed name

Cornell University .... accepted

Dartmouth College .... accepted

Harvard University .... denied

Johns Hopkins University .... accepted

Princeton University .... denied

Stanford University .... denied

Tufts University .... accepted

University of Chicago .... accepted

Washington University in St. Louis .... accepted

Wesleyan University .... accepted

Williams College .... accepted

Yale University .... denied

Stephanie Cross

Swarthmore College, Class of 2004

Applied to:

Swarthmore College .... accepted early decision

STEPHANIE WUN-LEE CHOW

Massachusetts Institute of Technology, Class of 2004

Applied to:

Massachusetts Institute of Technology.. accepted

Boston University... accepted

Brown University PLME Program .... denied

Columbia University... accepted

Cornell University... denied

Harvard College .... deferred early action, denied

Princeton University...deferred early action,

denied

Rensselaer Polytechnic Institute .... accepted

University of Connecticut... accepted

Yale University.. waitlisted, removed name

STUART PETER DEKKER

Georgetown University, Class of 2008

Applied to:

College of William and Mary .... waitlisted,

removed name

Georgetown University .... accepted

New York University .... accepted

Tulane University .... accepted

University of Illinois.. accepted

TRACY SERGE

Yale University, Class of 2004

Applied to:

Yale University.. accepted early decision

VICTORIA MARIEL BARONE

University of Notre Dame, Class of 2004

Applied to:

University of Michigan.. accepted

University of Notre Dame .... accepted

University of Southern California .... accepted

WENDY WEINERMAN

Whitman College, Class of 2007

Applied to:

Whitman College.. accepted early decision

WENJUN JING

Wellesley College, Class of 2005

Applied to:

Barnard College	accepted
Carnegie Mellon University	accepted
Columbia University	denied
Connecticut College	accepted
Harvard College	denied
Massachusetts Institute of Technology	denied
Rice University	waitlisted, removed name
Rutgers University	accepted
Tulane University	accepted
Washington University in St. Louis	accepted
Wellesley College	accepted
Yale University	denied

XUEYANG (SEAN) LI

Princeton University, Class of 2011

Applied to:

Cornell University	accepted
Dartmouth College	accepted
Duke University	accepted
Emory University	accepted
Georgia Institute of Technology	accepted
Northwestern University	accepted
Princeton University	accepted
Stanford University	denied
University of Georgia	accepted
University of Pennsylvania	waitlisted, removed name
Washington University in St. Louis	accepted
Yale University	waitlisted, removed name

ANONYMOUS 1

Duke University, Class of 2004

Applied to:

Clemson University	accepted
Davidson College	accepted
Duke University	accepted
Princeton University	denied

ANONYMOUS 2

Wesleyan University, Class of 2006

Applied to:

Wesleyan University	accepted early decision

Anonymous 3

Whitman College, Class of 2006

Applied to:

Lewis & Clark College	accepted
Kenyon College	accepted
Knox College	accepted
Oberlin College	waitlisted, removed name
Occidental College	accepted
Pomona College	denied
University of Puget Sound	accepted
Whitman College	accepted

Anonymous 4

Yale University, Class of 2006

Applied to:

Brown University	accepted
Columbia University	accepted
Cornell University	accepted
Dartmouth College	accepted
Harvard College	denied
Massachusetts Institute of Technology	denied
Princeton University	denied
Stanford University	denied
University of Pennsylvania	accepted
Yale University	accepted

Anonymous 5

Hamilton College, Class of 2010

Applied to:

Boston College	denied
Boston University	waitlisted, accepted
Brandeis University	accepted
Dickinson College	accepted
George Washington University	accepted
Georgetown University	denied
Hamilton College	accepted
The Johns Hopkins University	waitlisted, denied
Tufts University	denied
University of Massachusetts—Amherst	accepted
Wellesley College	denied

Appendix
THEY'RE, THEIR, AND THERE: GRAMMAR AND WRITING TIPS

GOOD GRAMMAR = GOOD FORM

You should strive to make your writing 100 percent grammatically accurate. Think of each essay you write as a building. If it doesn't have structural integrity, admissions officers will tear through it with a wrecking ball.

Let's face it: **Though a thoughtful essay that offers true insight will undoubtedly stand out, it will not receive serious consideration if it's riddled with poor grammar and misspelled words.** It's critical that you avoid grammatical errors. We can't stress this enough. Misspellings, awkward constructions, run-on sentences, and misplaced modifiers cast doubt on your efforts, not to mention your intelligence.

Most Common Grammar Mistakes

Chances are you know the difference between a subject and a verb. So we won't spend time here reviewing the basic components of English sentence construction (however, if you feel like you could use a refresher, check out our book, *Grammar Smart*.) Instead we will focus on problems of usage.

Below is a brief overview to the seven most common usage errors among English speakers. These are errors we all make (some more than others), and knowing what they are will help you snuff them out in your own writing.

Mistake #1: Misplaced Modifier

A modifier is a descriptive word or phrase inserted into a sentence to add dimension to the thing it modifies. For example:

Because he could talk, Mr. Ed was a unique horse.

Because he could talk is the modifying phrase in the sentence. It describes a characteristic of Mr. Ed. Generally speaking, a modifying phrase should be right next to the thing it modifies. If it's not, the meaning of the sentence may change. For example:

Every time he goes to the bathroom outside, John praises his new puppy for being so good.

Who's going to the bathroom outside? In this sentence, it's John! There are laws against that! The descriptive phrase *every time he goes to the bathroom outside* needs to be near *puppy* for the sentence to say what it means.

When you are writing sentences that begin with a descriptive phrase followed by a comma, make sure that the thing that comes after the comma is the person or thing being modified.

Mistake #2: Pronoun Agreement

As you know, a pronoun is a little word that is inserted to represent a noun (*he, she, it, they, etc*). Pronouns must agree with their nouns: The pronoun that replaces a singular noun must also be singular, and the pronoun that replaces a plural noun must be plural.

During your proofreading, be sure your pronouns agree with the nouns they represent. The most common mistake is to follow a singular noun with a plural pronoun (or vice versa), as in the following:

If a writer misuses words, they will not do well on the SAT.

The problem with this sentence is that the noun ("writer") is singular, but the pronoun ("they") is plural. The sentence would be correctly written as follows:

If a writer misuses words, he or she will not do well on the SAT.

Or

If writers misuse words, they will not do well on the SAT.

This may seem obvious but it is also the most commonly violated rule in ordinary speech. How often have you heard people say, *The class must hand in their assignment before leaving. Class* is singular. But *their* is plural. *Class* isn't the only tricky noun that sounds singular but is actually plural. Following is a list of "tricky" nouns—technically called collective nouns. They are nouns that typically describe a group of people but are considered singular and therefore need a singular pronoun:

Family
Jury
Group
Team
Audience
Congregation
United States

If different pronouns are used to refer to the same subject or one pronoun is used to replace another, the pronouns must also agree. The following pronouns are singular:

Either

Neither

None

Each

Anyone

No one

Everyone

If you are using a pronoun later in a sentence, double-check to make sure it agrees with the noun/pronoun it is replacing.

Mistake #3: Subject-Verb Agreement

The rule regarding subject-verb agreement is simple: singular with singular, plural with plural. If you are given a singular subject (*he, she, it*), then your verb must also be singular (*is, has, was*).

Sometimes you may not know if a subject is plural or singular, making it tough to determine whether its verb should be plural or singular. (Just go back to our list of collective nouns that sound plural but are really singular).

Subjects joined by *and* are plural:

Bill and Pat *were* going to the show.

However, nouns joined by *or* can be singular or plural—if the last noun given is singular, then it takes a singular verb; if the last noun given is plural, it takes a plural verb.

Bill or Pat *was* going to get tickets to the show.

When in doubt about whether your subjects and verbs agree, trim the fat! Cross out all the prepositions, commas, adverbs, and adjectives separating your subject from its verb. Stripping the sentence down to its component parts will allow you to quickly see whether your subjects and verbs are in order.

Mistake #4: Verb Tense

As you know, verbs come in different tenses—for example, *is* is present tense, while *was* is past tense. The other tense you need to know about is "past perfect."

Past perfect refers to some action that happened in the past and was completed (perfected) before another event in the past. For example:

I had already begun to volunteer at the hospital when I discovered my passion for medicine.

You'll use the past perfect a lot when you describe your accomplishments to admissions officers. For the most part, verb tense should not change within a sentence (e.g., switching from past to present).

Mistake #5: Parallel Construction

Remember this from your SATs? Just as parallel lines line up with one another, parallelism means that the different parts of a sentence line up in the same way. For example:

Jose told the career counselor his plan: he will be taking the MCAT, attend medical school, and become a pediatrician.

In this sentence, Jose is going to *be taking, attend*, and, *become*. The first verb, *be taking* is not written in the same form as the other verbs in the series. In other words, it is not parallel. To make this sentence parallel, it should read:

Jose told the career counselor his plan: he will take the MCAT, attend medical school, and become a pediatrician.

It is common to make errors of parallelism when writing sentences that list actions or items. Be careful.

Mistake #6: Comparisons

When comparing two things, make sure that you are comparing what can be compared. Sound like double-talk? Look at the following sentence:

Larry goes shopping at Foodtown because the prices are better than Shoprite.

Sound okay? Well, sorry—it's wrong. As written, this sentence says that the prices at Foodtown are better than Shoprite—the entire store. What Larry means is that the prices at Foodtown are better than the *prices* at Shoprite. You can only compare like things (prices to prices, not prices to stores).

The English language uses different comparison words when comparing two things than when comparing more than two things. Check out these examples:

more (for two things) vs. most (for more than two)

Ex.: Given Alex and David as possible dates, Alex is the more appealing of the two.

In fact, of all the guys I know, Alex is the most attractive.

less (for two things) vs. least (for more than two)

Ex.: I am less likely to be chosen than you are.

I am the least likely person to be chosen from the department.

better (for two things) vs. best (for more than two)

Ex.: Taking a cab is better than hitchhiking.

My organic chemistry professor is the best professor I have ever had.

between (for two things) vs. among (for more than two)

Ex.: Just between you and me, I never liked her anyway.

Among all the people here, no one likes her.

Keep track of what's being compared in a sentence so you don't fall into this grammatical black hole.

Mistake #7: Diction

Diction means choice of words. There are tons of frequently confused words in the English language and can be broken down into words that sound the same but mean different things (*there, they're, their*), words and phrases that are made up (*irregardless*) and words that are incorrectly used as synonyms (*fewer, less*).

Words that sound the same but mean different things are homonyms. Some examples are:

there, they're, their: *There* is used to indicate a location in time or space. *They're* is a contraction of "they are." *Their* is a possessive pronoun.

effect/affect: *Effect* is the result of something. *Affect* is to influence or change something.

conscience/conscious: *Conscience* is Freudian and is a sense of right or wrong. *Conscious* is to be awake.

principle/principal: *Principle* is a value. *Principal* is the person in charge at a school.

eminent/imminent: *Eminent* describes a person who is highly regarded. *Imminent* means impending.

Imaginary words that don't exist but tend to be used in writing include:

Alot: Despite widespread use, *alot* is not a word. *A lot* is the correct form.

Irregardless: *Irregardless* is not in anybody's dictionary—it's not a real word. *Regardless* is the word that you want.

Sometimes people don't know when to use a word. How often have you seen this sign?

Express checkout: Ten items or less.

Unfortunately, supermarkets across America are making a blatant grammatical error when they post this sign. When items can be counted, you must use the word *fewer*. When something can not be counted, you would use the word *less*. For example:

If you eat fewer French fries, you can use less ketchup.

Here are some other words people make the mistake of using interchangeably:

number/amount: Use *number* when referring to something that can be counted.

Use *amount* when it can not.

aggravate/irritate: *Aggravate* and *irritate* are not synonymous. To *aggravate* is to make worse. To *irritate*, is to annoy.

disinterested/uninterested: *Disinterest* means impartiality; absence of strong feelings about something, good or bad. *Uninterest*, on the other hand, indicates boredom.

Diction errors requires someone to cast a keen, fresh eye on your essay because they trick your ear and require focused attention to catch.

Here's a handy chart to help you remember the most common grammar usage errors:

GRAMMAR CHART

Grammatical Category	What's the Rule?	Bad Grammar	Good Grammar
Misplaced Modifier	A modifier is word or phrase that describes something and should go right next to the thing it modifies.	1. Eaten in Mediterranean countries for centuries, **northern Europeans** viewed the tomato with suspicion. 2. A **former greens keeper** now about to become the Masters champion, **tears** welled up in my eyes as I hit my last miraculous shot.	1. Eaten in Mediterranean countries for centuries, the tomato was viewed **the tomato** with suspicion by Northern Europeans. 2. I **was a former greens keeper** who was now about to become the Masters champion; **tears** welled up in my eyes as I hit my last miraculous shot.
Pronoun Agreement	A pronoun must refer unambiguously to a noun and it must agree in number with that noun.	1. Although **brokers** are not permitted to know executive access **codes, they** are widely known. 2. The **golden retriever** is one of the smartest breeds of dogs, but **they** often **have** trouble writing **personal statements** for law school admission. 3. Unfortunately, both **candidates** for whom I worked sabotaged their own **campaigns** by accepting **a contribution** from illegal **sources.**	1. Although **brokers** are not permitted to know executive access **codes, the codes** are widely known. 2. The **golden retriever** is one of the smartest breeds of dogs, but often **it has** trouble writing **a personal statement** for law school admission. 3. Unfortunately, both **candidates** for whom I worked sabotaged their own **campaigns** by accepting **contributions** from illegal **sources.**
Subject-Verb Agreement	The subject must always agree in number with the verb. Make sure you don't forget what the subject of a sentence is, and don't use the object of a preposition as a subject.	1. **Each** of the men involved in the extensive renovations **were** engineers. 2. Federally imposed **restrictions** on the ability to use certain information **has** made life difficult for Martha Stewart.	1. **Each** of the men involved in the extensive renovations **was** engineers. 2. Federally imposed **restrictions** on the ability to use certain information **have** made life difficult for Martha Stewart.

Grammatical Category	What's the Rule?	Bad Grammar	Good Grammar
Verb Tense	Always make sure your sentences' tenses match the time frame being discussed.	1. After he finished working on his law school essays he **would go** to the party.	1. After he finished working on his law school essays he **went** to the party.
Paralell Construction	Two or more ideas in a single sentence that are parallel need to be similar in grammatical form.	1. The two main goals of the Eisenhower presidency were a **reduction** of taxes and **to increase** military strength. 2. **To provide a child** with the skills necessary for survival in modern life is **like guaranteeing their** success.	1. The two main goals of the Eisenhower presidency were **to reduce** taxes and **to increase** military strength. 2. **Providing children** with the skills necessary for survival in modern life is **like guaranteeing their** success.
Comparisons	You can only compare things that are exactly the same.	1. The **rules** of written English are **more stringent** than spoken **English.** 2. The **considerations** that led many colleges to impose admissions quotas in the last few decades *are similar to the quotas* imposed in the recent past by large businesses.	1. The rules of written English are **more stringent than those of** spoken **English.** 2. The **considerations** that led many colleges to impose admissions quotas in the last few decades **are similar to those** that led large businesses to impose quotas in the recent past.
Diction	There are many words that sound the same but mean different things.	1. Studying had a very positive **affect** on my score. 2. My high SAT score has positively **effected** the outcome of my college applications.	1. Studying had a very positive **effect** on my score. 2. My high SAT score has positively **affected** the outcome of my college applications.

Using Punctuation Correctly

Now that we've got that covered, it's time to talk about punctuation. As a member of the LOL generation you might be great at turning punctuation into nonverbal clues, but colons and parentheses have other uses besides standing in as smiley faces at the end of your texts.

A formal essay is not like the notes you take in organic chemistry. "W/" is not an acceptable substitute for *with*, and neither is "b/c" for because. Symbols are also not acceptable substitutes for words (@ for *at*, & for *and*, etc.). (In fact, try to avoid the use of "etc."; it is not entirely acceptable in formal writing. Use "and so forth" or "among others" instead.) And please don't indulge in any "cute" spelling ("nite" for *night*, "tho" for *though*). This kind of writing conveys a message that you don't care about your essay. Show the admissions officers how serious you are by eliminating these shortcuts.

The overall effectiveness of your college application essay is greatly dependent on your ability to use punctuation wisely. Here's what you need to know:

Commas (,)

Very few people understand every rule for proper comma use in the English language.

This lack of understanding leads to two disturbing phenomena: essays without commas and essays with commas everywhere. Here is a quick summary of proper comma use:

Use Commas to Set Off Introductory Elements.

- Breezing through my SAT essay, I wondered if everyone were as well-prepared as I.

- Incidentally, I got a "4" on the Writing Sample section.

- Before you jump to any conclusions, I was only taking a mote out of her eye.

Use Commas to Separate Items in a Series.

- She made hot chocolate, cinnamon toast, scrambled eggs with cheese, and coffee cake.

[Note: There's always great debate as to whether the final serial comma (before the *and*) is necessary. In this case, the comma must be added; otherwise, there will be a question about the contents of the scrambled eggs. In cases where no such ambiguity exists, the extra comma seems superfluous. Use your best judgment. When in doubt, separate all the items in a series with commas.]

Use Commas Around a Phrase or Clause that Could Be Removed Logically from the Sentence.

- The Critical Reading section, the first section of the SAT, always makes my palms sweat.

- Xavier, the student whose test was interrupted by marching band practice, would have liked to have had ear plugs.

Use a Comma to Separate Coordinate (Equally Important) Adjectives. *Do Not* Use a Comma to Separate Noncoordinate Adjectives.

- It was a dark, stormy night.

- It was messy triple bypass.

***Do Not* Use a Comma to Separate a Subject and a Verb.**

- incorrect: My new ACT study group, meets at the local café.

- correct: My new ACT study group meets at the local café.

***Do Not* Use a Comma to Separate Compound Subjects or Predicates.**
(A compound subject means two "do-ers"; a compound predicate means two actions done.)

- incorrect: My best friend Xavier, and his brother Lou always tell me the truth about my practice essays.

- correct: My best friend Xavier and his brother Lou always tell me the truth about my practice essays.

- incorrect: Because of the strange tickling in the back of my throat, I stayed in bed, and gave myself a break from studying.

- correct: Because of the strange tickling in the back of my throat, I stayed in bed and gave myself a break from studying.

Colons (:)

Use a colon to introduce an explanation or a list.

- "I think you judge Truman too charitably when you call him a child: he is more like a sweetly vicious old lady." *Tennessee Williams*

- "When I am dead, I hope it may be said: 'His sins were scarlet, but his books were read.'" *Hilaire Belloc*

- "Everything goes by the board to get the book written: honor, pride, decency..." *William Faulkner*

Semicolons (;)

Use a semicolon to join related independent clauses in a single sentence (a clause is independent if it can logically stand alone).

- "An artist is born kneeling; he fights to stand." *Hortense Calisher*

- "Why had I become a writer in the first place? Because I wasn't fit for society; I didn't fit into the system." *Brian Aldiss*

Dashes (—)

Use a dash for an abrupt shift. Use a pair of dashes (one on either side) to frame a parenthetical statement that interrupts the sentence. Dashes are more informal than colons.

- "Like a lot of what happens in novels, inspiration is a sort of spontaneous combustion—the oily rags of the head and heart." *Stanley Elkin*

- "Writers should be read—but neither seen nor heard." *Daphne du Maurier*

- "Of all the cants which are canted in this canting world—though the cant of hypocrites may be the worst—the cant of criticism is the most tormenting." *Laurence Sterne*

Exclamation Points (!)

Use exclamation points sparingly. Try to express excitement, surprise, or rage in the words you choose. A good rule of thumb is *one* exclamation point per essay, at the most.

- "You don't know what it is to stay a whole day with your head in your hands trying to squeeze your unfortunate brain so as to find a word... Ah! I certainly know the agonies of style." *Gustave Flaubert*

Question Marks (?)

Use a question mark after a direct question. Don't forget to use a question mark after rhetorical questions (ones that you make in the course of argument that you answer yourself).

- "Why shouldn't we quarrel about a word? What is the good of words if they aren't important enough to quarrel over? Why do we choose one word over another if there isn't any difference between them?" *G. K. Chesterton*

Quotation Marks (" ")

Use quotation marks to indicate a writer's exact words. Use quotation marks for titles of songs, chapters, essays, articles, or stories—a piece that is part of a larger whole. Periods and commas always go inside the quotation mark. Exclamation points and question marks go inside the quotation mark when they belong to the quotation and not to the larger sentence. Colons, semicolons, and dashes go outside the quotation mark.

- "That's not writing, that's typing." Truman Capote on Jack Kerouac

WRITING CLEARLY

Now that you've gotten a refresher in the building blocks of good writing, it's time to talk about the other half of the equation: style. If grammar and punctuation represent the mechanics of your writing, style represents the choices you make in sentence structure, diction, and figures of thought that reveal your personality to admissions officers. We can't recommend highly enough that you read *The Elements of Style*, by William Strunk Jr., E. B. White, and Roger Angell. This little book is a great investment. Even if you've successfully completed a course or two in composition without it, it will prove invaluable and become your new best friend—and hopefully also your muse.

ELIMINATING WORDINESS

Remember: Good writing is writing that's easily understood. You want to get your point across, not bury it in words. Make your prose clear and direct. **If an admissions officer has to struggle to figure out what you're trying to say, there's a good chance he or she might not bother reading further.** Abide by word limits and avoid the pitfall of overwriting. Here are some suggestions that will help clarify your writing by eliminating wordiness:

Address One Idea at a Time

Don't try to put too much information into one sentence. If you're ever uncertain whether a sentence needs three commas and two semicolons or two colons and a dash, just make it into two separate sentences. Two simple sentences are better than one long convoluted one. Which of the following examples seems clearer to you?

Example #1:

Many people, politicians for instance, act like they are thinking of the people they represent by the comments made in their speeches, while at the same time they are filling their pockets at the expense of the taxpayers.

Example #2:

Many people appear to be thinking of others, but are actually thinking of themselves. For example, many politicians claim to be thinking of their constituents, but are in fact filling their pockets at the taxpayers' expense.

Use Fewer Words to Express an Idea

In a 500-word essay, you don't have time to mess around. In an attempt to sound important, many of us "pad" our writing. Always consider whether there's a shorter way to express your thoughts. We are all guilty of some of the following types of clutter:

Cluttered	Clear
due to the fact that	because
with the possible exception of	except
until such time as	until
for the purpose of	for
referred to as	called
at the present time	now
at all times	always

Test Yourself: Eliminating Wordiness Exercise

Another way in which unnecessary words may sneak into your writing is through the use of redundant phrases. Pare each phrase listed below down to a single word:

cooperate together_____

resulting effect_____

large in size_____

absolutely unprecedented_____

disappear from sight_____

new innovation_____

repeat again_____

totally unique_____

necessary essentials_____

Use Fewer Qualifiers

A qualifier is a little phrase we use to cover ourselves. Instead of plainly stating that "Former President Reagan sold arms in exchange for hostages," we feel more comfortable stating "*It's quite possible* that former President Reagan *practically* sold arms in *a kind* of exchange for people who were *basically* hostages." Over-qualifying weakens your writing. Prune out these words and expressions wherever possible:

kind of	basically
a bit	practically
sort of	essentially
pretty much	in a way
rather	quite

Another type of qualifier is the *personal qualifier*, where instead of stating the truth, I state the truth "in my opinion." Face it: Everything you state (except perhaps for scientific or historical facts) is your opinion. Personal qualifiers like the following can often be pruned:

to me

in my opinion

in my experience

I think

it is my belief

it is my contention

the way I see it

Use Fewer Adverbs

If you choose the right verb or adjective to begin with, an adverb is often unnecessary.

Use an adverb only if it does useful work in the sentence. It's fine to say "the politician's campaign ran smoothly up to the primaries," because the adverb "smoothly" tells us something important about the running of the campaign. The adverb could be eliminated, however, if the verb were more specific: "The politician's campaign sailed up to the primaries." The combination of the strong verb *and* the adverb, as in "the politician's campaign sailed smoothly up to the primaries," is unnecessary because the adverb does no work. Here are other examples of unnecessary adverbs:

very unique

instantly startled

dejectedly slumped

effortlessly easy

absolutely perfect

totally flabbergasted

completely undeniable

Test Yourself: Eliminating Wordiness Exercise (part 2)

Rewrite these sentences to make them less wordy.

1. It can be no doubt argued that the availability of dangerous and lethal guns and firearms are in part, to some extent, responsible for the undeniable explosion of violence in our society today.

_____

_____

_____

_____

2. Why is it always imperative and necessary for the teaching educational establishment to subdue and suppress the natural spirits and energies of adolescents in scholarly settings?

_____

_____

_____

_____

3. It seems to me that I believe one must not ignore the fact that Hamlet was a heroic character as well as a tragic and doomed character fated to suffer.

_____

_____

_____

_____

4. No one would deny the strong and truthful fact that young teenage pregnancy is on the rise and is increasing at unbelievable rates each and every single day of the year.

_____

_____

_____

_____

Eliminating Fragments and Run-Ons

Sentences with too few words are just as annoying to admissions officers as those with too many.

A fragment is an unfinished sentence. It may lack a subject or verb, or it may be a dependent clause. Use this test for sentence fragments: can the fragment logically stand alone, without the previous or following sentences?

- Fragment: My pencil broke during the last five minutes of the test. Pieces rolling beneath my chair.

- Correct Sentence: My pencil broke during the last five minute of the test, and the pieces rolled beneath my chair.

A run-on is an instance where two sentences run together when they should be separate. Sometimes the author forgets the necessary conjunction or the proper punctuation. Sometimes the two sentences are simply too long to fit together well.

- Run-on: Regardless of the weather, I will go spear fishing in Bali the water is as clear as glass.

- Correct Sentences: Regardless of the weather, I will go spear fishing in Bali where the water is as clear as glass.

Make sure your sentences don't contain these fatal errors.

Limiting Your Use of Passive Voice

Consistently writing in the active voice and limiting your use of the passive voice can make your writing more forceful, authoritative, and interesting. Look at the sentences below. They convey essentially the same basic idea, but they have very different effects on the reader.

- The tobacco industry deliberately withheld data about the dangers of second-hand smoke.

- Data about the dangers of second-hand smoke were deliberately withheld [by the tobacco industry].

The first sentence is in the active voice; the second, in the passive voice. The active voice has a clear subject-verb relationship which illustrates that the subject is doing the action. A sentence is in the passive voice when the subject of the sentence, instead of acting, is acted upon. By distancing the subject from the verb, the passive voice makes it appear that the action is being done to the subject. The passive voice uses a form of *be* (is, am, are, was, were, been) plus the main verb in past participle form. The "do-er" of a passive voice sentence is either absent or relegated to the end of the sentence in a "by" phrase.

Test Yourself: Eliminating the Passive Voice Exercise

Put each of the following sentences into the active voice:

1. The Constitution was created by the Founders to protect individual rights against the abuse of federal power.

_____

_____

_____

_____

2. Information about the Vietnam War was withheld by the government.

_____

_____

_____

_____

3. The right to privacy was called upon by the Supreme Court to form the foundation of the Roe v. Wade decision.

_____

_____

_____

_____

4. Teachers in many school districts are now often required by administrators to "teach to the test."

_____

_____

_____

_____

5. Residents of planned communities are mandated by Block Associations to limit the number of cars parked in their driveways.

_____

_____

_____

_____

6. Mistakes were made by the President.

_____

_____

_____

_____

7. The gaze of the tiny porcupine was captured by the headlights of the on-coming Range Rover.

_____

_____

_____

_____

Using Nonsexist Language

Pronoun agreement problems often arise because the writer is trying to avoid a sexist use of language. Because there is no gender-neutral singular pronoun in English, many people use *they*, as in the incorrect sentence above. But there are other, more grammatically correct ways of getting around this problem.

One common, albeit quite awkward, solution is to use *he/she* or *his/her* in place of *they* or *their*. For example, instead of writing, "If someone doesn't pay income tax, then they will go to jail," you can write, "If someone doesn't pay income tax, then he or she will go to jail." A more graceful (and shorter) alternative to *he/she* is to use the plural form of both noun and pronoun: "If people don't pay income tax, they will go to jail." Using nonsexist language also means finding alternatives for the word *man* when you are referring to humans in general. Instead of *mankind* you can write *humankind* or *humanity*; instead of *mailman*, you can use *mail carrier*; rather than stating that something is *man-made* you can call it *manufactured* or *artificial*.

There are a number of good reasons for you to use nonsexist language. For one thing, it is coming to be the accepted usage; that is, it is the language educated people use to communicate their ideas. Many publications now make it their editorial policy to use only non-gendered language. In addition, nonsexist language is often more accurate. Some of the people who deliver mail, for example, are female, so you are not describing the real state of affairs by referring to all of the people who deliver your mail as *men* (since it is no longer universally accepted that *man* refers to all humans). Finally, there is a good chance that at least one of your readers will be female, and that she—or, indeed, many male readers—will consider your use of the generic "he" to be a sign that you either are not aware of current academic conventions or do not think that they matter. It is best not to give your readers that impression.

Use of non-sexist language can feel awkward at first. Practice until it comes to seem natural; you may soon find that it is the old way of doing things that seems strange.

Avoid Clichés Like the Plague

Clichés are comfortable. When we're stuck for the next word, a cliché will suddenly strike us, and we'll feel lucky. We write something like "this *tried* and true method" or "he was one of the *best and brightest*." A cliché may let the writer off the hook, but the reader will be turned off. The reason a cliché is a cliché is because it is overused. Try something original instead of the following overused clichés:

"I've Always Wanted to Be a Doctor."

A great personal statement should clearly illustrate the applicant's commitment to and interest in professional goals. Even so, avoid throwaway lines and generic statements that could be repeated by any other doctor wannabe. Many students who choose to study something as specific as medicine truly feel the decision is the result of a long-term life calling, but making such statements will not distinguish you from the crowd. Instead, focus on illustrating how you have demonstrated that commitment to a long-term professional goal such as medicine—or even law—academically and through your activities.

"I Want to Help People."

Let's be clear: If you really want to spend your life saving lives, then by all means write about it. Just keep in mind that many other people will go this abstract route as well. Although some of these people really do want to make the world a better place, way down in the cockles of their hearts, most just say it because they want it to look good.

Here's the rub: Many essays about saving lives and healing will appear bogus and insincere. Even if you're heartfelt, your essay may get tossed into the same pile as all the insincere ones. Admissions officers will take your professed altruistic ambitions (and those of the hundreds of other applicants with identical personal statements) with a sizeable grain of salt. The key is to demonstrate your commitment to public service through examples of the work you have done. If you can in good conscience say that you're committed to a career in the public interest, you must show the committee something tangible on your application and in your essay that will allow them to see your statements as more than hollow assertions.

Speak from experience, not from desire. This is exactly where those details we've already discussed come into play. If you can't show that you're already a veteran in the good fight, then don't claim to be. Be forthright. Nothing is as impressive to the reader of a personal statement as the truth.

STYLE CHART

Style Category	What's the Rule?	Bad Style	Good Style
Wordiness	Sentences should not contain any unnecessary words.	1. The medical school is accepting applications **at this point in time.** 2. She carries a book bag that is made out of leather **and textured.**	1. The medical school is accepting applications **now.** 2. She carries a **textured, leather** book bag.
Fragments	Sentence should contain a subject and a verb and express a complete idea.	1. And I went to the library.	1. I went to class and I went to the library.
Run-ons	Sentences that consist of two independent clauses should be joined by the proper conjunction.	1. The test has a lot of difficult information **in it, you should** start studying right away.	1. The test has a lot of difficult information **in it, and you should** start studying right away.
Passive/Active Voice	Choose the active voice, in which the subject performs the action.	1. **The ball was hit by the bat.** 2. **My time and money were wasted** trying to keep www.justdillpickles.com afloat single-handedly.	1. **The bat hit the bat.** 2. **I wasted time and money** trying to keep www.justdillpickles.com afloat single-handedly.
Nonsexist Language	Sentences should not contain any gender bias.	1. A professor should correct **his** students' papers according to the preset guidelines. 2. From the beginning of time, **mankind** used language in one way or another. 3. Are there any **upperclassmen** who would like to help students in their Lit classes?	1. Professors should correct **their** students' papers according to the preset guidelines. 2. From the beginning of time, **humans** used language in one way or another. 3. Are there any **seniors** who would like to help students in their Lit classes?

Navigating the Minefield

Besides grammatical concerns, pre-meds should keep in mind the following points while writing their admissions essays:

Don't Repeat Information from Other Parts of Your Application

That is, don't repeat information from other parts of your application unless you can spin it to elucidate previously unmentioned facets of your personality and perspectives. The admissions staff already has your transcripts, standardized test scores, and list of academic and extracurricular achievements. The personal statement is your only opportunity to present all other aspects of yourself in a meaningful way. Even if you don't mind wasting your own time, admissions officers will mind if you waste theirs.

In General, Avoid Generalities

Admissions officers have to read an unbelievable number of boring essays. You'll find it harder to be boring if you write about particulars. It's the details that stick in a reader's mind. As Ludwig Mies van der Rohe wrote, "God is in the details."

Don't Go On at Length About Your Goals

Face it: You have only an imprecise idea of what college will be like. Everyone's goals change through the years. Your goals are especially likely to change because college will change you. So leave the 75-year plan out of your personal statement.

Maintain the Proper Tone

Your essay should be memorable without being outrageous and easy to read without being too formal or sloppy. When in doubt, err on the formal side.

Don't Try to be Funny, Unless What You Have to Say is Actually Funny

An applicant who can make an admissions officer laugh never gets lost in the shuffle. No one will be able to bear tossing your application into the "reject" pile if you garner a genuine chuckle. But beware! Only a select few are able to pull off humor in this context.

Stay Away from Anything Even Remotely Off-Color

Avoid profanity. It's not a good idea to be irreverent in admissions essays. Also, there are some things admissions officers don't need (or want) to know about you, so keep those things to yourself.

Circumvent Political Issues If Possible

Admissions officers don't care about your political perspectives as long as your viewpoints are thoughtful. They don't care what your beliefs are as long as you are committed to the preservation of human life. The problem is that if you write about a political issue, you may come across as the type of person who is intolerant or unwilling to consider other viewpoints. In college (and certainly in your professional career), you'll occasionally be challenged to defend a position with which you disagree—and you don't want to seem like someone who is so impassioned that you are incapable of arguing both sides of an issue. If you opt to write about politics, be very careful.

Consider Your Audience if You Want to Write About Religion

As a general rule, don't make religion the focal point of your essay unless you're applying to a college with a religious affiliation. Don't misunderstand us—religion is not taboo. It's totally fine to mention religion in any personal statement; just make sure to put it within the context of the whole, dynamic person you are.

Put the Fraternity Bake Sale Behind You

The same goes for the juggling club juggle-a-thon and the like. It's definitely worth noting on your resume if you were the president of your sorority or of any such institutionally affiliated organization. That said, achievements in a Greek organization or any club or student group are not the kind of life-changing events that have made you the person you fundamentally are today. **Make sure what you write about has had an actual impact on your life (and better yet, on the lives of others).**

No Gimmicks, No Gambles

Avoid tricky stuff. You want to differentiate yourself but not because you are some kind of daredevil. Don't rhyme. Don't write a satire or mocked-up front-page newspaper article. Gimmicky personal statements mostly appear contrived and, as a result, they fall flat, taking you down with them.

Excuses, Excuses...

Admissions officers have seen every excuse in the book for bad grades and lousy test scores. Rather than make excuses, you want to come across as resolute and capable of doing better.

"My Test Score Isn't Great, But I'm Just Not a Good Test Taker."

Don't dwell on a low standardized test score in your personal statement. If there were extenuating circumstances, you can briefly mention them or you can include a separate note in your application. If there were no such circumstances, it's best to avoid mention of your score. There's a reason for the test being taken before entrance to college—it's a primer, the first of many tests that you will take as a medical student. If you don't take tests well and the SAT or the ACT confirms it, don't make excuses for it; instead, resolve to do better. Consider also that a low standardized test score speaks for itself—all too eloquently. It doesn't need you to speak for it too. The test may be flawed, but don't argue the unfairness of them to admissions officers who use them as a primary factor in their admissions decisions. We feel for you, but you'd be barking up the wrong tree there.

"My College Grades Weren't That High, But . . ."

This issue is a little more complicated than the low test score. If your grades fall below average acceptance criteria to most medical programs, or if there are certain anomalous periods of low achievement on your transcript, it's probably best to offer some form of explanation—especially if you have a good reason for lower performance, such as illness, pregnancy, or a demanding work schedule. College admissions committees will be more than willing to listen to your interpretation of your college performance, but only within limits. Keep in mind that schools require official transcripts for a reason. Members of the admissions committee will be aware of your academic credentials even before they read your essay.

If your grades are unimpressive, the best strategy is to offer the admissions committee something else by which to judge your abilities. Many admissions committees say that they are willing to consider students whose grades or test scores fall slightly below the average acceptance criteria, particularly if they've demonstrated extraordinary altruism or service to the community. Again, the best argument for looking past your college grades is evidence of achievement in another area, whether it is your test score, extracurricular activities, overcoming economic hardship as an undergraduate, or career accomplishments.

READY, SET, WRITE!

Hopefully what you've read here will help guide you through the process of writing a great personal essay and stand-out secondaries. Though there's no magic recipe, we're confident that if you follow our advice about what to put in and what to leave out, you'll end up with a memorable personal statement that will differentiate you from the larger applicant pool and make you a more competitive candidate. Take our word for it and give it your best shot.

Index

Essay Themes

NOTES

NOTES

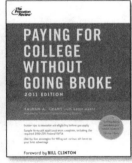